RICHARD B. RUSSELL

Biographies

IN AMERICAN FOREIGN POLICY

Joseph A. Fry, University of Nevada, Las Vegas
Series Editor

The Biographies in American Foreign Policy Series employs the enduring medium of biography to examine the major episodes and themes in the history of U.S. foreign relations. By viewing policy formation and implementation from the perspective of influential participants, the series humanizes and makes more accessible those decisions and events that sometimes appear abstract or distant. Particular attention is devoted to those aspects of the subject's background, personality, and intellect that most influenced his or her approach to U.S. foreign policy, and each individual's role is placed in a context that takes into account domestic affairs, national interests and policies, and international and strategic considerations.

Volumes Published

Lawrence S. Kaplan, *Thomas Jefferson: Westward the Course of Empire*

Richard H. Immerman, *John Foster Dulles: Piety, Pragmatism, and Power in U.S. Foreign Policy*

Thomas W. Zeiler, *Dean Rusk: Defending the American Mission Abroad*

Edward P. Crapol, *James G. Blaine: Architect of Empire*

David F. Schmitz, *Henry L. Stimson: The First Wise Man*

Thomas M. Leonard, *James K. Polk: A Clear and Unquestionable Destiny*

James E. Lewis Jr., *John Quincy Adams: Policymaker for the Union*

Catherine Forslund, *Anna Chennault: Informal Diplomacy and Asian Relations*

Lawrence S. Kaplan, *Alexander Hamilton: Ambivalent Anglophile*

Andrew J. DeRoche, *Andrew Young: Civil Rights Ambassador*

Jeffrey J. Matthews, *Alanson B. Houghton: Ambassador of the New Era*

Clarence E. Wunderlin, Jr., *Robert A. Taft: Ideas, Tradition, and Party in U.S. Foreign Policy*

Howard Jablon, *David M. Shoup: A Warrior against War*

Jeff Woods, *Richard B. Russell: Southern Nationalism and American Foreign Policy*

RICHARD B. RUSSELL

Southern Nationalism and American Foreign Policy

JEFF WOODS

ROWMAN & LITTLEFIELD PUBLISHERS, INC.
Lanham • Boulder • New York • Toronto • Plymouth, UK

ROWMAN & LITTLEFIELD PUBLISHERS, INC.

Published in the United States of America
by Rowman & Littlefield Publishers, Inc.
A wholly owned subsidiary of The Rowman & Littlefield Publishing Group, Inc.
4501 Forbes Boulevard, Suite 200, Lanham, Maryland 20706
www.rowmanlittlefield.com

Estover Road
Plymouth PL6 7PY
United Kingdom

British Library Cataloguing in Publication Information Available

Library of Congress Cataloging-in-Publication Data

Woods, Jeff, 1970–
  Richard B. Russell : Southern nationalism and American foreign policy / Jeff Woods.
    p. cm. — (Biographies in American foreign policy)
  Includes bibliographical references and index.
  ISBN-13: 978-0-7425-4497-0 (cloth : alk. paper)
  ISBN-10: 0-7425-4497-4 (cloth : alk. paper)
 1. Russell, Richard B. (Richard Brevard), 1897–1971. 2. United States. Congress.
Senate—Biography. 3. Legislators—United States—Biography. 4. United States—
Foreign relations—1945–1989. 5. United States—Politics and government—
1945–1989. 6. Southern States—Politics and government—1951– 7. Cold War—
Political aspects—United States. I. Title.
  E748.R944W66 2006
  327.730092—dc22
  [B]   2006020750

Printed in the United States of America

♾™ The paper used in this publication meets the minimum requirements of American
National Standard for Information Sciences—Permanence of Paper for Printed Library
Materials, ANSI/NISO Z39.48-1992.

To Cullen and Abigail

Contents

Acknowledgments ix

Chronology xi

Introduction xv

1 Region, Nation, World 1

2 Central Paradox 27

3 Power and Responsibility 51

4 Two Worlds 79

5 Dove's Lost Cause 113

6 Hawk's Lost Cause 137

Conclusion 161

Bibliographical Essay 165

Index 169

About the Author 173

Acknowledgments

It is customary to thank the series editor for his expert commentary and support. While I certainly owe Andy Fry my thanks, I owe him more than clichés. Andy is a friend and mentor. I can only hope to live up to his unwavering faith in me. It is less customary to thank one's father. My father's contribution to this work, however, merits special recognition. Like many fathers, he gave me his unconditional support, but unlike many, he shared with me thirty-five years of experience as a writer and professional historian. It was to my great advantage as well that he was writing a biography of Lyndon Johnson at the same time I began this work on Johnson's confidant, Richard Russell. I am truly blessed to have Randall Woods as a sounding board, editor, fan, and dad.

Marc Selverstone and Kyle Longley read drafts of the manuscript and made valuable suggestions. Richard McCulley and Sheryl Vogt helped tremendously in directing my research. Robert David Johnson gave me access to his work on Congress and the Cold War. And John Gaddis and Chester Pach first encouraged my study of Russell many years ago when I was a student at Ohio University. Thank you all.

Many others deserve recognition for their help in facilitating the publication of this book. The staff at Scholarly Resources first took the project on, and the staff at Roman & Littlefield completed it. Tom DeBlack and Michael Tarver at Arkansas Tech always did as much as they could to support my work. Students, colleagues, and friends too numerous to list inspired and tolerated me.

My deepest love and thanks to my wife, Andrea, and my children, Abigail and Cullen.

Chronology

1897

NOVEMBER   Richard Brevard Russell is born in Winder, Georgia.

1918

MAY   Russell graduates from the University of Georgia with a law degree.

SEPTEMBER   Russell joins the navy.

1920

NOVEMBER   Russell is elected to the Georgia House of Representatives.

1926

JANUARY   Russell is elected speaker of the Georgia House of Representatives.

1930

NOVEMBER   Russell is elected governor of Georgia.

1932

NOVEMBER   Russell is elected to the United States Senate.

1933

JANUARY   Russell is appointed to the Senate Appropriations, Naval Affairs, and Immigration committees.

1943

JULY   Russell investigates American bases overseas.

1946

AUGUST   Russell is made a member of the Armed Services Committee.

1950

JANUARY   Russell becomes chairman of the Armed
                 Services Committee.

1951

SPRING   MacArthur hearings.
JUNE   Universal Training Act becomes law.

1954

MAY   *Brown v. Board of Education* decision.
MAY   French surrender at Dien Bien Phu.

1957

MARCH   Congress approves Eisenhower Doctrine
                 without Russell substitute.
AUGUST   Congress approves Mutual Security Act.
SEPTEMBER   Little Rock crisis.
OCTOBER   Sputnik.

1960

JUNE   Congolese independence.

1961

APRIL   Bay of Pigs.
APRIL   Laos negotiations begin.

1962

OCTOBER   Cuban Missile Crisis.

1963

SEPTEMBER   Russell opposes Nuclear Test Ban Treaty.
NOVEMBER   Lyndon Johnson becomes president.

1964

JANUARY   Panamanian crisis.
JULY   President Johnson signs the Civil Rights Act.
AUGUST   Gulf of Tonkin Resolution.

1965

APRIL   Dominican crisis.

1966

FALL   Russell first supports anti–ballistic missile
                 system.

1967

MARCH   Russell leads largest defense appropriation
                 to date through Congress.

1968

	JANUARY	Tet Offensive.
	JULY	Russell out of Johnson inner circle.

1969

	JANUARY	Russell gives up leadership of Armed Services to lead Appropriations Committee.
	MARCH	Russell is diagnosed with cancer.

1971

	JANUARY	Russell dies.

Introduction

Richard Russell will be remembered more for what he represented than for what he accomplished in shaping American foreign policy. The Georgian served over thirty-five years in the Senate, amassing an impressive record, including the successful mediation of the MacArthur controversy, prescient warnings about American involvement in Vietnam, and consistent, steadfast support of a strong military. But the principles and causes that the senator from Georgia espoused were increasingly anachronistic. His support of a conservative, race-conscious, noninterventionist foreign policy had become passé in a world coming to embrace liberal internationalism. Russell was a powerful but failed dissident.

There is nevertheless much to be learned from the Georgian's dissent. His was the path not taken, for better and for worse. Had he been allowed to steer the nation's course, the country might have remained racially segregated, isolated from the outside world, and defensively militaristic, but it also might have been less imperialistic, more realistic about its interests and influence, and less likely to have entered the war in Vietnam. That his was the road not taken places Russell, like William Jennings Bryan or John C. Calhoun, in the negative space of American history. His career provides the contrast needed to fully recognize and judge the merits of the path taken.

Richard Russell was well aware that his views were misplaced in time. They were not so much old fashioned as they were slow moving, set at an almost preindustrial pace. As he would tell audiences in 1964, "The tempo of change is the crux of the whole matter." He suggested that the haste of the overzealous, the naive, and the unwise committed the federal government to ill-advised racial reforms, social justice initiatives, and cultural transformation projects at home and abroad. The expectation for liberal change brought by modern transportation and communication technology had put pressure on the state to solve problems it simply could not solve. "The tendency increases each day," Russell said, "to look to government for the cure of every ill, and a law to apply to every adjustment in our way of living." The danger was that power consolidated was power abused. "The shores of human history," he observed, "are littered with the wreckage of great civilizations which destroyed themselves by an undue concentration of power and authority over their citizens."[1]

Richard Russell was born on November 2, 1897. He entered the world at a time when anxiety over the modern pace of change consumed American culture. Frederick Jackson Turner bewailed the end of the frontier, Stephen Crane's bride ingloriously arrived in Yellow Sky, and Henry Adams lamented the moral force of the forty-foot dynamos found in the great hall of the Paris World Exposition. Only months after Russell's birth, the United States fought the Spanish American War, taking its largest, most anxious step to date in building an informal empire. Russell came of age when progress became the political catchword at home and big stick diplomacy gave way to the dawn of liberal internationalism. Then, in the fundamental formative experience of his generation, the momentum of the industrial revolution and America's rise to global power flung the nation into World War I. Like many of his contemporaries, Russell, the patriot, supported his country but came to see the conflict as avoidable, even regrettable. Oddly enough, the Georgian seemed to feel comfortable only during the Great Depression in the 1930s, when America temporarily turned inward and struggled to restrain its optimism for engineering a better world. A liberal in times of want, Russell was a champion of New Deal economic aid in the South, but as the economy recovered, as the country reasserted its influence overseas, and as new federal programs encouraged racial integration, his fiscal conservatism, noninterventionism, and reactionary racism resurfaced. The senator's anxiety was acute as the United States assumed new global responsibilities during World War II and the early days of the Cold War. He put his full weight to the brakes, hoping to slow the pace of change, but by the time he reached the height of his power in the 1950s and 1960s, he knew that he had failed. "We are living in a very troubled world," he confided to his mother in 1948, "and I fear that none of us will again ever see the relative peace and tranquility of the 1930s."[2]

Among Russell's greatest fears was that liberal internationalism, the foreign policy by-product of modernity that had led the United States to assert itself in global matters, rested on a naive sense of optimism, order, and control. Liberal internationalists, Russell intuited, made decisions under the misguided assumption that human society evolved in sudden fits of progress. It was a social Darwinian version of what evolutionary biologist Stephen Jay Gould has called punctuated equilibrium. Under certain complex conditions, liberal internationalists posited, the otherwise slow process of social change exploded in spasms of revolutionary development. The proliferation of democracy worldwide in the nineteenth and twentieth centuries, they felt, constituted that form of rapid human growth. They argued that the United States could help set, or even force, the conditions for punctuated change through the investment of capital, the inculcation of Western education, and the establishment of democratic capitalist institutions.

Russell shared many of the liberal internationalists' goals but questioned their assumptions about the nation's ability to achieve those goals. The Georgian believed, as did the liberal internationalists, that U.S. institutions of government, while not perfect, were certainly "by all odds the best yet devised." They had brought the country "more freedom, more happiness, and more material blessings" than any other in the history of humankind. He also agreed with the liberal internationalists that the future peace and security of the world depended to some degree on the promotion of democracy abroad. "We must strive for the ideal of a world," Russell wrote, "where *all* men are free to give expression to their talents and their thoughts as free men."[3]

But the Georgian doubted the liberal internationalists' supposition that the United States could set the conditions in which democracy might spread. He believed that societies that experienced accelerated change beyond their ability or will were doomed to disorder, destruction, and tyranny. Enlightened men, he agreed, would naturally seek liberty and democracy, the penultimate social compact, but Russell rejected the idea that social progress could be forced. The Georgian was a more traditional social Darwinist. He saw social evolution as a glacial process best left to its natural course. Stable, orderly human change only occurred over many generations, through experimentation and adaptation, not coercion. Russell's rejection of foreign aid, his cautious approach to foreign military adventures, and his generally noninterventionist

tendencies reflected his profound disagreement with liberal internationalist assumptions about rapid, managed, punctuated human
progress.

Russell's concept of a natural, slowly paced social development
was derived in no small part from his Southern roots. Reared in an
agrarian, rural setting, the Georgian understood time as cyclical and
absolute rather than as linear and relative. Furthermore, he saw history through a regional prism. It was the South's experience in the
Civil War and Reconstruction that convinced Russell that societies that
experienced accelerated change beyond their ability or will were
doomed to disorder, destruction, and tyranny. Southern blacks, in his
reading of his region's past, had not been culturally, historically, or
racially ready for their full transition to democratic citizenship, nor
had white Southerners who bore the burden of administering that
change. Russell believed that the federal government of the 1860s,
under assumptions anticipating those of liberal internationalists, had
invested its capital, introduced its social and political institutions, and
imposed its will through the force of arms, only to bring chaos, racial
animosity, Northern despotism, and a Southern sense of resentment
that remained unresolved some three generations later.

The senator's racism bolstered his pessimism about forced
change. While not a race-baiter, at a very basic level he was convinced
that blacks and other nonwhites, given some individual exceptions,
were inferior to those of "pure" Anglo-Saxon stock. Russell measured
that inferiority principally by a race's commitment to liberty and
democracy. It was of the utmost importance, he once wrote, that the
government of the United States should not risk its blood and treasure
"on peoples who are not willing to make substantial sacrifices to
assure for themselves the blessings of liberty." "Real love of democracy," Russell declared, "is a thing of the spirit. It must be generated in
the minds and hearts of those who seek it. It cannot be forced or pur-
chased from abroad."[4] Only whites, and especially Southern whites,
by Russell's reckoning, had generally achieved the "spirit" to be
responsible for their freedom. "The Southern devotion to principle,"
he wrote, had made the region "the bulwark of our democratic institutions." Indeed, the "future hope of this republic," he wrote, rested
"in the natural conservatism and loyalty of the Anglo-Saxon South."[5]
It was not that he believed that non–Anglo Saxon Southerners would
never acquire a "real love of democracy"; it was that in the course of
their social development, they generally had not yet been willing to
sacrifice for the blessings of liberty. It was a fool's errand, he insisted,
to attempt to force an acceptance of that responsibility.

Russell's vision of American foreign policy was thus selectively noninterventionist. He was not, as he wanted to think of himself, an isolationist or a strict proponent of "fortress America." He was willing, for example, to protect American interests abroad through the maintenance of overseas military bases acquired during World War II. Still, he defended a unilateralist position that avoided American economic or military intervention outside of the Western Hemisphere and Western Europe. He was also among the Senate's most virulent critics of foreign aid and military programs in Asia and Africa. And his support of immigration restriction and stronger deportation laws suggested that he not only hoped to reduce American influence abroad but to retard non-Western influence at home.

Russell's support for military preparedness complemented rather than contradicted his noninterventionist tendencies. The Southerner's siege mentality underlay his argument that only greater military strength would save the United States from foreign manipulation and the terrors of a third world war. As he famously told his colleague Milton Young, "You'd be more military minded too if Sherman had crossed North Dakota." It was in the name of deterrence that Russell literally led every measure to increase defense spending in the 1950s and 1960s, pushed for universal military training, and worked to expand the draft. If the modern world were becoming smaller, more interconnected, and more dangerous, Russell argued, only a large military would keep the enemies of the United States at bay. And enemies there were. Totalitarian aggressors posed a legitimate threat to the nation, according to Russell. The United States was in fact the "dike holding back the flood" of Nazi invasion and Communist revolution. He supported lend-lease, the Truman Doctrine, the Marshall Plan, and the North Atlantic Treaty Organization. But America's military efforts, he argued, must be limited to protecting its immediate economic and strategic interests rather than promoting democracy among those not yet ready to bear its responsibilities. America's mission, for Russell, was ecumenical but not evangelical.[6]

By the 1950s, Russell could muster tremendous power in support of his foreign policy views. He first chaired the Armed Services Committee in 1951, after having served on that committee since its origins in 1946 and on one of its precursors, the Naval Affairs Committee, since his first term in the Senate in 1933. He had also been a member of the powerful Appropriations Committee from his first Senate term. Additionally, Russell headed the Defense Appropriations Subcommittee and the Central Intelligence Agency Oversight Subcommittee, and he was a member of the Joint Committee on Atomic Energy. His power also came from his leadership of the Southern bloc. He swayed votes not only on civil rights issues but on many defense issues as well. Finally, his reputation for integrity, empathy, and subtlety earned him the respect and devotion of his colleagues, and his hidden-hand style of leadership protected his political flanks. Cumulatively this meant that Russell acted as a control valve for the knowledge and money necessary for the United States to wage the Cold War.

Despite his influence over American defense and foreign policy, Russell could never significantly alter the nation's course. The senator's power was in many ways constrained, even self-limited. As head of the Armed Services Committee, for example, he had little choice but to support the military; otherwise, he would lose influence in deciding how the military might be used. And his devotion to the separation of powers made him self-consciously accept the executive prerogative in making foreign policy. But most significantly, Russell was ideologically out of step with the liberal internationalists who dominated American foreign policy between 1945 and 1969.

Even as his friend and protégé Lyndon Johnson became president, Russell had only limited effect in persuading the administration of his vision of American interests and responsibilities. The pace of change that Russell had felt accelerating beyond reason only continued to build speed in the Johnson years. The president's escalation in Vietnam represented the breaking point. Russell, despite an impressive record of support for research, education, and economic development in his state, continued to see the world through the eyes of the "Old South." He valued traditional, agrarian, cyclical consistency and self-reliance. Johnson, on the other hand, was very much a disciple of the "New South." He prized modern, industrial, linear development and cooperation. The two had always managed to find common cause as Southerners, but when Johnson fully committed the United States to nation building in Vietnam, their fundamentally divergent perspectives became apparent. The Texan believed that with the help of the United States, sufficient advancements could be made in Vietnam in the short term to secure a capitalist, democratic government. The Georgian did not. Vietnamese peasants were as ready for change imposed from the outside, he thought, as rural Southerners. That he could not accept the president's assumptions about progress in Southeast Asia meant that Richard Russell truly lived in a world that for better and worse had passed him by.

Notes

1. "Senator Russell of Georgia: Does He Speak for the Whole South?" *Newsweek* 62 (August 14, 1963). Also found in *Congressional Record*, 88th Cong., 1st sess., 1963, 109, pt. 11:14864–66; Calvin Mcleod Logue and Dwight L. Freshley, eds., *Voice of Georgia: Speeches of Richard B. Russell, 1928–1969* (Macon, GA: Mercer University Press, 1997), 66; Gilbert Fite, *Richard B. Russell, Jr., Senator from Georgia* (Chapel Hill: University of North Carolina Press, 1991), 223.

2. Fite, *Russell*, 223.

3. Logue and Freshley, *Speeches of Richard B. Russell*, 58–60.

4. Logue and Freshley, *Speeches of Richard B. Russell*, 62.

5. Logue and Freshley, *Speeches of Richard B. Russell*, 42.

6. Fite, *Russell*, 282, 353.

1

Region, Nation, World

Richard Russell was a Southerner first and foremost. His regional identity shaped all that he did personally and professionally. It was the foundation of his sense of community, security, and order, and it framed his understanding of human history. It was as a Southerner that he approached the world.

Richard Russell was born on November 2, 1897, the year that William McKinley was elected president after trouncing Populist Democrat William Jennings Bryan, and the year that the revolution raging ninety miles from U.S. shores in Cuba reached a critical stage. Within just a few months, the United States fought and won a war that established a new relationship with the world. The nation acquired its first noncontiguous territories, began to build a network of naval and commercial bases, and aspired to great power status. Reacting to its passive, noninterventionist, amateur, and partisan roots, American foreign policy entered the twentieth century with a more active, internationalist, professional, and consensus-driven agenda. Born into the moment of this great transition, Russell would spend his life trying to unravel its mysteries and control its course for the benefit of his state, region, and country.

Richard Russell, called Dick by his friends, was born and raised near Winder, Georgia, a small farming community thirty miles northwest of Athens. His childhood was in some ways typical of a rural, white, reasonably affluent Southern boy. He worked on his father's farm chopping wood, hauling dirt, and mending fences, but he was at leisure to spend at least as much time in the red dust hunting, playing baseball, or pretending to fight Civil War battles from a homemade "Fort Lee." He attended the local Methodist church, and when old enough he courted most of the local girls close to his age. The black people he knew were tenants on his father's land. He was taught to treat them with neither disdain nor affection. "Negroes" or "colored people," as he called them, were human beings generally due a minimum courtesy, even respect, but they were also social and intellectual inferiors not to be trusted as intimates.

In other ways, though, young Dick's life was exceptional. He was the eldest son of thirteen children and was expected from an early age to rise above his peers. His father saw to that. Richard Russell Sr. was no ordinary farmer. A graduate of the University of Georgia, a lawyer, a reader of five languages, and committed to a life of public service, he was the kind of renaissance man Thomas Jefferson had lauded as the ideal citizen. He was elected to the Georgia House of Representatives at twenty-two years of age and became solicitor general and judge superior of the superior court of the western judicial district of Georgia. He edited and owned his own newspapers, founded the town of Russell, and eventually won election to the Georgia supreme court. Russell Sr.'s greatest commitment was to the education of his children, a sentiment shared by his wife, Ina, no slouch herself as a graduate of Emory College and a teacher in the Athens public schools. Suspicious of the public education their children might receive in Winder, Richard Sr. and Ina established their own school. Dick had no choice but to do well. His parents expected him not only to follow in his father's footsteps but to leave an even bigger imprint.

Though he was sometimes anxious and overwhelmed, the young man adapted well to his parents' high expectations. Mature beyond his age, he was at times a brilliant student. He excelled to the point that he was able to skip the fifth grade entirely. But Russell junior stumbled when his father sent him away to study at some of the best private schools in the state. Lonely and oppressed by his father's expectations, young Dick sought refuge in dates and parties. Still, he managed to earn marks sufficient to gain entry to the University of Georgia where he dutifully completed a law degree.

Richard Russell's most enduring quality was his intellectual curiosity, especially when it came to history. He reported reading a book on the Russo-Japanese War at the age of ten and was repeatedly caught skipping school, not to go fishing but to read his favorite books on the American Civil War. Compared to his fellow rural Georgians, he was well traveled. Atlanta, Athens, and Savannah were frequent destinations as young Dick accompanied his father on political trips. He even visited Washington, D.C., and Montreal before he completed high school; most of his contemporaries would never leave the state, much less the country. His father's expectations, his reading of history, and his exposure to travel afforded Russell a sense of place in the world and a certain cosmopolitanism that served him well throughout his life.

No matter how far Russell traveled or read, he never became a global citizen. His region always came first. As *Time* magazine put it in a cover story in the summer of 1957, "Dick was brought up to become nothing less than a repository of Southern traditions and an exemplar of Southern character." Family lore imbued him with a sense of reverence for the region's history. The Russells had lived in South Carolina and Georgia since colonial times, eventually settling in Marietta where Dick's great-grandfather had established a successful cotton mill. When General Sherman's troops approached on their march to the sea in 1864, the Russell men courageously joined the Confederate militia to confront the hated Yankees, only to be defeated. Northern troops burned the Russell mill to the ground and freed the Russells' thirty-five to forty slaves, one of whom went on to serve in the reconstructed Georgia state legislature. Though the family quickly rebuilt its textile business after the war, Dick's inherited memory of Reconstruction was bitter indeed. His favorite book on the subject was Claude Bower's *The Tragic Era*, which described Reconstruction as a disastrous time of carpetbagger and black control of state government. The history of home and family for Richard Russell, then, was one that embraced the heroic but futile efforts of the South in the Civil War and the region's tragic mistreatment in the years immediately after.[1]

It was thus with a loyal son's gut instinct to protect his own that Russell defended his beloved South. An overwrought speech delivered to the United Daughters of the Confederacy in 1930 accurately conveyed his sense of Southern history. When "the last waver of the bloody shirt of sectional hate" had passed, he said, and the "dispassionate judgment of America reaches a true verdict on the Civil War," the entire nation would "seek to share the glory which hallows the achievements of the Old South." It was an "epic story of the devotion to principle"—principle, he argued, that included "the cause of local self-government and home rule and defense of country, home and liberty." The South's commitment in the Civil War was the "brightest page of American history" and the "proudest tradition of our national life." Dixie, he insisted, could claim a heritage of "honor, chivalry, and devotion to ideals . . . without parallel in all the annals of history." Any who dared impugn that legacy and insult his heritage suffered Russell's quick, passionate, even vicious response.[2]

Russell never lost that defensive sense of Southernness, even after thirty-eight years of serving his country in the United States Senate. Indeed, Russell's patriotism, his devotion to the United States, was but a by-product of his regional identity. The South for him represented the "bulwark of democratic institutions" in the nation and the world. It was in the South that democratic health had been passed on like a gene. The commitment to responsible citizenship necessary to sustain democracy, according to Russell, had been handed from the Anglo-Saxons to Southern whites. But his "love of the memories of the stars and bars" did not mean "disloyalty to the stars and stripes." Rather, it was the South that would save democracy for the nation and the world. "The future hope of this republic," he sincerely told audiences of fellow Southerners, "rests in the natural conservatism and loyalty of the Anglo-Saxon South."[3]

Richard Russell was thus an odd mix of open-minded worldly wisdom and myopic regional pride. It left him endlessly interested in global affairs but profoundly distrustful of the world outside of the South, a romantic when his gaze turned toward home but a realist when focused abroad. With these predilections firmly ensconced during his formative years, Russell entered manhood and political life as a Southern exceptionalist committed to preserving his home and heritage in a hostile universe.

Ironically, it was a time when the South seemed once again poised to become a player in world affairs. In the spring of 1913, Dick, his father, and a contingent of Russell family members attended the inauguration of Woodrow Wilson. Born in Virginia and reared in Georgia and the Carolinas, Wilson was the first Democrat elected president in twenty years and the first native Southerner since before the Civil War. His inauguration represented for the Russells and most Southerners the region's return to greatness. In many ways, it was. The Democratic Congress placed Southerners in key leadership positions of both houses, and Wilson selected five native Southerners for his cabinet, including his closest adviser on foreign policy, Texas Colonel Edward M. House.

Wilson's approach to foreign policy, though, would veer away from the South's traditional noninterventionism in critical ways. He, more than any other president, established liberal internationalism as the driving force in U.S. foreign relations. Wilson sought world order through peaceful international cooperation organized around capitalist and democratic principles: self-determination, free trade, mutual defense, anti-imperialism, and representative government. Out of loyalty to the president and the Democratic Party, Southerners generally backed this agenda as manifested in the U.S. intervention in Mexico, the decision to join the battle in World War I, and, perhaps most surprisingly, the president's drive to establish the United States as a member of the League of Nations. Nevertheless, many Southerners, including Richard Russell, maintained foreign policy perspectives closer to the unilateralist, independent, cautious internationalism espoused by Wilson's principal adversary, Henry Cabot Lodge.[4]

Russell's sense of Southern exceptionalism, combined with his formative experiences in the 1910s and 1920s, influenced his initial responses to U.S. foreign policy. Russell was in his second year of college when the United States entered World War I. Admitting less courage than his forbears in the Civil War, Russell avoided service until the fall of 1918, after he had completed his law degree. Two months before the armistice and just short of his twenty-first birthday, he signed up with the U.S. Navy. For seventy-nine miserable days, Russell served as an apprentice seaman in Athens, far from any significant body of water. Though he would always be proud to call himself a veteran, his belated and brief participation spoke both to a then still-immature sense of public duty and to his reluctance to connect personally to global affairs.

Russell's early public life was dominated by local concerns. After his discharge, he returned home to join the family law practice. Under the ever-present demands of his father and a professed desire to meet clients and jury members in his community, Russell ran for and won a spot in the Georgia House of Representatives in 1920. At twenty-four years old, he was then the youngest member of the state legislature. He quickly hooked up with a group of "young Turks" committed to progressive reform and erasing the "redneck" image of Georgia. During a career in the Georgia legislature that lasted until 1930 and saw the young upstart elevated to speaker of the house, he served on the committees on rules, constitutional amendments, public property, higher education, agriculture, labor, the judiciary, taxes, and highways. No part of his early public life was significantly committed to affairs beyond his home state.

When Russell expressed himself concerning international affairs in this period, his remarks were fraught with a sense of foreboding and caution. When the elder Russell challenged Walter George for a U.S. Senate seat in 1926, for example, the campaign that Dick helped run made George's "dangerous internationalism" a key issue. The Russells would have voted to stay out of the League of Nations and the World Court. When Richard Jr. visited the capitols of Europe in

1927, he reported that the ongoing distrust among nations rendered another war likely. A strong defense and commitment to U.S. independence of action, he suggested, constituted the wisest response to a still hostile world.

Typical was the young state representative's 1928 Armistice Day address to the students and faculty of his high school alma mater, Gordon Military Academy. The United States had entered World War I with lofty, altruistic ideals to ensure "every people the right to determine for themselves the form of government they should have," and to bring a "day of universal peace among all of the nations of the world." Despite "the unselfish sacrifice of America, the world still gropes for a real peace based upon mutual understanding and good will." Selfishness and imperialism still dominated world politics, he suggested, regardless of the courageous attempts to outlaw war. Even among its closest allies, America had found only ingratitude. Its request for repayment of loans, Russell declared, had gained the appellation "Uncle Shylock" rather than "Unquestioned Saviors." In such a world, it behooved the nation to avoid the mistakes of the late world war by maintaining a strong military through universal training. Should war break out again, "then every resource of our country—men, material, wealth, industry, agriculture, commerce, all of talent and capacity and energy of every description—shall be drafted to make the supreme and united and unselfish fight for the national triumph." When "we enact this principle into law and national policy," Russell argued, "we will have less of war, if we do not abolish it altogether."[5]

Other than the occasional speech alluding to foreign affairs, Russell remained focused almost exclusively on state issues during the early 1930s. As was true for most Americans, the Great Depression concentrated his mind on the most pressing internal needs. Nevertheless, during those years, Russell developed political positions and styles that would contribute significantly to his later influence on foreign affairs. A commitment to populist/progressive reform had clearly become a part of the Georgian's political persona over the 1920s. In a successful bid for governor in 1930, Russell expressed a devotion to the people over parties, factions, and machines. He called for greater equality in public education and taxes and support for farmers whom he declared to be the backbone of the country. Russell retained this dedication to the plain folk as he later weighed the costs of foreign entanglements for the American public.

Russell also committed himself to greater efficiency and economy in government. As governor, he reorganized state administrative practices on a business basis, eliminating waste and balancing the budget. He understood that resources, especially in time of want, were limited. The costs of change would always need to be weighed against the benefits to his constituents, a calculation that he never failed to make when contemplating foreign affairs.

Though never a rabid, demagogic racist, Russell also believed strongly that the best safeguard for American democracy was Anglo-Saxon domination. In his 1931 inaugural address, the governor asserted that Georgia had rejected communism and socialism because it had held firm to the "ideals and institutions which have ever guided the Anglo-Saxon in government."[6] Conversely, he argued throughout his career that nonwhites were not yet ready to take responsibility for democracy, either at home or abroad.

Finally, Russell adopted a political style that won him supporters from all political camps. Publicly, he made a career of taking reasonable and compromising positions on issues, sometimes avoiding them altogether. In hidden-hand fashion, he left more controversial matters to his lieutenants and supporters. Preparing for his 1926 race for state speaker of the house, for example, Russell lay low while his supporters tackled the contentious education and road reform programs introduced by then governor Clifford Walker. His safe public persona worked only because of behind-the-scenes cajoling, encouraging, and manipulating in what might be called the Russell treatment. When Roy Harris, a powerful former ally in the state house, made plans to oppose him in the speaker's race, Russell's supporters informed Harris that the representative from Winder had already gathered enough votes to win. It was part of a ploy the young Turks had used on each house member: win by leaving the impression that "Dick is already elected," and the only reasonable choice was to "get on the bandwagon and enjoy the ride."[7] Whatever later influence he had on foreign affairs depended largely on this style of public and private maneuvering.

Only when he ran for a U.S. Senate seat in 1932 did Russell directly address American foreign policy. That year, Senator William J. Harris (D-GA) died of a heart attack, leaving an unexpired term that would end in 1936. Governor Russell and U.S. representative Charles Crisp (D-GA) jumped at the opportunity to fill the post. As the campaign turned to foreign affairs, Russell struck a cautious, nationalist, and even isolationist stance. He repeated his and his father's opposition to U.S. participation in the League of Nations and World Court and promised to fight any agreement or alliance that might result in the deaths of American boys sent to settle overseas conflicts. He then attacked his opponent for supporting a moratorium on the collection of foreign debts that cost the American taxpayer $10 billion. He also criticized Crisp's support of the Smoot-Hawley Tariff, which Russell argued had cost American farmers dearly. Promises to support further immigration restrictions and thereby defend American workers rounded out Russell's protectionist position.

Russell's defense of the American taxpayer and especially the American farmer resonated in Depression-era Georgia. His close association with Franklin Delano Roosevelt's presidential campaign also won support. Russell had attended and befriended Roosevelt when his fellow governor from New York traveled to Warm Springs, Georgia, for polio rehabilitation therapy. That friendship paved the way for the Senate candidate to deliver the seconding speech for FDR at the 1932 Democratic National Convention. Russell's populist, isolationist campaign on the coattails of Roosevelt's presidential victory gained him 58 percent of the popular vote and the vacant Senate seat.

When Russell entered the Senate in January 1933, he was, at thirty-five years of age, the youngest man in the chamber. At the same time, he could boast over ten years of political experience in some of the highest offices in his state. He knew how to build a power base. Russell approached Majority Leader Joe T. Robinson (D-AR) and insisted that he be assigned to the Appropriations Committee; with direct control over the nation's purse strings, it was arguably the most powerful committee in Congress. Hoping to keep Russell from joining a group of Senate insurgents led by Louisiana's Huey Long, Robinson granted the Georgian's wish. Although his position on the Appropriations Committee remained a source of Russell's power throughout his career, it was his other assignments—Naval Affairs, Immigration, and the Subcommittee on Agricultural Appropriations—that gained him his first influence over U.S. foreign policy.

Richard Russell was an agrarian. While never really a farmer himself, he grew up in rural Georgia, working occasionally for his father and neighboring farmers. More important than his work experience was his mythic attachment to agriculture. He respected, and even idealized, the independent yeoman's way of life. On the stump, he often referred to himself as a Jeffersonian Democrat, devoted to the idea that the citizens best equipped to decide the economic, social, and political welfare of the nation were rural, self-sufficient, and, of course, Southern farmers. Like Jefferson, Russell tied democratic virtue to those who by necessity generated for themselves the basics of life, such as food, shelter, and clothing, as well as the luxuries, like commerce, art, and education. Like William Jennings Bryan, Russell believed that farmers had been treated unfairly as the nation came to rely more on industry and finance in the late nineteenth century. As the backbone of America and the keepers of the nation's purity, stability, and economic strength, farmers needed and deserved the government's protection. Russell's worldview was also similar in many respects to the Southern Agrarians, particularly John Crowe Ransom, Allen Tate, and Donald Davidson. These men shared an antipathy toward centralized bureaucracy as an alternative to organic, slow-paced change. Russell, like the Agrarians, would argue against any societal change forced upon individuals by any other group, especially a group whose power emanated from outside the region. Southern farmers deserved economic aid, but never the social or moral guidance of their fellow citizens.

Russell's agrarian predilection made him a Southern exceptionalist, a nationalist, and a protectionist. Conspicuous among his commitments in the 1930s was the defense of Southern cotton farmers. Russell advocated stiff tariffs on jute, an import that competed with cotton for use in burlap bags, furniture lining, and carpet backing. In campaign speeches, he argued that he was protecting the average man against the powerful jute trust and international bankers seeking control through the federal government. In what would be a lifelong argument, Russell also began balancing foreign aid commitments against domestic farmers' needs. In 1940, for example, he voted against an eventually successful aid package to Finland after the Russian invasion. How could the government assist Finland, he asked, and do nothing for American tenant farmers and sharecroppers?

Russell's concept of white racial purity in the South dovetailed with his vision of an ideal Southern agrarian society. The relatively homogenous white South had inherited both agrarian and Anglo-Saxon democratic traditions by segregating nonwhites, who Russell believed were less inclined to adopt those traditions. Segregation was no less important in preserving the democratic purity of the South than farming. His decision on almost all legislative matters rested to some degree on its impact on farmers and segregation. His support for New Deal measures, for example, depended on how they benefited farmers. Like so many Southerners, Russell's allegiance to the New Deal wavered when programs threatened to change regional labor or racial practices. It is not surprising, then, that the Georgia senator's decisions on foreign policy were equally determined by his commitment to his farming and segregationist constituents.

Where Russell made tariffs and foreign aid part of his defense of farmers, he made immigration restriction part of his defense of white supremacy. The senator feared that if the waves of new Eastern European, Latin American, and East Asian immigrants were left unchecked, these newcomers, like assimilated blacks, could dilute the democratic spirit he deemed inherent in Anglo-Saxon culture. Throughout the mid-1930s, he introduced bills to further restrict immigration and strengthen the government's power to deport aliens. When the Truman administration called for the loosening of immigration restrictions to relieve Europe of refugees and homeless peoples in 1947, Russell revealed his ultimate intentions. Among the fiercest opponents of Truman's plan, he argued that the National Origins Act of 1924, which set stricter quotas for Southern and Eastern Europeans and banned immigration from East Asia, struck the perfect balance in controlling the flow of aliens. Even after Truman's Displaced Persons Act was reintroduced in 1948 with quotas reduced by half, Russell still voted against it.

It was not merely the long-term degenerative effects of immigrants that Russell feared. He consistently argued that aliens posed a direct threat to national security. In part, this was the result of genuine concerns about spies and saboteurs crossing open American borders. It was also part of a larger pattern of thought apparent in Russell's public utterances during the 1930s that efforts to fully assimilate nonwhites served the interests of the enemies of the state, namely Fascists or Communists. As the global threat increased during World War II, both considerations influenced his push for stricter deportation laws and registration requirements as ways to prevent spies from infiltrating the country. These apprehensions also drove his support of a bill to grant foreign service officers the authority to deny visas to aliens who might endanger the public safety. The Cold War only served to reinforce Russell's nativist tendencies. While arguing for quota restrictions in 1948, for example, he cited his concern that Communist agents could easily slip into the United States among the mostly nonwhite newcomers.[8]

Despite his efforts to restrict immigration and protect farmers, Russell ultimately understood that global trade and immigration were realities of the modern world. Strict isolationism was impossible, but the United States still needed to safeguard its interests in a dangerous world. For Russell, the only real protection of his home in such a world was a strong military. In one of his first trips as a Navy Committee member, Russell visited Haiti, the Panama Canal, and San Diego to inspect naval bases in late summer 1933. He found squadrons of planes taking off from the U.S. aircraft carrier *Saratoga* most impressive. From that point on, Russell unceasingly pushed the United States to become the world's greatest naval and air power.

Military power meant U.S. freedom of action for this advocate of rural independent yeomanry. It enabled the United States to chart its own course regardless of allies and international pressure. But a strong military, Russell sensed, must be almost entirely defensive in nature. During the period prior to World War II, he remained ambivalent about U.S. involvement in world affairs. Even cautious engagement, he understood, could change the nation's destiny in unexpected ways and accelerate its evolution beyond what he believed to be a safe, organic pace. So, while Russell argued for a strong defense and national preparedness, he remained a critic of wartime profiteering leading to overseas entanglements. Like Republican senator Gerald Nye of North Dakota, who famously led an investigation of the war industry in the early 1930s, Russell suspected that the entry of the United States in World War I had resulted in part from pressure from bankers, corporations, and the munitions industry.

The senator's reluctance to involve the United States in world affairs was evident in his first major foreign policy vote. Congress was considering a resolution that would pledge the United States to adhere to the decisions of the World Court. Russell considered the resolution "an abandonment of the time-honored foreign policy under which our country has prospered and grown great and populous." It was a step toward membership in the League of Nations and the commitment of American boys to "settling Asiatic brawls and European quarrels that are of no remote concern to us." He reminded his colleagues that neither the League, nor the World Court, nor any other international body had kept the peace. Mussolini and the Italian Fascists were at that very hour repudiating pacifism and denying the possibility and utility of perpetual peace in preparation for their invasion of Ethiopia. America must protect its interests, Russell asserted, but he "would not sacrifice the life of one American youth, in a quarrel in which he has no stake and which he does not understand, to save the lives of 10,000 citizens of another land."[9] Operating under the same assumptions, Russell voted for the Neutrality Act of 1936, which banned loans and credits to warring nations.

Like George Washington, the senator believed that "if we desire to secure peace, it must be known that we are at all times ready for war." On February 22, 1938, the first president's 206th birthday, Russell reflected on Washington's famous farewell address in which the president warned American leaders never to put another nation's interests above the United States. It was nearly two years after Germany reoccupied the Rhineland, a year and a half after the beginning of the Spanish Civil War, and six months after the outbreak of the

Sino-Japanese War. The war to end all wars had not lived up to its promise, Russell declared to his radio audience. "The devouring flames of war sweep parts of two hemispheres today. . . . Women and children are being blown to bits by artillery fire and aerial bombs." Americans were not a militaristic people and desired only peace, he proclaimed, but the "present-day spirit of imperialistic conquest can only be held in check by fear." "To insure peace," he advised, "our national forces must be strong enough to protect this country from any nation which may seek war." The navy and air force must be the first line of defense as the nation came to "depend on no allies for our protection." Russell's warnings came four months after President Roosevelt delivered his Quarantine Speech insisting that the United States fulfill its duty in checking the world's aggressors. It came seven months before the Munich Conference, where the European nations appeased Adolph Hitler, granting him occupation of the Sudetenland in return for the promise that Germany would refrain from taking further territory.[10]

Through 1940 and 1941, Russell voted for every piece of legislation designed to strengthen the military, including especially aircraft procurement measures and the draft. He also introduced an amendment to the Selective Service Act of 1940 that authorized the drafting of any manufacturing plant that refused national security contracts. Still wary of wartime profiteering, Russell hoped to tie business interests exclusively to U.S. defense while controlling the amount of money business could make from that relationship. Industry, like the individual citizen, Russell declared, must make sacrifices for the common defense. He wanted to ensure that in this war, business was behind the government rather than in front of it.[11]

And war was becoming a distinct possibility. Preparations were increasingly urgent after France fell to the Nazis and Britain's supplies ran dangerously low. Russell, like President Roosevelt, still hoped to avoid war if possible. The senator's vote to repeal the neutrality acts, ending the legal restrictions that prevented the United States from supporting its European allies, and his vote for lend-lease, the program to supply European allies with loans of military equipment and other commodities, grew mostly from a desire to show enough American force and solidarity with Britain to prevent further German and Japanese aggression. Russell did not act from any calculated scheme to involve the United States in the war, even though the realist senator recognized that American entry was a distinct possibility. Where other isolationists might deceive themselves concerning the seriousness of Axis expansionism, the descendant of Confederate

Georgians whose property had been burned by General Sherman could not. "We hope and pray that we may avoid sending our young manhood into the maelstrom of war," Russell told an audience on November 11, 1941, "but in calm common sense we may as well face the issue. The test is on." Every citizen, from the industrial worker, farmer, and draftee to the banker and business owner, he proclaimed, must "cheerfully sacrifice" in defense of his own freedom against "totalitarianism."[12]

Russell would later recall December 7 and December 8, 1941, as "the grimmest days of my lifetime." He recalled the "look of bewilderment" on the faces of his colleagues that he knew "was reflected from my own face" after the attack on Pearl Harbor. Unsure of the damage at Pearl or whether the attack would be carried to the West Coast, he "felt the strain of the responsibility which was imposed upon us as the representatives of the American people." It was with little reflection or doubt, however, that he and the Congress adopted declarations of war on Japan, Germany, and Italy. For Russell, it was clearly no less than a "great war for survival as a free people, into which we had been thrust by the treacherous action of our enemies."[13]

The war, like the New Deal, generated a multitude of economic benefits for the South, but the cost was greater federal control over the region's traditions and institutions, especially those having to do with race. Well-positioned Southerners like Russell could steer federal contracts for military bases and defense plants to their home states or others in the region. Georgia's war machine—the base at Fort Benning, the air depot in Macon, the shipbuilding facilities in Savannah and Bruswick, and after 1943 the Bell aircraft plant in Marietta—all experienced significant growth due to wartime contracts. But wartime pork brought with it a direct challenge to segregation. As the need for soldiers depleted the labor supply in the South, war industry looked to blacks to fill job openings. Seeing the need to increase production efficiency, and under pressure from civil rights advocates, the Roosevelt administration issued an executive order establishing the Fair Employment Practices Commission and outlawing employment discrimination on the basis of race, color, or religion in the defense industry.

Russell's national security priorities were, of course, different. He certainly saw the benefit of federal economic programs in his home state. He had been among the strongest advocates of government loans to small farmers and sharecroppers in the 1930s. His ideas, in fact, had contributed to the formation of the Resettlement Administration and the Farm Security Administration. A safety net for poor agricultural workers, black and white, he argued, would reduce political and social unrest as well as help prevent future depressions, but Russell also had long argued that segregation was necessary for order and democracy in the South. Federal efforts to chip away at the region's racial traditions, Russell maintained, generated animosity and resentment. At a time when farm prices were recovering and the war effort demanded a new unity of purpose, Russell decided that maintaining the status quo racial order was more important to the country's internal security.

When the House of Representatives passed a bill to eliminate the poll tax in Georgia and seven other Southern states, its proponents suggested that the tax unfairly disfranchised blacks as they and the nation were being called to fight for democratic principles on the battlefields of Europe and the Pacific. Russell responded angrily. The poll tax, he argued, had no bearing on an individual's willingness to fight. Citizens from poll tax states had bravely fought in every American war since the Revolution. While he admitted that the tax might be outmoded, he maintained that it was the state's prerogative to decide the issue. Federal intrusion in this case, Russell went on, amounted to an attack on the South not seen since Reconstruction. It was an insult mounted by the "professional South hater in the United States" and was designed to "tear down good relations which men of good will in both races have painstakingly and earnestly created." Indeed, Russell suggested, the reintroduction of the poll tax issue in Congress was part of a Communist plot "to array one race against the other." While he admitted that Russia was a powerful ally in the war and could follow the form of government it wished on its own land, Communist efforts to change race relations in the United States during the war amounted to an undermining of order and unity, an imposition of statist power, and a threat to national security. The 1942 poll tax bill eventually fell before a Southern filibuster, as did a subsequent attempt to pass the measure in 1944. Georgia repealed its poll tax only after the war had ended.[14]

During the early 1940s, Russell became obsessed with the fear that the extensive wartime powers granted to the executive branch were being used to upset Southern racial institutions. He expended more energy in fighting issues like the poll tax and the Fair Employment Practices Commission (FEPC) than anything else. The FEPC in particular, Russell felt, was an abuse of executive power under the guise of national security. Enforcing a ban on racial discrimination in war industries by executive order, he argued, unconstitutionally deprived a government contractor of the right of appeal and infringed upon the authority of Congress to legislate. Moreover,

Russell considered the FEPC to be "the most sickening manifestation of the trend that is now in effect to force social equality and miscegenation of the white and black races on the South." In this trend toward federal integration efforts, Russell foresaw the coming end of "Southern civilization," and with it, in his mind, republican virtue. While the United States might win World War II, it risked cutting out its own heart, the South, in the process.[15]

Russell biographer Gilbert Fite rightly pointed to the senator's central predicament as FEPC regulations were enforced over his objections: "His [Russell's] very success in helping to expand old federal facilities and to bring new ones into Georgia during the war worked against the status quo in race relations."[16] Russell sought to curb federal benefits to minorities. In 1944, for example, he attempted to limit the amount of money given to war industry workers who were "members of any race comprising less than 15% of the total population of the United States," in other words, any race but white.[17]

Regardless of his concerns about racial discord resulting from war industry regulations, Russell worked hard to tie his home state to the military effort. He actively recruited for the navy and helped establish Georgia's first aircraft production facilities. These were the kind of wartime projects that U.S. senators typically undertook. It was not until Russell's appointment to head a Senate committee investigating the foreign battlefields and military installations of the United States that his name became synonymous with American defense.

In July 1943, Democratic majority leader Alben Barkley of Kentucky asked Russell to lead a group of senators charged with investigating American bases overseas. The idea was to duplicate abroad the Truman Committee's oversight of domestic military production, distribution, quality, and spending efficiency. Russell, Albert Chandler (D-KY), Henry Cabot Lodge Jr. (R-MA), James Mead (D-NY), and Ralph Brewster (R-ME) took off from Washington on board a converted Liberator bomber. With dog tag, helmet, compass, knife, jungle survival guide, emergency rations, and extra cigarettes—a must for the chain-smoking Russell—the senators flew over Greenland and Iceland toward southwest England. Stretching over sixty-five days, the trip took them to Morocco, across North Africa to Egypt, and on to India, China, Australia, and New Guinea. Along the way, they met Winston Churchill, Dwight Eisenhower, Chiang Kai-shek, and Douglas MacArthur.

Exposure to the world outside of Winder and Washington, in the company of the globe's most powerful leaders, only accentuated Russell's provincialism and deepened his prejudices. His travel notes and letters mentioned the "squalor and different races" of North Africa, the "indescribably filthy" Arab cities, and the "no good" Chinese. He described black American soldiers in Calcutta as simply "chaotic."[18] The war had not only exposed the South to integration, but in Russell's eyes it had made the United States vulnerable to the decadence and corruption of the world.

Yet the Georgian recognized that American power was being used to tremendous effect. The productive capabilities of the United

Senator Richard Russell chats with a constituent, Andrew Boss, at Utah Beach, France, May 29, 1945. Courtesy of the Richard B. Russell Library for Political Research and Studies, Athens, Georgia.

States were turning the tide of battle in Europe and the Pacific. American troops, who according to Russell constituted "the best fed, best equipped, and best provided armed forces the world had ever seen," were bravely facing down the enemy across the globe. The realist in him understood that therein lay an opportunity for broadening U.S. power in the postwar world.

Russell's conclusions about his trip, outlined in his most important statement concerning the war and the future of U.S. relationships in the world, once again revealed a passive-aggressive approach to foreign policy. If not for the opportunism of committee members, especially Henry Cabot Lodge Jr., it was a statement that might never have been made publicly. Russell had planned to release a report agreed upon by the full committee in early October, after the members had met in executive session to discuss the language. But Lodge upstaged Russell and undercut the committee on September 30, when he delivered his personal account of the trip to the Senate. Other committee members took their cue from Lodge, speaking openly to the press about their own views following the executive session meeting on October 7, with some even quoting the chairman.

Russell dutifully delivered the findings of the full committee, but he seethed at his colleagues' violation of the secrecy agreement that protected executive session meetings. Some of his comments that had been leaked to the press had been frankly critical of America's allies, provoking editorial criticism. Russell was hurt and angry. On October 28, he publicly chastised his colleagues' disregard for the rules and the subsequent "confusion and distortion" of his views.

The statement, filling seven pages of the *Congressional Record*, amounted to a white paper on Russell's view of the conduct of the war and his vision of international relations in the postwar world. The global war had wrought changes in production, transportation, and communication previously undreamed of. Mobile factories and hospitals followed the army from China to North Africa as the American military coordinated action with allies from England to Russia. Russell acknowledged the emergence of a brave new world of interdependency in which American security depended on a sober assessment of the nation's strengths and limitations. He urged that the United States continue to supply its allies in China, especially General Claire Chennault's air forces, but Russell warned that the American investment would not ultimately buy stability or political reform in China. The Chinese "form of government lacks many of the elements of a democracy," he declared. Although Chiang Kai-shek embodied China's "last best hope of salvation as a free and unified democratic state," his efforts would continue to be met with "great difficulties." Russell also recognized the need to keep troops in India and work with the British there to maintain a strategic foothold, but again, any hope for political or social reform should be tempered by a clear understanding of conditions on the ground. Russell's initial reading of those conditions led him to the conclusion that "it would require unremitting investigation over many years to even faintly understand the so-called Indian problem." With a keen Southern sense of race, nationalism, and social evolution, he warned of the "complex problem posed by the conflicts between castes and creeds, Indian Nationalists and British Government, ancient ingrained habit and today's civilization."[19]

Russell, the cautious internationalist and fiscal conservative, coupled military spending with opposition to American efforts at nation building. The United States must help the poor and starving, Russell suggested, but it could not rebuild regions devastated by war or ravaged by colonialism. The expectations of its allies that the United States would "look after all of the needs of the world" and "restore the destruction wrought by this war" was great, he reported. Therefore, it was time to make clear that the government did "not consider it the responsibility of the United States to rebuild destroyed cities or embark upon any long-time program of relief." "Let them know in the last analysis they will be compelled to work out their own destiny and restore the destruction of war by their own efforts." While alliances with nations like Great Britain would be crucial in the postwar world, Russell believed the United States could not "afford to rely upon even so splendid an ally as the United Kingdom to protect all our interests." The nation must make its own way, beginning with the demand that it gain some return on its investments overseas. Sensible people understood that lend-lease would never be paid in full, he declared, but recipients of American aid such as Russia and Turkey must be made aware that the aid was coming from the United States and that their future support would be expected. Russell, the consummate politician, certainly understood the value of a favor. He also understood the value of natural resources. It was time, he said, that America's allies begin relying less on petroleum resources from the United States and more on oil from the Middle East and Russia. Most of all, Russell understood the value of raw power. In the new age of aircraft technology, he insisted, the United States must assert its permanent control of bases around the world, including those in Iceland, Dakar, and New Caledonia, as well as the western hemispheric holdings of Great Britain that had been leased to the United

States in 1940. It was not imperialism, he argued, but "a realistic step to prevent another generation of Americans who will undoubtedly still be paying for the present war from being compelled to pay again in blood and treasure." It was a day of realism, Russell maintained, where the "old type of kid-glove diplomacy" could not secure American interests. It was a day where "overoptimism" could destroy the nation's future.[20]

Russell was among those in the 1940s who would attempt to dampen Wilsonian enthusiasm for exporting American liberalism. Like Roosevelt, the Georgian understood the pledge to support democracy outlined in statements from the Atlantic Charter to the Declaration on Liberated Europe as a commitment to self-determination, not necessarily representative, constitutional, or liberal government. It was in the nation's long-term interest to promote a democratic world, but that process could not be forced. Rather, the U.S. operational procedure should be to check rival powers' attempts to carve out spheres of control that might threaten American interests or the efforts of weaker nations to achieve self-government.[21]

This new realism did not sit well with the keepers of the traditional Wilsonian vision. The *New Republic*, long the advocate of American global leadership, executive power, and democratic largesse, and a frequent critic of congressional drag on foreign policy, suggested that Russell's idea of maintaining air bases abroad smacked of imperialism. His committee's criticism of Britain and the other allied nations, moreover, would damage U.S. relations at a crucial time in the war effort. The rift between Russell's and the liberal internationalists' views on military power, foreign aid, and the promotion of democracy abroad widened and intensified during the last days of World War II and the first days of the Cold War.[22]

Russell's realist, nationalist, militarist approach to internationalism stemmed from views the senator had held about democracy, race, and the historic pace of change since his youth. His trip to the war theaters only intensified those views. The consequences of unpreparedness, the rapid pace of technological change, the new possibilities for human interaction, and the still vast differences between cultures were lessons Russell relearned during his junket. From those lessons, he derived a set of policies for postwar American security and self-interest that included most importantly a strong defense, tightly circumscribed foreign aid spending, and gradualism in the promotion of democracy. It was a set of axioms drawn from his prewar suspicion that the world was a scary place but catalyzed under the wartime realization that it was, in fact, terrifying.

What he learned about the "war without mercy" in the Pacific during his trip haunted him and reinforced his sense that America was an embattled island of democracy in the chaotic modern world. Unlike the "orthodox" war in Europe, Russell reported, the war in the Pacific was "a battle to the death" where tales of "incredible and shocking brutality by the Japanese in the treatment of our men, including the wounded, make it easy to understand why no quarter is now being asked or given."[23] The senator's anger over these atrocities publicly bubbled over three months later as news reached Washington of the aftermath of the surrenders at Bataan and Corregidor. Tales of the torture, starvation, and mutilation of several thousand American and Filipino prisoners of war did not surprise Russell but moved him to search for answers to explain the horror. Like so many of his fellow Americans, he instinctively fell back on the logic of race and civilization. The horrors carried out by the Japanese at Bataan, Russell declared in the Senate, were "indeed shocking to anyone who has any civilized instincts." But they were "not all of those which must be written in the Book of Doomsday." The soldiers he met while overseas had long been "imbued with such a personal hatred for all Japs that it is almost terrifying." Their experience with "Japanese bestiality" and "barbarity" had taught them that the "Japs are brutish beings without an instinct of humanity, though in human form." The American Indian "savage," he maintained, was a "chivalrous cavalier" in comparison. Those who knew firsthand the extent of Japanese cruelty, he insisted, would not "let us forget or forgive. They will demand vengeance for the blood of their comrades, an eye for an eye and a tooth for a tooth with compound interest." Russell demanded that punishment "be had for every drop of blood from the veins of American prisoners, including the wounded and sick who have been bayoneted or beaten while helpless to defend themselves." Punishment of the Japanese was retribution and vengeance that would serve "eternal justice," according to the senator, but it would also help "assure a permanent peace." Harsh treatment of war criminals would serve as an example to deter those similarly inclined "for a thousand years from the perpetration of such inhuman acts."[24]

Though he certainly learned of and even alluded to American atrocities in the Pacific, Russell's calls for punishment were for the Japanese only. They had initiated the war and had so debased the human instinct for civilization that the law of the jungle had to be invoked to ensure the survival of the nation and the preservation of peace. Russell knew well how means influenced ends. The means of fighting the war under FEPC rules, he understood, were a major step toward desegregation and what he considered the corruption of pure Southern white democracy. But he remained confident that while victory in the Pacific might be preserved through the total annihilation of the enemy, white American civilization would return and triumph over the cycle of bestiality the Japanese had initiated. What Russell had not recognized was the degree to which the means he suggested, both in maintaining segregation and in seeking vengeance against the Japanese, undermined the other values of "civilization" he held dear: social justice, individual responsibility, self-determination, and the rule of law.

Safely ensconced in the halls of power in Washington, D.C., Russell could adopt the libertarian's belief in ultimate free will while accepting the racists' and realists' mantras that some wills are freer than others. The war confronted every man—Japanese, American, black, or white—with the choice to accept the security of totalitarianism or the responsibility of liberty. But for Russell, these decisions were circumscribed by race, history, and power. Since blacks, "Japs," and other nonwhites were racially and historically less inclined to choose liberty, Russell believed, they must be kept at arm's length, with stern warnings that any attempt to encroach on the American white man's choice to be free carried severe, unmistakable punishment.

Thus wartime conditions confirmed Russell's worldview. He trusted that race, history, and power determined each man's decision to accept tyranny or demand liberty. Japanese atrocities only confirmed for him that the "Japanese race" would not responsibly defend individual liberty. It was a conviction the senator shared with many Americans, including President Roosevelt, who in 1942 authorized the army to "intern" Japanese Americans in what amounted to prison camps. Expressing little concern over the legality or morality of Japanese internment, Russell pressed the issue to its logical conclusion in the summer of 1944. That June, he sponsored a bill to strip Japanese Americans of citizenship if they declared their allegiance to the emperor of Japan. Those who made the choice to support the emperor, the bill implied, were unfit for citizenship in a democratic society. Under the bill, they would be taken out of the war relocation centers and interned as enemy aliens. Russell hoped that they could then be traded for Americans being held in territory occupied by the Japanese.[25] Those who remained loyal to the United States would continue to be held in the relocation centers for the duration of the war. The choice he offered Japanese Americans was to live in one kind of prison or another.

If Japanese Americans could not be completely trusted with the blessings of liberty, neither could the Japanese who had chosen to die for their emperor rather than surrender. Russell thus focused not on defeating and rebuilding Japan but on sending the Japanese a message of overwhelming American might, a message he thought even the uncivilized could understand. While American power, he believed, could not ensure democracy abroad, it could deter those who would threaten democracy at home. Japan was to be made an example. Russell welcomed the atomic bombing of Hiroshima as a step toward, but far from a completion of, that goal. A day after he and the world learned of America's new nuclear power, Russell sent a telegram to President Truman:

> Let us carry the war to them until they beg us to accept their unconditional surrender. The foul attack on Pearl Harbor brought us into war and I am unable to see any valid reason why we should be so much more considerate and lenient in dealing with Japan than with Germany. I earnestly insist Japan should be dealt with as harshly as Germany and that she should not be the beneficiary of a soft peace. . . . If we do not have available a sufficient number of atomic bombs with which to finish the job immediately, let us carry on with TNT and fire bombs until we can produce them. I also hope that you will issue orders forbidding the officers in command of our air forces from warning Jap cities that they will be attacked. These generals do not fly over Japan and this showmanship can only result in the unnecessary loss of many fine boys in our air force, as well as helpless prisoners in the hands of the Japanese, including the survivors of the march of death on Bataan who are certain to be brought into the cities that have been warned. This was a total war as long as our enemies held all of the cards. Why should we change the rules now after the blood, treasure, and enterprise of the American people have given us the upper hand? Our people have not forgotten that the Japanese struck us the first blow in this war without the slightest warning. They believe that we should continue to strike the Japanese until they are brought groveling to their knees. We should cease our appeals to Japan to sue for peace. The next plea for peace should come from an utterly destroyed Tokyo.[26]

Truman, just a few months in office after the death of President Roosevelt in April, and just returned from his first major foreign policy negotiation at Potsdam, replied on August 9, the day the United States delivered a second atomic bomb on Nagasaki:

> I know that Japan is a terribly cruel and uncivilized nation in warfare but I can't bring myself to believe that, because they are beasts, we should ourselves act in the same manner.

For myself, I certainly regret the necessity of wiping out whole populations because of the "pigheadedness" of the leaders of a nation and, for your information, I am not going to do it unless it is absolutely necessary. It is my opinion that after the Russians enter into war the Japanese will very shortly fold up.

My object is to save as many American lives as possible but I also have a humane feeling for the women and children in Japan.[27]

Russell's anger and fear did not subside. Weeks after the Japanese surrender, he continued to call for vengeance and retribution. On September 18, he stood before a full Senate to demand that the Japanese people be made aware of their defeat through the prosecution of Emperor Hirohito as a war criminal. Given the men, money, and resources sacrificed in the war effort and the onset of the atomic age, Russell declared that the "prevention of war is no longer merely desirable in our civilization. It is essential if the race is to survive." The senator cited reports suggesting that the Japanese had not recognized their complete military defeat; they chose to believe instead that peace had been achieved through the emperor's benevolence. Misinterpretations of Potsdam had weakened the policy of unconditional surrender, Russell argued, paving the way for a policy toward the Japanese that did not match the retribution then being visited upon the Germans. A complete psychological victory over Japan was crucial to the future peace. The flag of Texas from the First Cavalry Division should fly over Tokyo. The occupying forces should consist of the most direct victims of Japanese aggression, the Chinese, Filipinos, Koreans, and Australians. And Admiral Halsey should "ride the Emperor's white horse down the streets of Tokyo behind a brass band, even though it had been necessary to have four strong marines there to keep him in the saddle."[28]

Russell's obsession with retribution against the Japanese seemed to provoke him to new levels of hypocrisy. He argued that "any steps we may take to create a democracy in Japan are doomed to failure" if Hirohito was not tried as any other man and stripped of his status as an infallible god. "It is impossible for a democracy to grow and flourish in an atmosphere of absolutism that is embroidered with the myth of divinity which has been attached to him." Further, Russell claimed, the example of Nazi Germany had taught Americans that "where an entire people have been thoroughly indoctrinated with the idea that they possess some sort of superiority over all other peoples which destines them to rule the world by force and violence, they cannot be purged of such philosophy by weak and half-hearted methods." These were remarkable statements by the Southern advocate of white supremacy.[29]

Russell eventually introduced Senate Joint Resolution 94 declaring it the policy of the United States that Japanese emperor Hirohito be tried as a war criminal. The measure died quietly in committee. Meanwhile, a nearly identical plan suffered a similar fate in the Truman administration's inner circles. Fellow Southerner and secretary of state, James F. Byrnes, had made Russell's argument within the cabinet that the unconditional surrender terms agreed to at Casablanca and Potsdam could not be complete without the removal of the Japanese head of state. But Secretary of War Henry Stimson and others within the administration convinced Truman that the emperor could remain so long as the United States dictated the conditions of his retention. Japan, in the end, kept its leader, but Hirohito would remain subject to the supreme allied commander in the Pacific.

Richard Russell's travels to the theaters of war had brought to the surface his most deeply held prejudices and insecurities. He now had a concrete understanding of what family and regional lore had only allowed him to assume in the abstract: that the world was closing in and breaking down traditional definitions of community, security, and order that he considered most important to a virtuous society. Russell instinctively defended the South as the ultimate bulwark against this onslaught, but his attempt to convince the president that American security depended on further retribution against the Japanese represented a first, active move to make national security strategy his primary battlement. The effort established the senator among the principle advocates of a strong defense and a unilateralist foreign policy that would help frame America's approach to the Cold War, but it also established Russell as a dissenting voice to the liberal internationalism that was at the heart of the nation's postwar doctrine.

Notes

1. "The Rearguard Commander," *Time* 70 (August 12, 1957): 15; Gilbert C. Fite, *Richard B. Russell, Jr., Senator from Georgia* (Chapel Hill: University of North Carolina Press, 1991), 2.

2. Calvin Mcleod Logue and Dwight L. Freshley, eds., *Voice of Georgia: Speeches of Richard B. Russell, 1928–1969* (Macon, GA: Mercer University Press, 1997), 42–44.

3. Logue and Freshley, *Speeches of Richard B. Russell*, 42–43.

4. Joseph A. Fry, *Dixie Looks Abroad: The South and U.S. Foreign Relations, 1789–1973* (Baton Rouge: Louisiana State University Press, 2002), 174.

5. Logue and Freshley, *Speeches of Richard B. Russell*, 203–11.

6. Fite, *Russell*, 81–82.

7. Fite, *Russell*, 48.

8. *Congressional Record*, 75th Cong., 3rd sess., 1938, 83, pt. 1:1101–29; 80th Cong., 2nd sess., 1948, 95, pt. 4:6459–60, 6864; Fite, *Russell*, 179.

9. *Congressional Record*, 74th Cong., 1st sess., 1935, 79, pt. 1:1052–54.

10. *Congressional Record*, 75th Cong., 3rd sess., 1938, 83, app.: 737–38.

11. *Congressional Record*, 76th Cong., 3rd sess., 1940, 86, pt. 10:11090–92.

12. Logue and Freshley, *Speeches of Richard B. Russell*, 212–16.

13. *Congressional Record*, 79th Cong., 1st sess., 1945, 91, pt. 2:1900.

14. *Congressional Record*, 77th Cong., 2nd sess., 1942, 88, pt. 7:8901–3.

15. *Congressional Record*, 78th Cong., 2nd sess., 1944, 90, pt. 5:6022; Fite, *Russell*, 183–84.

16. Fite, *Russell*, 185.

17. *Congressional Record*, 78th Cong., 2nd sess., 1944, 90, pt. 5:5826.

18. Fite, *Russell*, 191.

19. *Congressional Record*, 78th Cong., 1st sess., 1943, 89, pt. 7:8859–66.

20. *Congressional Record*, 78th Cong., 1st sess., 1943, 89, pt. 7:8859–66.

21. Tony Smith, *America's Mission: The United States and the Worldwide Struggle for Democracy in the Twentieth Century* (Princeton, NJ: Princeton University Press, 1994), 118.

22. Richard H. Pells, *The Liberal Mind in a Conservative Age: American Intellectuals in the 1940s and 1950s* (New York: Harper & Row, 1995), 12–15; *New Republic* 109 (October 18, 1943): 503.

23. *Congressional Record*, 78th Cong., 1st sess., 1943, 89, pt.7:8861.

24. *Congressional Record*, 78th Cong., 2nd sess., 1944, 90, pt.1:872.

25. *Congressional Record*, 78th Cong., 2nd sess., 1944, 90, pt. 5:6616–17.

26. Russell to Truman, August 7, 1945, box 1, series 3, Russell Papers, Richard Russell Memorial Library.

27. Truman to Russell, August 9, 1945, box 1, series 3, Russell Papers, Richard Russell Memorial Library.

28. *Congressional Record*, 79th Cong., 1st sess., 1945, 91, pt. 6:8671–80.

29. *Congressional Record*, 79th Cong., 1st sess., 1945, 91, pt. 6:8671–80.

2

Central Paradox

In a speech at the University of Georgia in June 1946, Richard Russell declared that "isolationism is all but dead in this country," and it had become "our duty to see that it is not revived."[1] The world had changed for Russell and the generation that led the United States to victory in World War II. It had become smaller, increasingly interconnected, and more dangerous. The war had given birth to new weapons of unimaginable destruction, new nations struggling for their independence, new conflicts between democracy and totalitarianism, and new challenges to the values Russell held most dear. Lead the world, he advised, but carry the biggest sticks, trust no alliance to secure American interests, and understand the limits of American power.

The central paradox in Richard Russell's thinking about national security strategy developed in the early years of the Cold War: that the United States should vigorously build its military and economic power but should *not* use that power to promote democracy abroad. It was a profoundly defensive and conservative strategy. The ability to muster overwhelming military and economic strength, he insisted, would deter any aggressor's challenge, but no amount of money or force, he maintained, could change an individual's willingness to take responsibility for his own liberty. Russell thus supported the policy of containment and the huge defense budgets that would eventually go with it, but he simultaneously worked to reduce foreign aid, limit alliances, and prevent military adventures overseas.

Russell's strategy left him just outside the shifting center of American foreign relations politics and policy. He was far enough from that "vital center" that the label "independent" truly characterized his position in the Senate, but

27

he was close enough to gain a national following and an unmatched base of power in Congress. Russell's call for a strong defense but caution in using that power appealed to a consensus of the American right and left that recognized the need to confront the Soviet Union but avoid a third world war.

Ironically, while Russell's position left him at the center of popular sentiment concerning foreign policy, a principal factor in the senator's paradoxical calculus—racism—left him increasingly out of touch with the emerging national mainstream on civil rights. Russell's racial worldview fundamentally influenced his understanding of global security issues. Democracy and its defense were essentially the white man's burden, according to the senator. Asians, blacks, and other nonwhites were less inclined by blood and history to accept the individual responsibility for democracy that Russell found so crucial in avoiding totalitarianism. He held out hope that nonwhites would in time evolve a democratic spirit, but he believed firmly that the government's power could not be used to accelerate that evolution in the American South or anywhere else in the world. Such reasoning influenced his controversial arguments against the Fair Employment Practices Commission (FEPC), the postwar relaxation of immigration quotas on Asians, and the integration of the armed forces, but it also served as a foundation for his more popular positions on foreign aid spending, defense priorities, and global intervention.

Richard Russell longed for peace in the world and a return to some sense of normality and stability. He shared the concerns of politically powerful veterans in his home state and nationwide that space and time had shrunken under the pressure of communications, transportation, and weapons technology. The United States was now in a smaller, faster world where democracy could be more easily touched by totalitarian aggression. The hard-fought war had not earned the United States any respite. It was the "most costly and oft-repeated mistake of mankind," he told an audience in the spring of 1946, to assume that "victory in war brings peace." Indeed, the postwar challenges to order and freedom were for Russell "greater than they were even in 1918." Americans needed to strive for international cooperation, he insisted, but maintaining peace would require an ongoing commitment equivalent to war.[2]

By the time Russell spoke these words, a new totalitarian threat had emerged. Soviet control of Eastern Europe had already solidified, and challenges to Greece, Turkey, and Iran were in the offing. Soviet and American bickering had characterized the organizational meetings of the fledgling United Nations. George Kennan had written his "long telegram" to the secretary of state from the U.S. embassy in Moscow declaring that no permanent peaceful coexistence could occur between the Soviets and the Americans, and Winston Churchill had warned of the "Iron Curtain" descending between the Communist and the capitalist/democratic worlds.

Russell's suspicions of the Soviet Union were clear in his spring 1946 comments. The United States had "acceded" to Russian demands for security in Eastern Europe. Despite concessions that "hardly seem justified" to demonstrate America's good faith to the Soviets, no agreement on Germany, Italy, and Japan had emerged from the various wartime and postwar conferences, and the Soviet's use of its veto power in the UN had stalled that body's essential work. While wartime rhetoric had "clothed all of the allied nations with the cloak of democracy" in order to maintain some sense of unity, Russell made it clear that neither "the dictatorship of the communists in Russia" nor "the dictatorship of Chiang Kai-shek in China" were democratic. The "honeymoon" with its totalitarian allies, Russell declared, was over.[3]

Soviet subterfuge and aggression troubled the senator. He had warned of Communist attempts to undermine American religious and educational institutions since the early 1930s. He also experienced firsthand the coming tension between the Soviet Union and the United States when he was denied a visa for an official visit to Russia in June 1945. The Soviet postwar show of force rendered Russell's otherwise passing anxiety acute. Reflecting on the months just after the war's end, Russell declared that it had become "apparent almost immediately that our wartime Russian allies had no intention of disarming and of becoming a peaceful member of the family of nations." "On the contrary," he opined, "Stalin merely took up where Hitler had left off." The Soviets, like the Fascists, were bent on "the domination and enslavement of free men the world over."[4]

While those on the American left, most notably former vice president and soon-to-be presidential candidate Henry Wallace, stressed the similarities between U.S. and Soviet goals and sought some postwar agreement between the nations, Russell highlighted the dissimilarities. There was a "basic difference between the spurious democracy proclaimed by the Politburo and the real democracy we enjoy as citizens of the United States," Russell asserted. It was a "cold fact" that "in Russia a handful of masters dominate the masses in an absolute slave state." The "Communist program" was "destroying all property rights, striking down the essential freedoms of speech, of press and to worship according to the dictates of individual con-science." It would "strip the individual of any pretense of dignity and chain him to the wheel of state." The Bolsheviks had even abandoned Marx's communal dreams in their pursuit of total power, according to the senator. Russell found it "unforgivable for any intelligent American to defend as democratic the form of government imposed by Russia on the satellite states, and which they seek to impose upon the rest of the world."[5]

Russell also highlighted the differences between capitalist and socialist economies. Collectivized agriculture was a testament to the waste and inefficiency of Communism: "In the Communist bloc of nations, shortages of agricultural output are the rule rather than the exception," he said. The failure of government-operated collective farms in Communist countries was so great that "in order to enable the people to live, it has been necessary to allow each farmer a free acre or two from which he might sell on his own account anything that he produced." This minimal amount of capitalism, he argued, was keeping people alive. The "scanty provisions in the state stores" of the Communist world simply could not provide for the people.[6]

Russell's views of Communism in the early Cold War resembled George Kennan's. A career foreign service officer and the father of American containment strategy, Kennan concluded at the end of World War II that cooperation with the Soviets was hopelessly naive. Stalin and the Soviet leadership viewed the West as a capitalist, impe-rialist enemy that would continue to threaten Communism's future. The Soviets would seek to expand the Communist empire at every opportunity. Soviet attempts to do so, Kennan declared, should be met with counterforce at shifting geographic and political points around the world. The United States and its Western allies, in short, must contain Communism. But Americans should also be patient. The Soviets would only be passively aggressive, and Marxism as a political and economic system was doomed to ultimate failure. Checking Soviet power while maintaining the stability and prosperi-ty of capitalist democracies would yield victory without total war. Russell essentially agreed with this analysis, but, much more than Kennan, the senator would use this understanding to conclude that a defensive posture backed by a huge military force would best check Soviet expansion while the United States waited for Communism to collapse.

In the meantime, Russell also sought advantage in the new Cold War political center. As early as January 1946, he called for unity in confronting the new enemy. Americans must be unequivocal in supporting their country against Soviet aggression. They must build an economic and defensive system capable of withstanding any threat and remain vigilant against domestic enemies who would distract from those purposes.

The first great distraction in America's quest for security against the forces of Marxism-Leninism, Russell contended, arose not from spies, saboteurs, or strikers, but from supporters of the Fair Employment Practices Commission. Issued as an executive order in 1941, the FEPC policed racial discrimination in the defense industry. Russell saw it as a direct challenge to segregation by the president and as an opening wedge to broader civil rights reform for Southern blacks. When Congress moved to renew the commission in early 1946, Russell blatantly associated the action with Communism. The FEPC debate and the Southern filibuster that would inevitably follow would stifle Washington and stir national disunity at a time when Congress needed to deal with more pressing world problems, he argued. The bill to continue the FEPC was a "dangerous and revolutionary" measure that not only promoted race and class conflict and threatened the "American way of life," but was an "entering wedge to complete state socialism and communism." "I do not say that every man who is supporting this bill is a Communist," he proclaimed, but "I do say . . . that every Communist and every Socialist in this land . . . is ardently supporting this bill."[7]

Russell had felt the political currents shifting around what were becoming the two most important issues in postwar America: civil rights and anti-Communism. The FEPC debate focused his attention on their interrelationship. Russell knew that while an anti-Communist consensus had begun to form nationally, support for racial segregation was mostly regional. As his January 1946 speech suggested, the senator hoped that by tying Southern Democrats' racial concerns to the national anti-Communist consensus, he could muster a conservative coalition to defeat the FEPC. Anti-Communism would help anchor segregation from drifting too far from the political middle.

The senator's argument that continuation of the FEPC and federal civil rights reform in general amounted to state socialism and an appeasement of Communism gained some support, though just as important in the ultimate defeat of the FEPC were Republican concerns about regulation of the economy and Southern Democrats' ability to filibuster. Russell nevertheless had joined a popular, effective, centrist, conservative political alliance. Anti-Communists and civil rights liberals, however, had also begun to build a powerful coalition that challenged the South's traditional position of power within the Democratic Party. Harry Truman's successful nomination in 1948 over the arch-segregationist Strom Thurmond and the Soviet-coddling Henry Wallace, and the party's adoption of an anti-Communist, pro–civil rights platform, suggested a new party center. Increasingly, its leaders in the new administration mounted a powerful counterargument to Russell's. Domestic racial reform, they argued, would serve the nation's security interests by challenging Soviet propaganda suggesting that the United States was a racist, imperialist juggernaut and by bolstering American support in the Third World.

Liberal calls to tie racial reform to national security moved Russell from arguments tempered by sound legal principle to positions that were shrill and extreme. In 1949, for example, he introduced a bill to relocate blacks out of the South as a solution to the nation's racial problems. With his tongue only loosely planted in his cheek, he said that when compared to the money spent on relocation programs abroad, the cost would be insignificant.[8] Even where he was tempted to support alliance building in Europe, racial considerations were paramount. Russell once suggested to *Atlanta Constitution* editor Ralph McGill in 1947 that a great federation of English-speaking countries could "beat back the tide of communism and so stabilize affairs as to bring a long period of world peace." Though he knew that such an idea would not be met with "universal approval," he told a constituent that he believed "that without consolidation of the whole Anglo-Saxon race we will either be undermined internally or swamped by external attack with forces who could not secure world domination if confronted with unified Anglo-Saxon opposition."[9]

Russell's reactionary apogee came in his response to the integration of the armed forces. President Truman's executive order to integrate the army in 1948 pitted Russell's most entrenched political commitments—to segregation and a strong military—against one another. The president's announcement came just as Russell was beginning to work on legislation that would require compulsory military service of all American males after they completed high school. Russell actually considered withdrawing his support if soldiers were not granted "the very modest right to serve with members of their own race." The president's order would "intermingle the races in the most intimate relations of life," he argued. "The morale and health of the men is sure to be adversely affected," since World War II statistics showed that "crime in Negro organizations was approximately twice that of white units" and that "syphilis among nonwhite males was 19 times greater than among white males." Both crime and syphilis, the usually careful Russell implied, were easily communicable diseases in all-male barracks. The senator further stated without elaboration that integrated units would threaten the "morals" of American boys called to serve.[10]

When the senator failed to amend the 1948 legislation to allow those who registered under the act to state their preference for joining an integrated or segregated unit, he faced a tough decision: accept the increase in troop strength on an integrated basis or reject the increase in protest against the president's desegregation order. Ultimately, Russell "resolved the grave doubts" he entertained about the bill and supported it. It was a telling moment for the Georgian. National defense trumped segregation, but not by much. Russell resubmitted his amendment two years later amid the debate over universal military training (UMT). It remained his contention that the fighting man's "faith in our American civilization" rested in his "pride of community, State, and Nation, and of race."[11]

Russell's ability to reestablish segregation in the armed forces and improve the defensive posture of the United States increased markedly in the immediate postwar years. In 1946, the senator was the third-ranking Democrat on the Naval Affairs Committee and was situated solidly in the middle ranks of the Appropriations Committee. He also became one of the original members of the Joint Committee on Atomic Energy. With the Legislative Reorganization Act of 1946, Russell's position on the Naval Affairs Committee was transferred to the new, powerful Armed Services Committee. The transition turned out to be among the most fateful events in Russell's political career. By 1949, Russell was second in seniority only to Democrat Millard Tydings of Maryland on the Armed Services Committee, a position that earned the Georgian an important spot on and eventual leadership of the Central Intelligence Agency Oversight Subcommittee. Then, when Tydings was defeated and Senate Democrats retained a majority in the midterm elections of 1950, Russell advanced to chairman of the Armed Services Committee.

Russell's committee assignments afforded him a great deal of control over military planning and spending. Once he became chair of Armed Services, requests for money and troops to fight the Cold War had to go through him. Russell did what he could to grant them all, and he frequently called for more. Demobilization after World War II had been "folly," a "wasteful and extravagant process" that left the nation "impotent," according to Russell, and it would cost American taxpayers a great deal to rebuild. But that rebuilding had to occur. American security could only be preserved with a strong defense.

While he hoped the United Nations and international cooperation might help reduce conflicts, "power," Russell argued, was "still the dominant factor in world politics." America's diplomatic obligations as well as its leadership in the UN depended on a "strong military establishment."[12]

Russell took over Armed Services at a crucial time in the Cold War. China had only recently fallen to the Communists, Russia had exploded its first nuclear weapon, the Korean War had begun, and the Truman administration had changed the course of containment strategy to a track Russell found more to his liking. National Security Council Memorandum 68 (NSC-68) called for a hardening of the defensive perimeter around the Western democracies and huge increases in defense budgets. Russell thus assumed control of a committee in late 1950 that controlled some $50 billion, up from $13 billion the previous year. NSC-68 brought about essentially what Russell had asked for: a wartime defense budget.

Russell oversaw more than eighty pieces of legislation in his first term as chairman of the Armed Services Committee during the 82nd Congress. He became a parent, human resources manager, cruise director, and legal representative for military personnel. Everything from uniform lapel buttons to mess hall operations, to pay scales and promotions, to medical care and health benefits, to funeral arrangements, to transportation and recreation programs fell under his scrutiny. He also controlled budgets and contracts for material procurement, base openings and closings, and research and development of large-scale defense systems—such as missiles and submarines. And he oversaw CIA appropriations, prisoner control policies, aerospace programs, civil defense organization, real estate contracts in the Panama Canal, and the establishment of the U.S. Air Force Academy.[13]

Above all of these, Russell made the passage of a Universal Military Training Bill his greatest priority. On January 8, 1951, he and nine members of the Armed Services Committee introduced Senate Bill 1, which would require all eighteen-year-old men to register for selective service and undergo four months of military training after high school. The senator offered it as an alternative to the expense and social disruption of maintaining a large standing army. UMT also dovetailed nicely with his view that democracy demanded individual responsibility. It was only fair, he reasoned, that the burden of defending the United States be shared by all those who benefit from its institutions. The universal commitment would "serve notice on the mad masters of communism" that the United States was prepared for any attack. Its power was a "pledge to freedom," a "symbol of our determination to maintain ourselves against the forces of tyranny and aggression." Under Russell's leadership, both branches of Congress agreed to, and the president signed, a universal training measure in June 1951. The House and Senate, however, never issued an implementation plan; all but the registration portions of the legislation died with the end of hostilities in Korea.[14]

Universal military training embodied the Russell paradox. The senator could justify universal training in part because it was his intention that the U.S. armed forces only be used defensively. The U.S. possession of a mass of trained manpower along with its superior nuclear arsenal and technological prowess, he hoped, was enough to deter the Communists from taking aggressive action. Russell understood that winning the Cold War depended as much on the perception of power as its reality. UMT, by his calculation, reduced the number of Soviet imperialist ventures by increasing Moscow's fear of a grand American military retaliation. Fewer Communist uprisings meant that the United States was relieved of the need for overseas troop deployments and nation-building efforts that Russell believed to be so fruitless and wasteful.

Economy of resources was a key component of the Russell paradox. The senator consistently pushed for a larger and larger military, but he did not believe that the nation's assets were unlimited. Large standing armies, he understood, could bankrupt the nation and undermine its capitalist system. UMT generated a huge pool of trained fighting men that could be called in times of need, but it eliminated the expense of keeping those men perpetually in uniform.

Russell sought savings elsewhere as well, particularly in foreign aid spending. Russell was a lifelong opponent of foreign aid for three basic reasons. First, democracy depended on individual responsibility. It could not be forced on a people or bought for them by another nation. Second, America could not and should not depend on others to secure its interests. Russell trusted neither enemies nor allies with American technology or money. Third, U.S. resources were limited and must be invested wisely to secure America's future against totalitarian enemies. It was a better investment, Russell argued, to build U.S. military might than to enrich others at American taxpayers' expense.

Such was Russell's reasoning in rejecting the $3.75 billion British loan in 1946. The senator told his colleagues that he could only support the bill if the United States gained rights to British overseas bases in exchange. Even with America's closest allies, he insisted, the United

States must come first. Internationalists like J. William Fulbright (D-AR) charged that the strings Russell had attached to the loan smacked of imperialism, but Russell considered it common sense to try to guarantee a return on the nation's investments. England, he trusted, would take care of itself, and such an acknowledgment would be a sign of respect for its sovereignty.

Russell's aversion to making investments abroad did not mean he opposed all foreign aid and military alliances. For example, in early 1947, he backed the Truman Doctrine, which included aid money to Greece and Turkey. He also supported the Marshall Plan, a massive foreign aid package to rebuild Western Europe and prevent Communist expansion there, and the creation of the North Atlantic Treaty Organization, a multilateral defense pact designed to check Soviet military power. These were telling exceptions to Russell's rules. In all of these instances, he convinced himself that American interests were paramount. With Great Britain unable to maintain its power in the Middle East and the Eastern Mediterranean, U.S. support for Greece and Turkey was needed to stop Communist expansion in key geographic areas, separating the Soviets from strategic resources like oil and restricting their access to warm water trade routes through the Bosporus and the Suez Canal. Support for Western Europe in the Marshall Plan and NATO would ensure that Germany, the nation central to the stability of the European economy and to the containment of Russian power, remained strong and able to secure the front line against Communist aggression. World War II, the senator had to admit, had changed his philosophy. "There was a time when I suppose I was as much of an isolationist as ever served in this body," he told the Senate in 1951, "but I have changed my views." International cooperation in confronting Communism would "reduce the sacrifices of American resources and American manhood and American blood."[15]

But Russell's new trust in international cooperation had limits. The financial burden had to be considered. Though he voted for them, Russell considered the initial outlays for the Marshall Plan and NATO too expensive and worked to reduce them. And in approving the aid package accompanying the Truman Doctrine, he warned that the money sent to Greece and Turkey would not promote democracy. The world, he declared, would ultimately have to stand on its own without the financial assistance of the United States. It was unfair to American taxpayers to pay for other nations' security, and pure folly to think money could buy a democratic spirit. Race, of course, was also a factor. Except for Turkey, all of the nations that received aid with Russell's blessing had capitalist, democratic histories and/or the racial makeup, according to the senator's worldview, predisposed to capitalist democratic institutions. The investment in whites, simply put, was more secure than the investment in nonwhites. Politics, furthermore, was a key. Russell supported only the most popular of the foreign aid programs deemed crucial to the fight against Communism by a nearly unanimous domestic consensus.

No consideration was more important to Russell, though, than a demonstrated commitment to self-defense. "I am one of those who have sought to have the nations who would fight with us make contributions of their own to the common cause," he told his colleagues. A man who "puts something of his own into a given project, if he puts his heart and his soul and his energies into that project, he will fight harder for it."[16] The United States and its allies, while they cooperated, should never depend on the other states for its own defense. He questioned, moreover, whether any amount of aid could really protect Western Europe from a Soviet onslaught should it come to that. A degree of cooperation was fine, Russell concluded, but only a strong U.S. military could deter Soviet aggression against America's interests around the globe.[17]

Russell's dedication to the military over foreign aid redoubled after the United States committed itself to greater defense budgets in 1950. Increasingly it became a zero-sum equation for Russell: the more money that went to defense, the less that could be spent on foreign aid. President Truman and then NATO commander Dwight Eisenhower tried to convince Russell that both defense spending and foreign aid were necessary in securing American Cold War interests by sending him to inspect military bases in Europe in 1951. The senator returned with advice that disappointed both men. "I don't know whether we are getting our money's worth," Russell told an interviewer with *U.S. News & World Report*. "We have not generated as great a will to resist and sacrifice as I would like to see. Dollars won't buy that. They simply won't buy will to work, will to resist, will to fight." While he did not advocate pulling out of Europe, Russell suggested that the wisest course was a gradual withdrawal of support. There were "undoubtedly many things that our friends in Europe could do for themselves that they are not doing at the present time," he said. "Self-help," he advised, should be the mantra. In a statement that might have applied equally to his view of domestic welfare spending, Russell concluded, "We can't make a go of things in Europe if we permit those people to become completely dependent upon us, any more than we could if we pulled out tomorrow." He promised not to support spending in the coming year unless directly related to defense concerns abroad.[18]

Russell's support for defense spending and opposition to foreign aid led many to label him a conservative whose views were closer to the Republican than the Democratic Party. Perhaps too committed to the Democratic Party to be truly part of a "conservative coalition," Russell's recommendations did fit most closely with Republican protectionist policies that stressed self-reliance and rugged individualism and shunned government dependencies. His advice was also conservative in the traditionalist sense of that term. Other than lend-lease, the United States had consistently rejected peacetime foreign aid programs prior to World War II, and Russell was among those clamoring for a quick end to lend-lease after the war was over. Russell did not join with the Robert Taft (R-OH) and John Bricker (R-OH) wing of the Republican Party in advocating neoisolationism. The world was too interconnected. "What happens in Asia unquestionably affects . . . Europe," he argued, and "Europe has a great deal of bearing on what policy might be applied in the Far East."[19] But he did often align himself with Republican opponents of foreign aid like Everett Dirksen (R-IL), John Vorys (R-OH), and his colleague on the Senate Armed Services Committee, Leverett Saltonstall (R-MA). The Georgian was surely to the right of Republican internationalists like Douglas Dillon and Senator Henry Cabot Lodge Jr. (R-MA).

Among the Democrats, Russell could not be considered a foreign policy extremist either. He was firmly in the mainstream of Southern Democratic thought on America's relationship with the world and no farther right of center than J. William Fulbright (D-AR) was to the left. At the end of World War II, he was arguably as centrist as Mike Mansfield (D-MT), Hubert Humphrey (D-MN), or Wayne Morse (D-OR), and he was certainly closer to the middle than either Henry Wallace or Strom Thurmond. But the center within the Democratic Party was changing. Russell resisted the Democrats' trend toward liberal internationalist policies. Foreign policy makers in the Truman administration and powerful Senate Democrats like Fulbright pushed hard in the early postwar years for nonmilitary aid to struggling nations. American money, they argued, could win friends and resolve the social and economic problems that led to instability and Communist exploitation. Taking the New Deal and Fair Deal abroad would also free up trade and contribute to the general prosperity of the non-Communist world. With the Democrats in control of Congress until 1952 and the majority of party members supporting liberal internationalist programs, Russell lost nearly all of his battles against foreign aid.

It was not a lack of faith per se in liberal institutions that separated Russell from the liberal internationalists in his own party. He believed, like Harry Truman and others of his generation, in the eventual triumph of a universal world order based on liberal values. But Russell saw this triumph as much farther in the future than did his fellow Democrats. The evolution toward a free world would come, but at a glacial pace. Attempts to accelerate that pace were either futile or as likely to produce totalitarian as democratic results. Russell believed in liberal institutions, but unlike the liberal internationalists, he did not believe that most members of the international community were ready to embrace them. This absence of trust drove the Russell paradox. It led him to conclude that it was necessary to protect American democracy into the distant future by preventing the spread of Communism, but to do so with limited military confrontation and without wasting immediate resources in the hopes of accelerating the pace of democratic change elsewhere. As the senator would discover in Asia, this proposition was akin to trying to preserve a leaf of rice paper under the treads of a tank.

Russell held little hope of securing Asia for the capitalist, democratic world. The senator's allusions to a "Yellow Peril" and his casual use of the term "coolie" revealed his generalized concept of Asians as devious, lazy, and selfish. Like late nineteenth-century nativists and anti-imperialists, Russell argued that such traits made Asians less likely to assimilate democratic institutions. This reasoning led the Georgian, as the postwar Immigration Committee chairman, to push for a return to the National Origins Act of 1924, setting higher quotas for nonwhite immigrants and establishing an absolute ban on Asians.[20] It also shaped his concept of the Cold War in Asia. Asians, culturally and perhaps genetically predisposed against democracy, were multiplying at an alarming rate, Russell declared after visiting the region during World War II, and they did not have "enough money to bring a measure of security to the rapidly exploding population."[21] Thus his persistent fear that Asians would envelop the world and dilute democracy by procreation alone. In 1965, he wrote to constituents that even though the "Russians do not want a nuclear war, . . . I do not think that China really fears one. It may be to their advantage to lose a couple of hundred million so they could feed the rest."[22]

Russell's solution to the Asian problem was never to fight "a conventional campaign on the land mass of Asia" or "propose to swap any fine American boys for any Chinese coolies."[23] And, he might have added, never invest American money in promoting democracy in Asia, where democracy was unlikely to succeed in the immediate future. Asia, Russell was predisposed to say, just was not worth risking a global conflict. The senator was thus less disturbed than most by the "loss of China" to Communism in 1949. The United States, he was convinced, could really have done very little about it. After visiting China in 1943, he reported that "order and decency," even "in the Nationalist Government," was unlikely to materialize. Russell opposed using U.S. resources to save Chiang Kai-shek in 1949 and thereafter contested any suggestion of going to war with China to defend Formosa.[24]

The Korean War moved the senator closer to supporting confrontation with Communism than any other conflict in Asia during his lifetime. But Korea also served as a test of the limits of Russell's paradox. Russell sought to place strict limits on American involvement there from the start and ultimately concluded that even limited engagement had been folly.

In the weeks following the June 24, 1950, Communist North Korean invasion of the South and the subsequent commitment of U.S. troops to reinforce what remained of the South Korean army, Russell wrote that he would insist "that all of the United Nations join in the effort to restore peace in Korea." Failure to repulse North Korea would result in the United States "losing what friends we have in the world." The senator also suggested that the invasion was a trap: "There is, of course, a strong possibility that the Russians hope to bleed us white in the far corners of the earth before they drop their atomic bombs on us."[25]

For the reluctant internationalist, Korea would be an important test of collective security in the face of Communist aggression. Those who bore "an equal stake in resisting Communism" in Korea would be demonstrating the "proper sense of responsibility" necessary to join the "free nations of the earth." Russell understood the already significant Cold War burdens the British were bearing in the Middle East, Germany on the edge of the Iron Curtain, and France in Indochina, but those closer to the fight—Australia, New Zealand, and Canada—should be asked to contribute more. The Korean conflict should be an even greater test for the Asians. Let Chiang Kai-shek's forces join the battle, he suggested. Arm and equip the South Koreans. Let us see who will stand with the United States against Communism and who will not. It would be a test of domestic consequences as well, according to Russell. The fight for freedom would be "one of the most difficult tests of the fiber of our people." Embracing Joe McCarthy's rhetoric, Russell observed that America would see at last who was and who was not soft on Communism.[26]

The senator knew that with the United States assuming some "ninety percent" of the cost of the war in both money and human resources, few could deny its commitment, but Russell had little confidence that the world would pass the test in Korea. His worldview predetermined the fate of nonwhites seeking to claim the privileges and responsibilities of democracy. He was convinced from the beginning, moreover, that even American success would be limited. His apprehensions were confirmed after General Douglas MacArthur, commander of the UN forces in Korea, pushed north to the Korean-Chinese border along the Yalu River in October 1950. With MacArthur poised to cross the river, Chinese forces invaded en masse and pushed the UN troops back into the South. UN forces abandoned Seoul in January 1951, and only with the greatest difficulty did they reestablish a front line in the proximity of the 38th parallel. Several days after the fall of Seoul, Russell expressed his fear that the whole venture had been a mistake:

> Many mistakes have undoubtedly been made in our international relations, and I have not always been in accord with the decisions which have been made. The decision to go into Korea was largely based on political considerations rather than military judgement. It was a gamble as to whether the Chinese would come into Korea and we have evidently lost that gamble. I am strongly opposed to undertaking to fight a land war with China and think our troops should be drawn from Korea.[27]

To protect American forces and hold the line as they withdrew, Russell suggested "bombing some important section of China every day and notify them that we were going to continue that until they got out of Korea."[28]

What Russell had feared most was coming to pass: a quagmire in Asia. If his fears of the Yellow Peril were strong before the Korean conflict, they were doubly so after a quarter of a million Chinese soldiers joined the fray. Confronting Communism was necessary, but Russell as always was keenly aware of the costs. Reflecting on the lessons of his region's past, the Georgian was determined not to sacrifice the sons of his homeland in a war where victory could not be assured.

The Chinese offensive marked a low point in the Korean War and the Cold War. The nation's leaders scrambled to reassess the strategy of global containment as U.S. casualty rates soared. They did so in a political atmosphere supercharged by the accusations of Senator Joe McCarthy (R-WI) that the loss of China, and by implication the stalemate in Korea, was a result of the Truman administration's coddling of domestic and foreign Communists. Under already tremendous pressure, in March 1951 the president decided that the time had come to deescalate the conflict, and he ordered his representatives to seek truce talks with North Korea. His actions only added ammunition to those who labeled him soft on Communism.

Truman acknowledged the need to hold the line against Communist expansion in Korea. A Communist Korea would upset the balance of power in Asia and pose a unique threat to Japan and Formosa, America's new keys to regional security. Truman had committed American soldiers to contain northern aggression. His instinct, however, was to limit their mission. He did not want a potentially cataclysmic confrontation with the Soviets or the Chinese. To this end, Washington prevailed on Chiang Kai-shek not to escalate the fight by joining the South Koreans. After MacArthur regained the ground lost to the North Koreans with his famous amphibious attack at Inchon, Truman authorized American forces to push across the dividing line of North and South Korea, but only "provided that neither China nor the U.S.S.R. intervened in the war." If Chinese or Soviet troops moved into Korea, he added, American forces were to remain south of the 38th parallel. When the Chinese invaded, U.S. troops retreated across the line.[29]

Increasingly suspicious of the administration's commitment to fight Communism, and with an eye to the 1952 Republican presidential nomination, General MacArthur balked at the order from Truman. Since mid-1950, MacArthur had publicly disagreed with the president's strategy. The hero of the war in the Pacific could not fathom a limited conflict. A southerner himself, he, no more than Russell, did not want to lead another lost cause. He advocated extending the bombing directly to China and asked that Chiang Kai-shek's forces be allowed to join the fight. In one of the greatest miscalculations of his career, MacArthur assumed that the Chinese would not invade. That he had misjudged Beijing did little to shake the "American Caesar's" confidence. As Truman pushed for peace talks in March 1951, MacArthur undercut the president by declaring that the Chinese and Koreans must surrender or face annihilation. Then, in early April, Republican congressional leader Joseph W. Martin of Massachusetts released a letter from the general declaring that the United States "must win" and accept "no substitute for victory." Truman fired MacArthur for insubordination, igniting another political firestorm.

Russell's position on the proper strategy in Korea differed from both Truman and MacArthur. He was as willing as MacArthur to bomb China and unleash Chiang's soldiers. Russell was committed to military victory as a deterrent to future Communist aggression. But the senator was even less willing than Truman to risk escalating the ground war once the Chinese entered the fray. Where Russell called for a full troop withdrawal, the administration left American troops in place to help defend South Korea. Such was Russell's paradox in Asia: quick and total victory or complete extraction of U.S. forces.

Russell's recommendations on Korea were never really seriously considered by the administration. This is not to say that his position did not serve the senator well. Indeed, Russell's Asian strategy left him in the politically advantageous place between being hard on Communism and soft on war. This stance earned him the respect of right and left, isolationist and internationalist, Asia-firster and Europe-firster, and made him the ultimate arbitrator of centrist policy in Korea.

Richard Russell's career changed dramatically when he was called to head the "MacArthur hearings" in the spring of 1951. The negative reaction to Truman's firing of MacArthur was at first nearly universal. The general's mystique remained strong despite his mixed military record. He returned to the United States not in disgrace but as a conquering hero. MacArthur addressed a joint session of Congress, and no member dared to criticize him. Perhaps worst of all for the administration, MacArthur's firing played into the hands of Joe McCarthy, who told reporters that "the son of a bitch [Truman] should be impeached."[30] Congressional Republicans demanded an immediate investigation. The hearings would fall naturally to the Armed Services and Foreign Relations committees in the Senate.

Russell and the Armed Services Committee made plans to hold independent hearings in mid-April, but after he and Senator Tom Connally of Texas, a fellow Southerner and chairman of the Foreign Affairs Committee, discussed the matter, they agreed to a joint inquiry of the two committees. Since military matters would dominate, Russell would preside over the hearings.

Both the Democrats and the Republicans were comfortable with Russell's chairmanship. Truman had already begun to establish public support for his position and rebuild his base in the Democratic Party. Among his first steps, apparently, had been to make peace with Southern Democrats by secretly backing Richard Russell for the Democratic leadership. Russell declined, but his position as Armed Services head and chairman of the MacArthur hearings served the president's and the Democratic Party's interests well. Congressional Democrats supported Russell almost to a man. Lyndon Johnson and J. William Fulbright went so far as to entrust their proxies to the Georgian. Republicans, too, liked Russell. None could accuse the senator of being a yes-man for the administration. They knew well of Russell's disagreements with the president and the party over civil rights and noted that he had run against Truman as the alternative Southern candidate within the Democratic Party in the 1948 presidential election. In announcing the hearings, Russell had demonstrated his impartiality in praising MacArthur as one of the "great captains of history." Committee Republicans like Henry Cabot Lodge Jr. and Leverett Saltonstall regularly deferred to Russell throughout the hearings. Marquis Childs of the *Washington Post-Dispatch* predicted that the senator would be judicious, calm, and objective.[31]

Russell delivered on these expectations. The senator established tight security to prevent leaks and closed the questioning of witnesses to reporters to prevent a media circus and the release of military secrets. He also authorized the hourly distribution to the press of edited transcripts of each day's session. He enforced executive privilege in protecting conversations between the president and the Joint Chiefs and blocked Republican attempts to use the hearings to bash Truman for being soft on Communism. Finally, he avoided issuing a politically charged committee report, instead stressing American unity and inviting all parties to comment on the testimony as individual members of Congress.

Most importantly, Russell steered the committee members away from making statements, allowing the witnesses for the most part to speak for themselves. As *U.S. News & World Report* would declare in the midst of the hearings, Russell's only problem was "being scrupulously fair to both sides." Of the committee's fist witness, Douglas MacArthur, Russell was "searching" but "unhostile" in his questioning.[32] The senator also gave MacArthur a full three days to make his argument that the administration's restraint on his actions in Korea amounted to appeasement. The general voiced the military's frustrations at being expected to achieve victory without being allowed the firepower to do so, but he came across as arrogant and either ignorant of or unconcerned with global realities. If a world war resulted from his actions, he famously said, it was not his responsibility. Nor did he admit any error in judgment, blaming his miscalculation of Chinese intentions on the CIA. MacArthur, the putative hero, was passing the buck.

When Secretary of State George C. Marshall and Chairman of the Joint Chiefs Omar Bradley took the stand, the tide turned against MacArthur. Marshall, Bradley, and the Joint Chiefs fully supported the president. The administration was not appeasing Communists, Marshall testified; it had engaged the enemy as fully as it could given the resources at hand and had held the line against Communist expansion. The reunification of the Korean peninsula was simply not worth the risk of atomic war. Bradley then delivered the most quoted line of the hearings. Had MacArthur's engagement of China been approved, it would involve the U.S. "in the wrong war, at the wrong place, at the wrong time, with the wrong enemy." Marshall, Bradley, and all of the Joint Chiefs agreed, too, that the firing of MacArthur was more than warranted. Civilian control of the military must remain sacrosanct.[33]

Men of such stature, ego, and intellect could not exactly be steered to predetermined answers through clever questioning, but Russell and his Democratic colleagues on the committee, especially his protégé Lyndon Johnson, organized the hearings in such a way as to give MacArthur his day in court while demonstrating that the president's actions had been sound. It was Johnson's aides, George Reedy and Gerald Siegel, who supervised the staff work and summarized the testimony for the press. Reedy and Siegel also formulated questions for the committee members each day. Johnson took Reedy and Siegel's questions to Russell every morning before the hearing. The questions, Siegel remembered, showed that MacArthur was "wrong in his analysis of the policies that should have been implemented in the Korean War." Russell later denied using questions from the staff, but that was only because the senator had already thought of the same questions himself. Russell, Johnson, and the staff collectively erected the main bumps over which MacArthur would stumble: how did the general know how Moscow and Peking would respond to aggressive American action, and would the world continue to support the United States if it ignited a wider war?[34]

As the MacArthur hearings indicated, Russell was becoming a master of a kind of passive, almost hidden-hand politics. While he asked many of the toughest questions, he allowed his lieutenants, like Johnson, to follow up and share the political fallout, whether good or bad. He also defused rhetorical hyperbole by seeming to defer to the wisdom of experts, in this case the most respected military leaders in the country. Finally, and perhaps most effectively, he stretched the hearings out to allow public passions to subside. Even in an age before the Internet and cable television, seven weeks of summarized hearings were too much to sustain the attention of most Americans. With truce talks getting under way in late June and early July, public support for MacArthur began to erode.

At the close of the testimony, Russell appeared on the cover of *U.S. News & World Report*. He told the periodical that no one had gained politically from the hearings. No one, he might have added, except himself. Both sides felt they had gained under his leadership. The hearings had clearly revealed the weaknesses in MacArthur's arguments and had saved the foreign policy center for Truman and the Democrats, but Russell's evaluation did not spare the administration. He hoped the hearings would push the White House to reverse its policy and consider a blockade of North Korea as a way to move negotiations forward. He also openly reevaluated the administration's, and indeed his own, stance on putting Europe above Asia in global containment strategy, and he questioned U.S. reliance on the UN. Russell, in addition, criticized Secretary Marshall for statements suggesting that Chinese bases in Manchuria might have been bombed in response to Chinese intervention in Korea but for fear of Russia's entrance into the war. The senator had come to endorse a wedge strategy in Asia and suggested that such statements served to drive China and the Soviets closer together rather than further apart. Finally, Russell suggested that the hearings had pointed to administrative difficulties in setting arms aid priorities. Assistance outlays, he predicted, could be limited in the next legislative session by those who believed that the "U.S. has borne an unequal share of the Korean burden."[35]

His skillful, seemingly nonpartisan handling of the MacArthur hearings gained Russell a national following. Talk about a vice presidential or presidential run naturally followed. Russell initially resisted the idea. A political realist, he knew full well the difficulties he faced as a candidate from the Deep South. The 1948 election had proved that the Democrats could oppose Southern issues, namely segregation, and still win. Truman and the liberal wing of the party had accepted a civil rights platform that year, causing a walkout of delegates from several Southern states. The so-called Dixiecrats went on to form the States Rights Party and run their own candidate, Strom Thurmond of South Carolina. Despite the Dixiecrat revolt, Truman won the general election. Southerners, it seemed at first glance, were no longer as crucial a piece in the Democratic coalition. A failed Russell candidacy would prove that point all the more.

Upon further reflection, though, Russell saw a vigorous, even if an ultimately unsuccessful run as an opportunity to bring the South back into the Democratic fold and increase its power within the party. The South had actually been split in 1948. Russell had been among a group of powerful Southern political leaders who remained loyal to the Democratic Party, believing that the region's best political hope still resided with it rather than the Dixiecrats. The Georgian's and the other Southerners' loyalty was a crucial factor in helping Truman win what was ultimately one of the closest elections in American history. A legitimate Russell candidacy in 1952 would easily gain the backing of Southerners and bring many, if not all, of the Dixiecrats back to the Democratic Convention. He might lose the nomination, but the Georgian would gain the opportunity to tell his Southern backers that since they had expected the support of the Democratic Party if he had won, they were honor bound to support the Democrats now that he had lost.[36]

Russell, though he knew he would probably lose, resented the notion that a Southerner could not win the presidency. Throngs of people in the North told him he was the best candidate but would not get their vote because of his regional roots. Russell squirmed under the perceived injustice, but the senator deserved much of the blame. It was not simply that Russell was from the South; it was that he openly and vigorously supported racially discriminatory institutions and helped them become synonymous with Southern identity. While he cushioned his racism with calls for states rights and free enterprise, his strident rhetoric in opposition to the FEPC and integration of the armed forces came back to haunt him.

Few, however, argued with the kind of cultural relativism, negative though it was, that accompanied Russell's racial worldview. Russell's argument against the integration of the armed forces in 1950 touched on a popular premise:

> Differences in customs and habits exist and are a part of the heritage of each community. These conditions are, of course, not completely static. Through the process of evolution changes are occurring. Some of these changes are wholesome and are to the benefit of all. But these changes take time. They must be based upon mutual understanding and good will. Their success depends upon voluntary cooperation. They cannot be forced and efforts to coerce people by law will fail.[37]

Abroad, the United States had "undertaken to apply American methods to systems and cultures that are entirely different from our own," Russell told an interviewer during the campaign. This, he said, "has resulted in some waste in our foreign aid programs." Russell pledged to continue the programs, "but not at the high expenditure levels proposed by the present administration." Such sentiments appealed to a nation disenchanted with the high cost in lives, money, and resources involved in fighting the Korean War. Two years of conflict had resulted in nothing better than a stalemate. Russell offered to better balance the nation's "assistance to other free people" against American "ability to pay and produce."[38]

Russell sounded much like the eventual victor in the 1952 presidential election, Dwight D. Eisenhower. Like Ike, Russell warned of the dangers of power centralized in the federal government and the inadequacy of U.S. responses to Communist threats around the world. Russell, also like Eisenhower, called for a reliable internationalism that carefully weighed resources against commitments. The Georgian declared himself a "middle-of-the-road man," supportive of the new and fair deals, but cautious of creating government dependencies; for government protection of collective bargaining rights, but also for states rights to enact "right-to-work" measures; committed to defending segregation, but determined to protect "the rights of every American citizen without regard to race, creed, or national origin"; committed to collective security against Communism, but devoted to rearmament and "independence of action."[39]

Russell may have been correct when he claimed that he was the only Democratic candidate who could beat Eisenhower. But the senator had to win the nomination first. Harry Truman identified the crux of the problem when he told Russell that he would be elected hands down if he hailed from Indiana or Missouri. Labor and civil rights supporters in the North simply would not vote for a Southerner. On the first ballot, Russell received 268 votes to Estes Kefauver's (D-TN) 340 and Adlai Stevenson's (D-IL) 273. That was as close as he would come. Stevenson gained enough ground on the next two ballots to ensure the nomination and the Democrats' loss to Eisenhower in the fall.

The Russell paradox—strong defense but limited intervention—helped establish the senator as a centrist on foreign policy and defense issues in the early years of the Cold War. It earned him the support of the left and the right, helped him successfully mediate the MacArthur controversy, and gained him a national following as a presidential candidate in 1952. However, the paradox also contained within it the fundamental assumptions that would leave Russell on the margins of influence. Racism and protectionism, the fundamental motivating forces behind the paradox, were increasingly out of favor within the senator's own party. The Democrats would commit to civil rights at home and liberty abroad as mutually reinforcing foundations for social stability and peace. Russell's views, they argued, were anachronistic, contradictory, and counterproductive. Americans might agree with the senator that there were "literally hundreds of millions of people throughout the world who would gladly subject themselves to the so-called great discrimination" in the United States, but Democrats were convinced that social injustice was real and at the heart of the nation's and the world's ills.[40] A man virtually without a party, Russell was relegated to the margins of electoral if not congressional politics. "Jim Crow," as Lyndon Johnson later put it, had placed a political "collar" on smart men like Russell, as sure as if "they were sentenced to a chain gang in Georgia."[41]

Notes

1. Calvin Mcleod Logue and Dwight L. Freshley, eds., *Voice of Georgia: Speeches of Richard B. Russell, 1928–1969* (Macon: Mercer University Press, 1997), 248.

2. Logue and Freshley, *Speeches of Richard B. Russell*, 246–47.

3. Logue and Freshley, *Speeches of Richard B. Russell*, 248–50.

4. Logue and Freshley, *Speeches of Richard B. Russell*, 264–65.

5. Logue and Freshley, *Speeches of Richard B. Russell*, 61, 65; *Congressional Record*, 81st Cong., 2nd sess., 1950, 96, pt. 5:6695.

6. Logue and Freshley, *Speeches of Richard B. Russell*, 177–78, 280.

7. *Congressional Record*, 79th Cong., 2nd sess., 1946, 92, pt. 1:178–82.

8. *Congressional Record*, 81st Cong., 1st sess., 1949, 95, pt. 1:570–72.

9. *Congressional Record*, 79th Cong., 2nd sess., 1946, 92, pt. 6:7458; Russell to Stevenson, March 11, 1947, box 8, series 16, Russell Papers, Richard Russell Memorial Library; "Georgian's Plan for England," *U.S. News & World Report* 22 (March 14, 1947): 68.

10. *Congressional Record*, 80th Cong., 2nd sess., 1948, 94, pt. 5:5665–66; pt. 6:7355–65.

11. *Congressional Record*, 80th Cong., 2nd sess., 1948, 94, pt. 6:7355–65 and 7676–77; 81st Cong., 2nd sess., 1950, 96, pt. 7:8973, 8991–93, 9073.

12. *Congressional Record*, 82nd Cong., 1st sess., 1951, 97, pt.2:2013; Logue and Freshley, *Speeches of Richard B. Russell*, 251.

13. Index by author: Russell, 82nd Congress, 1951–52, box 2, 80th–94th Congressional Committee Calendars, Records of the United States Senate, RG 46, National Archives.

14. *Congressional Record*, 82nd Cong., 2nd sess., 1952, 98, pt. 1:232–35.

15. *Congressional Record*, 82nd Cong., 1st sess., 1951, 97, pt. 3:3169.

16. *Congressional Record*, 82nd Cong., 1st sess., 1951, 97, pt. 3:3170.

17. Gilbert C. Fite, *Richard B. Russell, Jr., Senator from Georgia* (Chapel Hill: University of North Carolina Press, 1991), 218–19, 248–49.

18. "Europe's Need: More Self-Help," *U.S. News & World Report* 32 (December 2, 1968): 28–33.

19. *Congressional Record*, 82nd Cong., 1st sess., 1951, 97, pt. 3:3947.

20. *Congressional Record*, 80th Cong., 2nd sess., 1948, 94, pt. 5:6459–60, 6864.

21. Russell to Neff, December 1, 1965, and Russell to East, June 22, 1965, box 36, series 16, Russell Papers, Richard B. Russell Memorial Library.

22. Russell to Giglio, August 16, 1965, and Russell to Wolfson, January 4, 1966, box 36, series 16, Russell Papers, Richard B. Russell Memorial Library.

23. Russell to Wolfson, January 4, 1966, box 36, series 16, Russell Papers, Richard B. Russell Memorial Library.

24. Fite, *Russell*, 251.

25. Russell to Gravey, July 12, 1950, and Russell to Hunnicutt, July 26, 1950, box 21, series 16, Russell Papers, Richard B. Russell Memorial Library.

26. Logue and Freshley, *Speeches of Richard B. Russell*, 68–69.

27. Russell to Davis, January 12, 1951, box 21, series XVI, Russell Papers, Richard B. Russell Memorial Library.

28. "Europe's Need: More Self-Help," 28–33.

29. Alonzo Hamby, *Man of the People: A Life of Harry S. Truman* (New York: Oxford University Press, 1995), 542.

30. Hamby, *Man of the People*, 558.

31. Fite, *Russell*, 256.

32. "Man on a Tightrope," *U.S. News & World Report* 30 (May 18, 1951): 28–29.

33. David McCullough, *Truman* (New York: Simon & Schuster, 1992), 854.

34. Robert Dallek, *Lone Star Rising: Lyndon Johnson and His Times, 1908–1960* (New York: Oxford University Press, 1991), 399–400; George Reedy Oral History, 4, May 21, 1982, Lyndon Baines Johnson Library.

35. "Senator Russell, the Man Who Heard 2 Million Words, Thinks MacArthur Inquiry Did Some Good, Some Harm," *U.S. News & World Report* 30 (June 29, 1951): 28–33.

36. George Reedy Oral History, 4, May 21, 1982, Lyndon Baines Johnson Library.

37. *Congressional Record*, 81st Cong., 2nd sess., 1950, 96, pt. 7:8993.

38. "Quizzing Russell," *U.S. News & World Report* 32 (June 13, 1952): 54–62; *Congressional Record*, 82nd Cong., 2nd sess., 1952, 98, pt. 2:1587.

39. "Quizzing Russell," *U.S. News & World Report* 32 (June 13, 1952): 54–62.

40. *Congressional Record*, 81st Cong., 2nd sess., 1950, 96, pt. 5:6695.

41. Bill Leuchtenburg, *The White House Looks South* (Baton Rouge: Louisiana State University Press, 2005), 300.

3

Power and Responsibility

By the early 1950s, Richard Russell was one of the most powerful and respected men in the Senate. In 1953, he ranked third overall in seniority, he was the ranking Democrat on the Armed Services Committee and the second-ranking Democrat on the Appropriations Committee, and he controlled subcommittees on defense appropriations, CIA oversight, and atomic energy. Serious contenders for his Senate seat had all but disappeared in Georgia, and he led the Southern bloc in Congress on civil rights, agriculture, and defense issues. He was a master of Senate rules and procedure and had a keen sense of that body's constantly shifting political tectonics. His daily life was dominated by Senate work. He was not so much lonely as a loner. He was aloof from his staff, he had few close friends, and though he maintained a long-term relationship with Patricia Collins, an Atlanta native and lawyer with the Justice Department, he remained a bachelor. Russell retained ties to his siblings in Georgia, but he would reach the height of his power without the guidance of his parents. When his father died in 1938, he drew closer to his mother, who remained his most trusted confidant until her death in 1953. In the end, his family and his life was the Senate.

Russell's reputation for integrity, hard work, and fair play contributed to his power. He arrived at work early, took meals daily in the Senate cafeteria, and went home late to his empty apartment. He knew the Senate inside out, its members, its traditions, and its procedure. He was a master compromiser and soother of egos. He respected others' ideas and became famous for his ability to put himself in the political shoes of others, even his worst enemies. But his capacity for empathy also gave him the ability to respectfully pick apart his opponents. Nobody was better at getting his political victims to smile as he eviscerated them. Russell's harshest critics appreciated him, and his closest allies venerated him. For John Stennis, he was a mentor. For Lyndon Johnson, he was a father figure. For both, he was a conduit to political power. Russell's hidden-hand style allowed his protégés to rise in the ranks. Rather than taking the public lead, the Georgian instead gave his charges the reins. When they succeeded, Russell shared the credit. When they failed, they shielded him from blame.

But Russell knew in the end that hard work, the respect of his colleagues, and the perquisites of seniority would only go so far. Ultimately, only knowledge and money mattered in Washington. Russell made certain that he was a control valve for both. He directed defense spending at a time when it constituted on average more than 50 percent of the federal budget. He shut off or opened the flow of dollars for the production of everything from missiles to combat boots. If a state relied on defense facilities, it needed Russell's support. The senator also kept at least one step ahead of his peers by mastering the information that informed procedure and policy. George Reedy remembered being surprised as Russell led "one of the most brilliant discussions of international politics" he had ever heard at a NATO conference in Paris in 1956. His understanding of the political intricacies of the member nations at that event, Reedy concluded, was the key piece in allowing the United States to work with socialist allies to pass a resolution denouncing the Soviet invasion of Hungary. Russell, an amateur diplomat, effectively outmaneuvered the world's foremost professionals.[1]

Russell's power to ensure his vision of U.S. foreign and defense posture was never greater than during the Eisenhower, Kennedy, and Johnson administrations. Yet that power had limits. Indeed, the senator largely conspired to check his own influence. He accepted that the direction of both foreign and defense policy was largely an executive prerogative, and he obsessively guarded against making the most important national security secrets public and political. Also limiting his influence was the fact that the independent senator's vision of foreign and defense policy never fully meshed with those of the Eisenhower, Kennedy, and Johnson administrations. Russell found common cause with each president but at the same time maintained positions more closely associated with their opponents. He believed, for example, more like Ike than JFK or LBJ, that U.S. resources were limited and must be used wisely in the pursuit of national defense. But more like Kennedy and Johnson than Eisenhower, Russell supported the maintenance of conventional forces to provide for a flexible response to Soviet aggression. On some issues,

Russell remained completely independent. Savings, Russell argued to the dismay of every administration, must come from the foreign aid programs. Thus, at the height of his power, Russell was never able to fully convince the executive branch that his vision of priorities better met the security interests of the nation. At most, the Georgian offered a dissenting voice that helped define the limits of American defense and foreign policy.

Of all the sources of Richard Russell's influence over policy, his access to and control of classified information were among the greatest. His daily review of the *Congressional Record*, his encyclopedic knowledge of Senate rules and procedure, his deep understanding of the nation's history, and his expertise in one of the most important functions of Congress—funding and oversight of military affairs—set him apart from most of his colleagues. But his critical ability to control the flow of privileged information to which only a few had access made him absolutely indispensable. Nowhere was this more apparent than in his leadership of the CIA Oversight Subcommittee.

In establishing the Central Intelligence Agency under the National Security Act of 1947, Congress retained almost no power to check the agency. The act provided that the CIA answered to the president alone, could protect its own sources and methods from unauthorized disclosure, and could perform any "other functions and duties related to intelligence affecting the national security" that the president and National Security Council deemed necessary. The enabling act for the CIA that passed in 1949, moreover, left the agency's director solely accountable for its expenditures and free to keep the purposes of those expenditures secret. Congress created only House and Senate subcommittees to rubber-stamp the appropriations.[2]

Russell was ideally positioned to hold a seat on the Senate subcommittee. CIA oversight in the Senate fell to the Armed Services Committee, of which Russell was then second in rank. Russell also ranked fourth on the Appropriations Committee and served on the Joint Committee on Atomic Energy. These assignments, plus his reputation for discretion, garnered him a place on and eventual chairmanship of the CIA Oversight Subcommittee.

Russell jealously guarded national secrets from foreign enemies as well as his colleagues who he thought could not be trusted to keep classified information confidential. Most famously, Russell protected the agency from what he saw as congressional efforts to limit the CIA's independence through expanded scrutiny. He was also, of course, protecting the power inherent in monopolizing access to the CIA for himself and the other members of the subcommittee.

The first such attempt came in 1953, when the young upstart senator from Montana, Mike Mansfield, proposed the establishment of a joint Senate-House committee to oversee the activities of the CIA more aggressively. Over the following three years, Mansfield pushed hard for a more "responsible" scrutiny of the agency, arguing that once "secrecy becomes sacrosanct, it invites abuse."[3] He gained the cosponsorship of fifty-four senators on the resolution in 1956, setting up what seemed to be its easy passage. But Russell and CIA director Allen Dulles resolutely opposed the Mansfield resolution. Russell declared to the Senate that nothing "should be held so sacred behind the curtain of classified matter" as "the activities of this agency."[4] The more who knew about its vital operations in the interest of national security, he argued, the more likely it was that those operations would fail. Trust me, he said in effect, and I will protect the nation's interest through the existing subcommittee. In the end, the Senate's esteem for Russell and its respect for the prerogatives of the Cold War won out. The resolution was defeated 59 to 27.

The second attempt to expand oversight of the CIA came in 1966, when Russell's friend and rival Senator J. William Fulbright of Arkansas moved to add three members of the Senate Foreign Relations Committee (SFRC) to the CIA subcommittee. Fulbright at first hoped to privately persuade Russell to adopt the change, but the Georgian refused. Fulbright, Mansfield, and others then moved to create a Full Committee on Intelligence Operations to replace the subcommittee. Russell, with the help of former CIA subcommittee member and then president Lyndon Johnson, moved to convince the press and members of the Senate that the SFRC under Fulbright had consistently leaked information affecting national security in the midst of crises in the Dominican Republic and Vietnam. The Senate effectively killed the Fulbright measure by a vote of 61 to 28.[5]

Russell's ability to limit oversight, protect his subcommittee, and guard CIA interests earned him favors. Though the senator's tight lip makes it difficult for any historian to gain the full picture of his access to CIA information, there is ample evidence in public sources that the agency kept him consistently abreast of its operations. In the congressional debates over Fulbright's intelligence committee resolution, for example, Russell admitted to knowing about and keeping secret CIA construction of U-2 surveillance aircraft and agency plans for the Bay of Pigs invasion.[6] He also admitted in an interview toward the end of his career that he knew about Soviet attempts to put nuclear missiles in Cuba before White House congressional briefings had taken place.[7] But perhaps the best evidence of his access to CIA information comes from recorded telephone conversations between Russell and President Johnson and the journal of the CIA's legislative counsel. On the phone with Johnson, Russell made repeated references to classified information, including one conversation in which the senator cited details that the CIA had directly divulged to him regarding Vietnam and Laos.[8] The legislative counsel's records also revealed that the agency frequently briefed him on its operations.[9] An open line with the senator, CIA officials knew, helped sustain his protection and generosity.

Russell's access to classified information sometimes extended even beyond the CIA's. On one occasion, when the senator claimed publicly that large Soviet transport aircraft flew Kremlin advisers to North Korea to exploit captured intelligence equipment from the *U.S.S. Pueblo*, an American warship captured by the North Koreans in January 1969, the CIA scrambled to verify the information. A follow-up confirmed that Russell's account was accurate, if subtly differing from and adding to CIA intelligence. Investigators reported being unable to discover the senator's sources, a revealing confession given the agency's and Russell's close relationship.[10] The senator, as its main protector, was a constant worry for the CIA. He controlled its purse strings and knew things that no other person in Washington was in a position to know. Russell thus leveraged the CIA in the same way he leveraged Congress and the White House: with insider access to information. Over time, that power redoubled as policy makers simply assumed that Russell knew as much or more than they did. By the mid-1950s, his opinion became indispensable to nearly all defense or foreign policy makers.

Russell's leadership of the Armed Services Appropriations Subcommittee had a similar effect. While Russell could not politically withhold or dispense money with a completely free hand, his perceived ability to do so allowed him to steer the general course of defense spending. He was among the first to criticize the Eisenhower administration's policy of cutting expenses by reducing conventional forces. When the president and Secretary of State John Foster Dulles called for a defense budget that was $5 billion less than Truman's and cut significantly into air force allocations, Russell castigated the administration. In September 1953, he told a national television audience on *Meet the Press* that he, too, wanted a balanced budget, but not at the expense of adequate security. Eisenhower could not cut $5 billion from the defense budget, Russell argued, and properly defend the United States from a Soviet attack. He then reiterated his lifelong mantra that a reduction in foreign aid would help cover the cost.

Russell's suggestions offered a balance to Republican leader Robert Taft's (R-OH) criticism that the Eisenhower cuts were "puny" and added an important voice to the long line of Democrats lamenting the defense decrease. Russell's badgering arguably had some effect. Eisenhower admitted in his diary that he was more concerned with those like Russell and Stuart Symington (D-MO), who were calling for increases, than with Republicans like Taft calling for further reductions. Though the Eisenhower administration did not in the end go as far as Russell hoped, defense expenditures remained relatively high throughout the decade, while the combined economic and military foreign aid expenditures abroad actually decreased between 1953 and 1957.

When the Democrats regained control of Congress in 1956, Russell's influence mushroomed. The senator's impact on the Suez crisis and subsequent mutual security debate provide key examples of the extent of Russell's power in defense and foreign affairs.

In 1952, Egyptian nationalist Gamal Abdel Nasser headed a military junta that forced the abdication of King Farouk. Over the next

Senator Richard Russell, Secretary of Defense Charles E. Wilson, and Senator Leverett Saltonstall, January 5, 1955. Courtesy of the Richard B. Russell Library for Political Research and Studies, Athens, Georgia.

two years, Nasser solidified his one-man rule and rallied nationalists by condemning the vestiges of British and French colonial rule in the Middle East, denouncing Israel, and calling for the withdrawal of British troops from Egypt. Hoping to protect American interests, maintain stability in the region, and set a course that coincided with the rising tide of nationalism, the Eisenhower administration sought to cultivate Nasser by offering him nonmilitary aid. But Nasser needed arms, especially after Israel launched a raid in February 1955 on an Egyptian army camp in the Gaza Strip. When the United States refused to provide weapons, the Egyptian leader struck a deal with Czechoslovakia. Eisenhower saw the move as a sign of Communist penetration in the Middle East.

In early 1956, Eisenhower moved to negotiate a peace between Egypt and Israel that would defuse another potential Cold War flashpoint. Presidential aide Robert Anderson shuttled between Cairo and Tel Aviv for weeks to no avail. Nasser, Anderson reported, was the main stumbling block. He labeled the Egyptian leader a threat to American interests in the region as Nasser imperiled non-Communist Europe's access to Middle Eastern oil. As punishment for his cooperation with Communists, the administration moved to isolate Nasser by cutting off his aid and wooing his neighbors—Libya, Saudi Arabia, Lebanon, and Ethiopia—with economic assistance.

Washington's decision to punish Egypt for the Czechoslovak arms deal posed a mortal threat to Nasser's Aswan Dam project. The dam was to be the crowning achievement of his reign, providing water to more than a million acres of farmland and generating half of Egypt's electricity requirements. Nasser responded by threatening to go to the Soviets for the necessary money.

Congressional leaders like Russell had already objected to the rising cost of foreign aid earlier in the year. In January, he had complained that the Department of State was "so sterile of ideas that the only answer they have to the Russians is to ask for more money."[11] Russell and other Southerners also understood that aid diverted to the dam project would indirectly subsidize Egyptian cotton and hurt agriculture in their home region. Nasser's wooing of the Soviets only added to administration opponents' lists of complaints. When in mid-July Republican Senate minority leader William Knowland (R-CA) told Dulles that Congress was ready to prohibit the use of American funds to finance the dam, Dulles halted negotiations with the Egyptians. In a strikingly bold response, Nasser nationalized the Suez Canal, arguing that he needed to make up the lost revenue for the Aswan Dam project. The British and French, who together owned most of the stock in the canal, made plans for military action. Secretary of State Dulles explained the situation to members of Congress in mid-August. The administration would act to counter Nasser's move to take over the canal as well as block any use of force by the French and British before diplomatic solutions were exhausted.

Russell doubted Nasser's willingness to cooperate. He also doubted the ability of the United States to control its allies or mediate a successful conclusion to the conflict. The White House, he suggested, was avoiding the underlying problem: that money would not buy a solution to the problem. The recent American trouble with Egypt, he reminded his colleagues, was evidence that the basic assumptions behind foreign aid were flawed.[12] Nevertheless, Eisenhower was convinced that strangling Nasser through negotiation and economic pressure would work far better than abandoning aid altogether.

Through the fall of 1956, Britain and France refrained from the use of force and took their dispute to the United Nations. Behind the scenes, however, they made preparations to oust Nasser from the canal zone by force of arms. In mid-October, the French and British moved their militaries into position and conspired with Israel to trigger the action. Israel would invade the Sinai and push on to the Suez Canal, giving the Europeans a pretext for intervention.

On October 29, Israeli forces invaded the Sinai, and French and British paratroopers dropped into the canal zone, ostensibly to "protect" the international waterway. The Eisenhower administration immediately submitted a resolution to the United Nations General Assembly condemning the invasion. The president did not want to completely alienate America's allies, but he could not resist seeing the crisis in Cold War terms. The military conflict prematurely initiated by the French, British, and Israelis would destabilize the region, giving the Soviets an opportunity to gain allies as it backed Arab nationalism. The resolution was not unsympathetic to the reasons for British and French action, but its condemnation of the use of force was intended to garner support in Africa, Asia, and the Arab world and blunt any Soviet attempt to label the United States a sponsor of European imperialism. In early November, as Eisenhower won a sweeping reelection victory, the British and French agreed to a UN-brokered cease-fire.

With winter's arrival, the violence in the Middle East subsided, but the issue of long-term American commitments in the region became a hot topic of debate. Conditions had changed. With the U.S. relationship with Britain and France strained and Europe's influence in the Arab world eroded in the wake of the Suez crisis, the country could no longer rely on its allies to check Russian ambitions in the region. Hoping to thwart any advantage the Soviets might take in the Middle East, President Eisenhower articulated a new doctrine in early 1957 that pledged U.S. military and economic aid, and, if necessary, armed intervention to stop Communist aggression and slow subversion in the Middle East. At the same time, the administration asked Congress for the authority to allocate at the president's discretion $200 million in aid to the region during each of the next two fiscal years.

The Eisenhower Doctrine drew immediate criticism from Democratic congressional leaders like Hubert Humphrey (D-MN), who worried that it was a "predated declaration of war." Russell, too, voiced concerns about the "shadowland between the president's authority to use Armed Forces and the necessity for a declaration of war."[13] But Russell was more troubled by the appropriation. While he grudgingly recognized the commander in chief's authority to deploy troops without a declaration of war, he insisted that the expenditure of public funds came under the sole jurisdiction of Congress. Over the years, Russell argued, along with most of his colleagues in the Senate, that Congress had been far too generous in granting foreign aid appropriations and almost completely uncritical of the ways in which they had been spent. Congress had thus granted the executive a "blank check" for a "pig in a poke." The legislature might decide to appropriate Eisenhower's aid request, Russell declared, but not before demanding and receiving an outline of how the money would be used. If Congress did not use its only real source of power to check the executive's foreign policy, it would be derelict in its duty.[14]

At stake, according to Russell, was the whole direction of America's foreign aid program, and indeed the overall future of the American economy and its national security. The $200 million, he argued, was just "the entering wedge," "the camel's nose," "the foot in the door." If the current trend continued of granting aid to trouble spots around the world without thought to limits on objectives, time, and resources, the Middle East grant will be "merely a down payment or 'earnest money' on a program that could run into billions of dollars over the years." It was not the idea of spending money itself that most troubled Russell. Indeed, he had supported the Marshall Plan and the rebuilding of Europe after World War II. It was the idea of using money "to cure the troubles of the world" and "to placate people," without concern for costs. Given the hazards, Russell contended, "we must start tapering off the foreign-aid program if we ever hope to have a program of fiscal responsibility at home." All federal programs needed trimming, according to Russell, but indiscriminate increases in foreign aid made it politically impossible for senators to cut elsewhere. To turn down "Grandma" for a "$10 increase in her old age assistance" while voting for aid overseas, Russell argued, would end the political careers of every legislator in Washington. Spending reductions must start with foreign aid. Any ongoing aid should be directed to countries that could help themselves through efforts such as the Truman administration's Point Four programs that delivered U.S. science and technology to underdeveloped areas.[15]

Russell deemed keeping the U.S. economy strong as far more important than wooing allies with American money. The logic down home in Georgia, Russell told his colleagues, was that a person cannot "spend himself rich" or "drink himself sober." The same logic applied to foreign aid. Spending overseas was not making the nation more prosperous or secure. Only economic strength at home coupled with overwhelming military might protected the national interest. Eisenhower's promise to use military force in the Middle East, Russell asserted, would do enough to prevent the spread of Communism on its own. The senator had concluded from the Suez crisis that the Russians were not in a bidding war in the Middle East. "It seemed that the United States was almost ready to build the Aswan Dam, on the theory that if the United States did not build it, the Russians would build it," Russell told his fellow senators. "But then, when one day it was announced that the United States would not contribute to the building of the Aswan Dam, within 24 hours the Soviet Union announced, 'We have never seriously considered building the Aswan Dam.'" Indeed, where the Russians were selling their wares in the area, making both money and friends, Russell contended, the United States delivered grants, lost money, and had yet to gain a reliable ally in the region.[16]

Russell's opposition to the Eisenhower Doctrine aligned him with senators like J. William Fulbright (D-AR), who was then pushing for a new Democratic foreign policy offensive castigating the administration's amateurish efforts to deal with the Suez crisis. For nearly two months following the White House's introduction of the Eisenhower Doctrine, Russell, Fulbright, and Democratic members of the Senate Armed Services and Foreign Relations Committees held hearings and offered modifications to the administration's proposed course of action. Russell, with cosponsors Harry Byrd (D-VA) and John Stennis (D-MS), proposed the most politically potent of the substitutes. It placed two principal restrictions on the president's resolution. The first retained notice that U.S. troops would be used, if necessary, against Communist aggression in the Middle East, but it limited the president's power over such a commitment. It stipulated that the joint resolution authorizing the use of force could be terminated by a concurrent resolution of the two houses of Congress. A concurrent resolution did not need the president's signature to take effect. The second restriction limited the president's authority in distributing aid by insisting that Congress be given time to collect information and vote on specific economic projects under the appropriation proposed by the White House.[17]

Russell defended his substitute resolution in the Senate chamber on February 27, 1957. He asserted that his amendments should not be construed as a vote of no confidence in President Eisenhower, but they were necessary to preserve Congress's power over the purse and prevent the trend toward an overreliance on foreign aid in American policy. There was no emergency in the Middle East, he argued, that outweighed the larger systemic concerns. There was time enough to review the specifics of the appropriation more closely before a decision was made.[18]

Meanwhile, the simmering Suez crisis had come to a diplomatic head. King Saud of Saudi Arabia, Eisenhower's new choice to be America's chief Arab ally, had visited Washington and reluctantly endorsed the doctrine. The leaders of Iraq, Libya, and Lebanon had also voiced support for the American initiative. But continued Arab support for the Eisenhower Doctrine would depend on Israel's willingness to leave Egyptian territory. While France and Britain had withdrawn their military forces, Israel had not, hoping to expand its navigation rights in the Gulf of Aqaba. In retaliation, Nasser had blocked traffic through the Suez Canal, shutting off oil to Europe. The administration came under immediate pressure to help end the ongoing conflict by forcing Israeli evacuation of the Sinai. Washington supported a UN sanction cutting off some $100 million a year in U.S. aid for Israel. Russell voiced no dissent when he and other congressional leaders were briefed on February 20. Rather, the Georgia senator urged the president to "make a statement to crystallize public opinion" in support of the UN action.[19]

Russell was not at all confident, however, that the administration could balance the emerging nationalist tensions in the Middle East with aid money. To act without careful consideration was to "risk an arms race in the Middle East." The administration should not assume that it could calibrate aid to Saudi Arabia, Egypt, and Israel so as to win those countries' support against Communism while providing a lasting deterrent to war. The "elimination of arms assistance," he insisted, "will do more to help the United Nations create a peaceful atmosphere in the Middle East than will any other single step we might take."[20] Eisenhower considered Russell's argument shortsighted. He countered that the elimination of economic and military assistance from the resolution would specifically impair the Middle Eastern nations' ability to deter internal subversion.[21] Russell's amendments worried administration supporters more than the other democratic versions. "This is gong to be our toughest vote," Republican senator from California William F. Knowland told Secretary of State Dulles on February 27; "R[ussell] thinks he has 40–41 votes."[22] Dulles and others immediately moved to counter Russell. The secretary of state, Assistant Secretary Robert Hill, and the president delivered letters to the Senate denouncing Russell's resolution and defending their own. Events conspired against Russell as well. On March 1, Israel gave in to UN pressure and announced plans to withdraw. With that, support for the Russell substitution began to fade. While the Southern bloc, committed to the fight against foreign aid and increasingly at odds with the administration over civil rights, generally stayed with Russell, the Georgian lost some key Southern supporters, including Foreign Relations Committee chairman J. William Fulbright; the powerful senator from Tennessee, Albert Gore Sr.; and Majority Leader Lyndon Johnson. While Johnson later claimed that "it was the hardest thing he had ever done" given Russell's sponsorship of the Texan for majority leader, Johnson voted against the Russell substitute, fearing that too much congressional opposition to the Eisenhower Doctrine would undermine U.S. prestige in the Middle East and weaken the president's ability to deal with the Soviet Union.[23] Given the Israeli withdrawal, other Democrats, including John F. Kennedy (D-MA), joined Johnson in affirming the Eisenhower Doctrine.[24] On March 3, the Senate overwhelmingly voted down the Russell substitute, 58 to 28. Two days later, it passed the administration's resolution, 72 to 19.[25]

On March 9, the president signed the resolution into law, and by the end of the month, the Suez Canal had reopened. Europe was out of a bind, and the United States had reaffirmed its commitment against Communism in the region. As Russell predicted, though, the long-term problem would be balancing aid issues amid the ongoing conflict between Israel and its Arab neighbors. Ten years later, on the eve of the 1967 war, Russell would wonder aloud with his constituents what American aid and involvement in the Middle East had really bought.[26]

Just days before the March 3, 1957, vote on the Russell substitution to the Eisenhower administration's Middle East resolution, White House legislative liaison Bryce Harlow predicted that "we will win on the Russell res[olution]," but "life will be grim on Mutual Security" given the resulting "bad spirit" among senators.[27] Harlow was right. Numerous congressmen had been calling for an overhaul of this pioneering aid program to the Third World. Isolationist Republicans lamented the unnecessary involvement in overseas affairs, fiscal conservatives complained about the cost, liberal internationalists called for a more open accounting of specific goals under the program, and hard-line anti-Communists demanded an end to aid for nations unwilling to take sides in the Cold War. Russell agreed with them all and became part of the "foreign aid revolt" in Congress that constituted one of the most important checks on executive foreign policy during the Cold War.[28]

In response to congressional pressure for mutual security reform, President Eisenhower introduced major changes to the program in late May. He returned to arguments for increased aid to the Middle East, explaining that American investments in foreign aid bolstered the nation's defense. Building the Third World's military strength while helping to raise its standard of living prevented successful Communist subversion and gained crucial allies for the United States. To this end, the president proposed a Developmental Loan Fund that would receive $500 million in fiscal 1958 and $750 million in each of the following fiscal years. In addition, he asked for $300 million for an emergency fund to be used at his discretion for technical assistance abroad. The total cost of the programs would come to $3.87 billion.

As the debate raged over the summer on mutual security and its place in the administration's proposed budget, Russell offered few public remarks about the plan. When he did, he voiced particular concern about the emergency fund, "which removes all the economic aid from any real congressional control."[29] However quiet Russell was in public, administration operatives recognized that Russell was a major behind-the-scenes voice in building opposition to the mutual security program.

At a breakfast meeting with President Eisenhower, Lyndon Johnson told the president that it was important to "see Dick Russell off the record." Russell, Johnson understood better than perhaps anyone, represented the voice of the white South. His opposition to foreign aid was shared by most Southerners and indeed was tied to the region's sentiments on civil rights. The "increasing responsibilities of the Federal Government in the field of international relations," Russell often repeated the common Southern assumption, "creates a threat to the rights of States and our dual system of government." In this calculation, the enhanced federal/executive power necessary to meet the threat of Communism came at a cost to state and local control of a range of issues, most importantly race relations.[30]

Johnson was a committed Southerner, as well as Russell's friend and protégé, but they disagreed on both civil rights and foreign aid. Though reticent to do so publicly, Johnson supported civil rights in principle and was the driving force behind the 1957 Civil Rights Bill. Russell disagreed with Johnson's position but understood. The Georgian could not give his blessing to his colleague from Texas, but he knew well that the South needed Johnson and that the majority leader's success and chance to move on to the presidency depended on his support of civil rights reform. Johnson also generally backed foreign aid spending. He had taken the president's side over Russell's in the debate on executive control of aid to the Middle East, and, while helping to reduce defense and foreign aid spending overall, he basically hoped to meet the president's request in both departments.[31]

Seeking to craft a compromise civil rights bill and balance liberal and Southern needs in the Democratic Party while at the same time following his convictions on national security and racial issues, Johnson provided the president at their breakfast with ammunition to use against his friend. Russell was "very anti-economic aid" but would go along with military appropriations, Johnson advised. Further separating personal affection from political expediency, Johnson added details about Russell's personality that could be useful. Russell, he intimated, was "shy, reticent, sensitive personally." A show of empathy, concern, and personal friendship might go a long way in winning him over. Johnson then suggested giving a little on the pending civil rights legislation to encourage Russell "to be helpful with respect to mutual aid appropriation." If that failed, the president ought to be prepared to talk about closing military installations in Georgia.[32] When Eisenhower called Russell that evening armed with Johnson's advice, Russell said that he would continue to avoid speaking publicly on the foreign aid bill and would support the president generally on defense matters. But he would not alter his fundamental opposition to foreign aid and would vote against the appropriation bill funding it. There was no need, apparently, to waste time even discussing civil rights.[33]

The Mutual Security Act of 1957 in the end authorized $500 million less than Eisenhower requested and allowed for only a two- rather than a three-year Developmental Loan Fund. Later, at Russell's instigation, Congress cut the appropriation bill even further, giving Eisenhower only $2.8 billion for mutual security and only $300 million for the first year of the Developmental Loan Fund. Still, the overall trajectory of American foreign policy was running against the Georgian. Economic aid steadily increased during the later Eisenhower years despite Russell's continued dissent, going from $1.5 billion in 1956 and 1957 to $1.8 billion in 1958 and $3.3 billion in 1959. And, closer to home, the 1957 Civil Rights Bill, while severely weakened under Russell's and the Southern bloc's pressure, passed, marking a radical and lasting change in Congress's posture toward racial issues.

Russell continued to use his power to try to change the course of both foreign and domestic policy in the late 1950s. His greatest opportunity to demonstrate to the administration and his own party that it was time to change directions came in the fall of 1957. The coincidental occurrence of the Little Rock crisis and the Soviet Union's launching of Sputnik put Russell's and other Southerners' arguments in a new perspective. His position that the nation had mistakenly spent its money and energy on foreign aid and civil rights rather than defense and the protection of states' rights gained at least a temporary resonance. That, in turn, fueled one of the Democrats' and Russell's principle indictments of the Eisenhower administration: the missile gap.

Richard Russell's argument that federal and executive power had stripped the states of their rights reached a fevered pitch in late September 1957. On September 24, President Eisenhower sent federal troops to Little Rock, Arkansas, to enforce a federal court's order to desegregate Central High School. Publicly, Russell declared that the president's actions demonstrated the "folly and danger of politically dictated federal power from Washington." It was, according to Russell, an indication of the executive's willingness to use "overwhelming military might to take over functions of the state," and constituted a long step toward "totalitarian rule." Privately, Russell vented to Eisenhower in a long telegram. The senator told the president that his methods were "high-handed and illegal," resembling the tactics formed in "the office of Hitler's Storm Troopers." Eisenhower resented Russell's accusations but calmly explained that he had done what was necessary to keep order and enforce the court's ruling.[34]

Both Russell and Eisenhower were still fuming when, just days later, on October 4, the Soviet Union launched a missile that placed Sputnik, the world's first artificial satellite, into orbit. Suddenly the nation's confidence in the foundation of its national security, superior American science and technology, was shaken to its core. Democratic partisans like Senate Armed Services Committee member Stuart Symington of Missouri saw the chance to attack the administration. He wrote to Russell that the Soviets had clearly demonstrated their superiority over the Americans in missile technology while the government, for fiscal reasons, continued "to cut back and slow down its own mis-sile program." The chairman of the Armed Services Committee, Symington insisted, must hold hearings. Russell assured the former air force secretary that he had already asked Senator Johnson's Preparedness Subcommittee to look into the matter.[35]

Symington had hoped his powerful colleague from Georgia would chair the hearings himself, but Russell left the task to Majority Leader Johnson. Despite their differences, Russell still considered Johnson a friend and the best hope to put a Southern-friendly candi-date in the White House in 1960. Both men's political instincts imme-diately told them that this was Johnson's opportunity to cash in on his own version of the MacArthur Hearings. If he could restrain the par-tisanship of Symington and other Democrats and keep the question-ing of American science and defense experts behind closed doors so that his subcommittee might avoid being labeled unpatriotic, Johnson could still portray the White House as soft on defense and prepare the way for a presidential run. As significant as the chance to further Johnson's political career was to Russell, even more important was the opportunity to bring Johnson back in line with his vision of American defense priorities. If Johnson was to be president, Russell needed him committed to military spending rather than foreign aid or domestic welfare programs. If all went well for Russell, he would have his own man in the White House, a leader who would help reverse the direction of American foreign and domestic policy.

Having Johnson lead a moderate, bipartisan, measured evalua-tion of the lagging American missile policy also afforded Russell the opportunity to join Symington in bashing the administration about Sputnik. Responding to Eisenhower's claim that the missile launch posed no new or significant threat to American security, Russell told an audience in Augusta, Georgia, that he was "dumbfounded by the apparent indifference of those in charge of our national government to the shocking news that Russia had successfully launched Sputnik, the amazing earth satellite." The American people, he asserted, should not be "lulled into a false sense of security by unrealistic assurances that this event is of no importance." "American prestige," he continued, had "suffered a disastrous blow." The nation's security was at direct risk from the "long range ballistic missile of tremendous strength and great accuracy" that had delivered the satellite into space. Such a missile was "capable of delivering atomic and hydrogen explosives across continents and oceans." The security of the nation demanded that "the Administration take the American people into their confidence and tell the truth." The White House, he insisted, must take the advice consistently given in Congress and his committee to reverse the "cutbacks and stretch-outs in research and development" of missiles and invest in a defense budget that was "an insurance policy upon the American way of life." American prosperity, he suggested, was in danger of fostering "complacency" and "neglect" in defense that threatened "our system of self-government." With a not-so-veiled reference to what Russell saw as the administration's extraconstitutional actions in Little Rock, he concluded that "we must join in demanding that the Federal Government exercise the duty placed squarely upon it in the Constitution of providing an adequate defense" rather than interfering in state and local matters.[36]

Russell's call to reinvigorate America's missile program gained further momentum on November 3, when the Soviets launched Sputnik II, displaying their ability to deliver not only nuclear warheads across continents but live beings, this time a small dog, into the outer atmosphere. The following day, Russell, Johnson, and the Republican minority leader in the Senate, Styles Bridges of New Hampshire, attended a seven-hour briefing in the Pentagon. Secretary of Defense Neil McElroy reviewed the missile and satellite situation. Washington was fully aware of the Soviet satellite and ICBM program and had taken actions to keep pace. The United States held the lead in the number and design of nuclear weapons as well as accurate solid-fuel long-range missiles. The Soviets were ahead in overall ICBM development, but U-2 intelligence made it clear that they did not yet have the ability to launch a missile attack on the United States. By the time they did, the administration knew, the American missile force would be larger and more reliable. Russell and Johnson were more cautious in their responses after the briefing but remained convinced that the Republicans had failed in allowing the Soviets to be the first to demonstrate their missile technology.[37]

Despite the administration's attempt to reassure him in the Pentagon briefing, as well as its mid-November promises to invest in American science and technology, Russell continued to blast the Republicans' "hemming and hawing." He and Johnson knew that for security reasons the administration could not make public all it knew about the supposed missile gap. The Soviets "were far ahead of us," Russell told an audience in Valdosta. The problem was that the administration was focused on integration rather than the missile crisis. The federal government, he declared, must end its "undeclared war on the South and face the real threat—that of Communist superiority in the ultimate weapons of warfare." The troops must be trained to fight the Soviets, not integrate the schools. From late November through the end of January, Johnson added testimony from the Preparedness

Subcommittee hearings to the call for reform. Witnesses, including Edward Teller, leader of the U.S. hydrogen weapons project, insisted that it was necessary to commit larger sums and better organization to the nation's missile research and development program. The explosion of the Americans' Vanguard satellite rocket and the subsequent humiliating offer by the Soviets' UN representative to make available to the United States its program of technical assistance for backward nations reinforced the Democratic indictment. Russell and Johnson had found the issue that would destroy the Republicans in 1960.[38]

Russell broadened his accusations against the administration over the months that followed. Again, for Russell it was a question of prioritizing spending to ensure the economic and military strength of the nation. The president's efforts to control spending by lowering price supports for farmers, to reduce waste through a reorganization of the Defense Department, to strengthen American alliances through foreign aid, and to invest in a National Defense Education Act (NDEA) to improve the country's security through improved science, math, engineering, and foreign language training missed the mark, according to Russell. While he supported and ushered through his committee the administration's Defense Department reorganization and backed the NDEA, Russell considered the president's farm policies to be an assault on the nation's economy and his support for foreign aid to be seriously misguided. White House complacency and incompetence, he told audiences in the spring of 1958, extended beyond the missile issue. The recession then gripping the nation resulted from administration indifference. The Republicans' obsession with balancing the budget had resulted in defense cutbacks that reduced American power and stifled the growth of the overall economy.[39] Russell also accused the State Department of allowing a once useful reciprocal trade program to lapse into a distribution center for foreign aid that did little for the American people. Investment in American jobs and entire industries, especially American cotton, he declared, had been sacrificed to support a foreign aid program that had not increased American prestige or power.[40] As Russell understood it, the nation must find the wisdom to be both strong and efficient. The Eisenhower administration's efforts had yielded only weakness and waste.

Even at their most aggressive, Russell's criticisms had a limit. The senator always understood that his dissent on foreign policy issues fell under the advice and consent role of Congress. As he repeated over and over again to constituents, it was ultimately the executive's role to decide the course of foreign policy. Behind the scenes, Russell actually protected the executive prerogative in making policy. In June 1959, he, Johnson, and Fulbright met with Eisenhower concerning a resolution introduced by Democratic senator Henry "Scoop" Jackson of Washington that called for an investigation of the government's overall fight against Communism. Eisenhower argued that it would open the National Security Council (NSC) up to congressional interference and make public vital, confidential information. Russell, with Johnson in tow, agreed. Russell suggested that while Johnson held up the measure in a steering committee, Eisenhower should write a letter to the majority leader implying that national security dangers made it currently ill advised for Congress to investigate the NSC. When Jackson eventually settled for a study that did not include the NSC, the administration thanked Russell.

The complex dance between the president, the senator, and his congressional colleagues yielded mixed results for Russell. Defense appropriations increased for fiscal 1959 to $2 billion, and both Defense Department reorganization and the NDEA contributed to American needs in missile research and development. But foreign aid also increased by $1.6 billion from 1958 to 1959. That money, Russell once again asserted, was better spent on improving the missile program. With every step that it seemed the country took toward the Georgian's ideal of an impregnable garrison state, it took another step back.

Politically, however, Russell and the Democrats had found the issue that would launch the race for the presidency in 1960. Despite efforts to improve the public image of America's missile defense posture, the Republican administration and its candidate, Vice President Richard Nixon, could not shake the accusation that the nation had slept while Russia took the lead in ICBM technology. Russell's candidate, majority leader and head of the subcommittee investigating the nation's missile problems, Lyndon Johnson, was in a good position to ride the issue into the White House. Johnson, though, presented himself as a reluctant candidate and was quickly overshadowed in the primary race by the young upstart war hero and ostensible foreign policy expert from Massachusetts, John F. Kennedy. Johnson reluctantly settled for the Democratic nomination for vice president. Russell was disappointed in Johnson's lackluster run for the presidency and felt that his protégé's decision to give up his majority leader's post to accept the largely powerless vice president's position was foolish. He liked Kennedy personally but despised what he saw as the Democratic Party's commitment to a second reconstruction in the South. The Georgian thus stayed largely on the sidelines during the general election, reluctantly agreeing to campaign for the Democratic ticket in Texas only after Johnson begged for his assistance.

Kennedy's victory marked a new direction in American foreign policy that matched Russell's desire for an enhanced defense posture. Conventional forces, Kennedy argued, had been woefully neglected. In his first year, the new president increased the regular military budget by 15 percent, adding to the number of combat and reserve units while committing to exponential increases in American counterinsurgency efforts. The president also sought to change the international perceptions of American missile strength by announcing a plan to increase the U.S. nuclear arsenal to one thousand ICBMs.

Russell had called attention to these very needs in late January 1959 when he accepted the Reserve Officers Association's Minute Man Award, given to the man who had "contributed most to provide national security in the United States." Echoing his criticisms of the Eisenhower administration's complacency in defense policy, Russell reflected on the state of the national defense. Sufficiency could only be determined by the nation's power relative to its greatest enemy. Under Eisenhower, the public's access to that measurement had been hidden. Once it was entrusted with this information, Russell was confident the American public would "support whatever defense measures are needed to preserve our freedoms." They would support, in particular, "a potent retaliatory force capable of deterring overt aggression and use of force by the Kremlin." Such a program, Russell argued, would of necessity include "conventional forces" to meet the enemy in "less than total" conflicts. To reduce the likelihood that such conflicts would expand into larger wars, America's nuclear strength needed to be mighty enough to serve as a deterrent to all-out war with the Communists. To this end, Russell suggested, the nation must reverse the trend to reduce the size of American active duty and reserve forces and outfit both with the training necessary to meet the threat of limited as well as total war.[41]

After the election, the Kennedy administration worked closely with the Armed Services Committee chairman to expand and make flexible the American defense posture. On January 15, 1961, Russell announced a comprehensive review of the nation's military program with a specific eye to manpower and missile research, development, and deployment in comparison to the "best estimates available of the military potential of the communist bloc." The committee and the nation, he declared, were "in complete agreement with the president on the need for maintaining a high degree of military effectiveness while we negotiate with the Russians on a workable and enforceable disarmament plan." In particular, the committee would explore the feasibility of "expediting our missile program in order to narrow what has been described as the 'missile gap.'"[42]

With the groundwork for cooperation in place, Russell and the administration pushed for significant increases in national defense. After a meeting in February between Russell, Vice President Johnson, CIA director Allen Dulles, and President Kennedy on the defense budget, the Armed Services chairman announced his support of a $2.1 billion increase in defense spending that would mostly go for additional bombers and missiles. In May, the Armed Services Committee called for another $525 million for long-range bombers, and a billion more in July. By August, the military budget for fiscal 1962 approached $46.7 billion, $6.4 billion over Eisenhower's final submission.

While working with Russell to build a stronger military, President Kennedy repeatedly disappointed the Georgian on the foreign aid front. More attuned to Eisenhower's idea of limited resources, Russell had hoped to reduce foreign aid expenditures to help pay for defense. Kennedy, however, operating under Keynesian economic philosophies adapted by his adviser John Kenneth Galbraith, saw no such need. Federal spending, he reasoned, reduced unemployment, fueled economic growth, and provided enough additional tax revenue to more than pay for the boosts in both defense and foreign aid.

Over time, Russell's doubts about this economic course led him to openly question Kennedy's ability to maintain U.S. security interests. Russell also questioned the Kennedy administration's willingness to maximize the effects of its increased defense posture with the Eisenhower-Dulles tactic of confronting the Soviets with American power. As his concern over the missile gap revealed, Russell was keenly aware of the relationship between the perception of a strong defense and deterrence. Sound nuclear policy, he understood, depended both on the actual relative strength between the United States and the Soviet Union and on global assumptions about that relative strength. Military might was only a deterrent if coupled with corresponding negotiating strength. Thus, Russell resisted any initiative that might call into question or compromise U.S. nuclear superiority.

To this end, throughout the Eisenhower years, Russell had opposed the sharing of atomic equipment or information under the UN, NATO, or any other international agreement. He had voted against amendments to the 1954 Atomic Energy Act and the 1957 Statute of the International Atomic Energy Agency Treaty that he feared unnecessarily disseminated American nuclear secrets. Any proliferation of nuclear technology, Russell insisted, would "weaken the Free World."[43]

Guaranteed nuclear superiority was the key. The senator demanded that all American nuclear arms negotiation treaties meet two mutually reinforcing standards: that the treaties maintain U.S. nuclear superiority over the Soviets and that adequate inspection protocols ensure this status. The United States, he argued, had set the proper course in insisting on these standards when it demanded licensing and full inspection to sustain its nuclear monopoly under the Baruch Plan in 1946.[44] Subsequent disarmament negotiations had failed to meet one or the other condition. This was true for the Antarctica Treaty in 1960. This multilateral treaty, which went into effect over Russell's objections in 1961, preserved Antarctica for peaceful scientific purposes by prohibiting the establishment of bases and testing of weapons on the continent. Under the treaty, open, on-site inspections could be carried out by any of the participating countries at any time. According to Russell, the treaty failed "to meet the test of the national interest." Specifically, it gave the Soviet Union a role equal to the United States in controlling and developing the territory "notwithstanding a total absence of any legitimate Russian rights and of any legitimate interest in that continent." The United States had established itself in Antarctica by right of exploration and discovery, Russell argued. The Soviets had not. The Monroe Doctrine, Russell further insisted, extended to Antarctica, and the United States must protect its strategic interest by keeping open the Drake Passage in the event of nuclear attack on the Panama Canal. For Russell, to sign the treaty was to "give away all" to the Soviets and "gain nothing" in return. This was an "affront to the national pride and the national prestige" and encouraged an entering wedge to Soviet claims in the Western Hemisphere.[45]

Underlying Russell's insistence on ensured American nuclear superiority over the Soviets was his ongoing belief that Russia could not be trusted. "Every person of intelligence in this country knows that Russia is a ruthless, conscienceless, atheistic, Communist society whose pledges are absolutely worthless, and are used only to achieve an end, without any intention of being honored," Russell declared while attacking the Antarctica Treaty. The senator would never surrender America's security "on the pledged word of Russia."[46]

Richard Russell feared that the Kennedy administration displayed too much trust in Soviet good intentions and seemed less and less willing to guarantee American nuclear superiority. This was never more evident than when the Kennedy administration began preparations for the negotiation of a Nuclear Test Ban Treaty. The main provisions of the treaty outlawed nuclear weapons tests in the atmosphere, in outer space, and under water and provided for regular on-site inspections to enforce the ban. At first, Russell expressed his cautious support.[47] A new treaty might help prevent the spread of nuclear weapons to China, France, and other nations while preserving U.S. nuclear power relative to the Soviets. But when Khrushchev insisted that on-site inspections be limited to only three per year, Russell's overriding distrust of the Soviets reemerged. He precluded any support for the treaty without guarantees that Russian compliance could be fully monitored. When the administration presented its final draft to Congress without provisions for on-site inspections, Russell's cautious support disintegrated.

On September 17, 1963, just days before the final vote ratifying the Nuclear Test Ban Treaty, Russell voiced his dissent. Despite his desire "to take any step, however short, in the direction of world peace," Russell declared that he could not "in good conscience" vote to ratify the test ban. The senator opposed "any program of disarmament . . . that did not provide for onsite inspections"; the Soviet's "long record of broken promises" and "impressive evidence that this treaty gives Russia a military advantage" was decisive. The Russians had demonstrated their bad faith repeatedly, most recently during the Cuban Missile Crisis, when the Soviet foreign minister, Andrei Gromyko, had lied to President Kennedy about the placing of offensive nuclear weapons in Cuba. That the Soviets would not concede to full, on-site inspections was evidence that they had only feigned interest in a real atmospheric test ban. Their real purpose, Russell insisted, was to make permanent their lead in the atmospheric testing of high-yield nuclear weapons while maintaining their ability to catch up to the American lead in small-yield nuclear weapons that could still be tested underground. Furthermore, the treaty surrendered too much sovereignty to an international community that did not care a fig for American interests. "If we are to endure as an independent nation," the senator argued, "we must have patience, diligence, the will to sacrifice and to live dangerously, for this is a dangerous world, and those who cower or flinch are lost."[48]

In the end, Russell found Kennedy's trajectory in defense policy no less discomforting than Eisenhower's. Although he was not exactly an isolationist, Russell nevertheless chafed at internationalism's requirement that America surrender a portion of its sovereignty and power. Like Henry Cabot Lodge before him, Russell's profound distrust of the international community underlay his insistence on relative strength and independence of action.

No administration or change in international conditions would change Russell's mind. Even as his friend and political protégé Lyndon Johnson ascended to the presidency after the assassination of John F. Kennedy, Russell continued to insist on an aggressive, independent strategic program that ran counter to the liberal internationalist approach of each successive Cold War administration. This again became clear as the senator's support for an American anti–ballistic missile program clashed with the Johnson administration's priorities in 1968.

Russell had originally opposed the deployment of an anti–ballistic missile system. In 1963, he had rejected legislation authorizing the program, arguing that research and development in the field had not advanced far enough to justify the expense. But by 1966, the senator had begun to believe that an anti–ballistic missile program was both viable and worthwhile. Russell understood that no defensive missile network would be successful enough to save all Americans, but a "thin" system could protect the United States against accidental or limited attack. It would also be worth the expense to save the lives of even a few million Americans in an all-out attack. "If we have to start over again with another Adam and Eve," Russell insisted, "I want them to be Americans and not Russians, and I want them on this continent and not Europe."[49]

Russell helped secure nearly $300 million for an ABM system in fiscal 1967 and 1968, but none of the funds were spent. Secretary of Defense Robert McNamara opposed the system. Reeling from the cost of the Vietnam War, McNamara instead favored offensive missile strength as the best deterrent to enemy attack. With McNamara's departure from the Pentagon in early 1968, Russell moved to ensure that the Defense Department spent the ABM money in 1969. The ensuing debate, however, came on the heels of the Tet Offensive, a massive and costly attack by Communist forces against key South Vietnamese cities under American and South Vietnamese government control. It also coincided with the Johnson administration's efforts to negotiate the Nuclear Nonproliferation Treaty, a pact designed to keep nonnuclear countries from attempting to develop nuclear weapons. Suddenly the longstanding conflict between Russell and the executive branch over budgetary priorities resurfaced. Of the "$80 billion a year" then being spent on defense, Russell thought it "much better to take some of the money we are spending for other purposes and apply it to this [missile defense] system." Foreign aid was predictably at the top of his list of "spending for other purposes," with Great Society domestic programs not far behind. Russell also very nearly included the war in Vietnam. While the senator would not have taken money from

Vietnam to fund ABMs, he used that conflict to argue for financing the missile network. Compared to the "catastrophic $20 billion-odd we are spending in Vietnam, which I did everything within my power to avoid," Russell told his colleagues, the cost of the ABM system was "relatively small."[50]

It was again Russell's distrust of the Soviets and the perceived need of the United States for an effective deterrent that drove his priorities. The danger was that the United States was moving toward "unilateral disarmament," Russell told the Senate. While he desired "as much as any man to see that day come when we can disarm," it was more important that the nation's potential enemies "be convinced that we are capable of destroying them if they see fit to disturb the peace." Russell simply did not trust Russia. The Soviets had not "entirely abandoned the idea that communism is good for the entire world and that they have a holy mission to spread communism all over the earth." Even if they had, he insisted, their nuclear power and national self-interest would still make them a legitimate threat. American missile and antimissile technology must keep pace. Despite unprecedented foreign and domestic spending for Vietnam and the Great Society, the Senate refused to delay the ABM procurement by a vote of 45 to 34.[51]

Throughout his career, Russell occasionally paused to reflect on his support for an ever-stronger defense. On one occasion in 1952, he told audiences "that inexorable fate has thrust upon us the responsibility of world leadership." Though the nation had not sought or desired this role, it bore the "costly responsibility" to "keep alight the lamp of human liberty on this globe." The "threat of world Communism," he contended, made it necessary "to organize the free peoples of the earth, many of whom are tired and listless, into a force strong enough to deter armed aggression and spare mankind the horrors of an atomic war." There were costs. The United States had departed from "century-old tradition" and taxed itself "to a degree unheard of in peacetime to rebuild the economies of peoples on other continents." The nation must "find ways and means to give the Federal Government power to meet the common danger without vesting all power of government in Washington."[52]

The balancing act between power and responsibility was a constant in Russell's life. Toward the end of his career in 1969, the senator accepted the National Security Industrial Association's highest honor, the James Forrestal Award. He reiterated the basic dilemma as he reflected on the military-industrial complex he helped to create. The nation certainly owed its strength and security to "a close working relationship between government and industry," and that relationship must continue as the world remained uncertain and threatening. "The Atlantic and Pacific Oceans that so long served as protective moats around our homeland have—defensively at least—shrunk to puddles and the once friendly skies are now broad avenues of approach for massive missiles of destruction." But "with power comes responsibility." The government, he insisted, "must continue to maintain close supervision and control over operations involving the military and defense oriented industry."[53]

Richard Russell used his tremendous power in the Senate to help frame and influence the foreign and defense policy debates of the 1950s and 1960s. His knowledge and control of the nation's purse strings led to some significant successes: increasing defense budgets, limiting foreign aid spending, reining in executive initiatives, and opening political avenues for his allies. Yet Russell never fully achieved his vision of American foreign and defense policy. Indeed, foreign aid spending increased overall, executive branch programs continued despite his protest, and liberal internationalism was still the overwhelming trend in American foreign policy. In attempting to balance federal power and responsibility, Russell placed limits on his own ability to control policy. While he criticized the national security strategies of both Republican and Democratic presidents, he respected and even protected executive prerogatives in making foreign and defense decisions. Actually, as the protectionist Armed Services chairman from a conservative Southern state that benefited mightily from the military-industrial complex, he had very little room to maneuver. He consistently supported defense increases as a matter of course. To do otherwise would be to relinquish power, compromise his most heartfelt convictions, and sacrifice the economic interests of his constituents. Truly, Russell was left in an odd position. He had too much power to give up on what he believed was the responsible course, but too little power to actually get the nation to follow his lead.

Notes

1. Gilbert C. Fite, *Richard B. Russell, Jr., Senator from Georgia* (Chapel Hill: University of North Carolina Press, 1991), 370.

2. Arthur Darling, *The Central Intelligence Agency: An Instrument of Government to 1950* (University Park: Pennsylvania State University Press, 1990), 183–92.

3. Don Oberdorfer, *Senator Mansfield: The Extraordinary Life of a Great American Statesman and Diplomat* (Washington, DC: Smithsonian Books, 2003), 144–45.

4. Fite, *Russell*, 369.

5. Randall Woods, *Fulbright: A Biography* (Cambridge: Cambridge University Press, 1995), 430–31; Frank J. Smist Jr., *Congress Oversees the United*

States Intelligence Community (Knoxville: University of Tennessee Press, 1990), 6–7.

6. *Congressional Record*, 89th Cong., 2nd sess., 1966, 112, pt. 8:10623 and pt. 12:15687.

7. *Richard Russell, Georgia Giant*, documentary script number 3, 1970, box 1, Russell Personal Papers, Lyndon Baines Johnson Library.

8. Johnson Tapes, WH6405.10, PNO3–5, 5/27/64, 1055A, 3519–21 and WH6507.08, PNO12–13, 7/26/65, 546P, 8399–8400, Lyndon Baines Johnson Library.

9. "Journal—Office of Legislative Counsel, 24 January 1969"; "Journal—Office of Legislative Counsel, 12 March 1969"; and "Journal—Office of Legislative Counsel, 28 January 1969," in CREST [database] (College Park, MD: National Archives, 2005 [cited June 23, 2005]).

10. "Clarke Memo for Assistant Deputy Director for Intelligence, 3 January 1969," in CREST [database] (College Park, MD: National Archives, 2005 [cited June 23, 2005]).

11. Russell Baker, "Congress Begins a Crucial Session in Friendly Mood," *New York Times*, January 4, 1956.

12. Notes on Presidential Bipartisan Congressional Leadership Meeting, August 12, 1956, box 2, Legislative Meeting Series, Whitman Files, Eisenhower Papers, Dwight D. Eisenhower Library.

13. Chester Pach and Elmo Richardson, *The Presidency of Dwight D. Eisenhower* (Lawrence: University of Kansas Press, 1991), 161.

14. *Congressional Record*, 85th Cong., 1st sess., 1957, 103, pt. 2:2678–86; Robert David Johnson, *Congress and the Cold War* (New York: Cambridge University Press, 2006), 71.

15. *Congressional Record*, 85th Cong., 1st sess., 1957, 103, pt. 2–3:2678–86, 2921–22.

16. *Congressional Record*, 85th Cong., 1st sess., 1957, 103, pt. 2:2678–86, 2796–97.

17. *Congressional Record*, 85th Cong., 1st sess., 1957, 103, pt. 2:2678–86.

18. *Congressional Record*, 85th Cong., 1st sess., 1957, 103, pt. 2:2678–86.

19. Notes on Presidential Bipartisan Congressional Leadership Meeting, February 20, 1957, box 2, Legislative Meeting Series, Whitman Files, Eisenhower Papers, Dwight D. Eisenhower Library.

20. *Congressional Record*, 85th Cong., 1st sess., 1957, 103, pt. 2:2678–86.

21. "Text of Note to Knowland," *New York Times*, March 3, 1957.

22. Notes on Telephone Call with Senator Knowland, February 27, 1957, 2:10 P.M., box 6, Telephone Calls Series, Dulles Papers, Dwight D. Eisenhower Library.

23. Robert Dallek, *Lone Star Rising: Lyndon Johnson and His Times, 1908–1960* (New York: Oxford University Press, 1991), 512–13.

24. John D. Morris, "7 Democrats Aid G.O.P. on Mideast," *New York Times*, March 2, 1957.

25. John D. Morris, "Israel Now Balks at Withdrawal; Eisenhower Appeals to Ben-Guiron; Senate Backs Mideast Aid, 58–28," *New York Times*, March 3, 1957; Stephen Ambrose, *Eisenhower Volume 2: The President* (New York: Simon & Schuster, 1983), 382–88.

26. Russell to Emmons, June 20, 1967, and Russell to Cordes, June 1, 1967, box 23, series 16, Russell Papers, Richard Russell Memorial Library.

27. Notes on Telephone Call from Mr. Harlow, February 28, 1957, 8:32 A.M., box 11, Telephone Calls Series, Dulles Papers, Dwight D. Eisenhower Library.

28. Johnson, *Congress and the Cold War*, xviii–xix.

29. *Congressional Record*, 85th Cong., 1st sess., 1957, 103, pt. 7:8914.

30. Calvin Mcleod Logue and Dwight L. Freshley, eds., *Voice of Georgia: Speeches of Richard B. Russell, 1928–1969* (Macon, GA: Mercer University Press, 1997), 67–68, 74–75, 82–83. See also Joseph A. Fry, *Dixie Looks Abroad: The South and U.S. Foreign Relations 1789–1973* (Baton Rouge: Louisiana State University Press, 2002), 222–29.

31. Dallek, *Lone Star Rising*, 513–15, 518–21.

32. Notes on President's Breakfast with Johnson, August 26, 1957, box 26, Dwight Eisenhower Diaries, Eisenhower Papers, Dwight D. Eisenhower Library.

33. The President's Interview with Senator Russell, August 26, 1957, 5:30, box 26, Dwight Eisenhower Diaries, Eisenhower Papers, Dwight D. Eisenhower Library.

34. Fite, *Russell*, 343–44.

35. Telegrams Exchanged between Symington and Russell, October 8, 1957, box 382, Senate Armed Services Committee Papers, RG46, National Archives.

36. Remarks of Richard Russell in Augusta, Georgia, October 15, 1957, box 382, Senate Armed Services Committee Papers, RG46, National Archives.

37. Fite, *Russell*, 363; Pach and Richardson, *Eisenhower*, 171–73.

38. Fite, *Russell*, 363–64.

39. Wilton Hall, "Ike's Recession: Senator Russell's Analysis of the Cost of Indifference," *Anderson South Carolina Independent*, April 12, 1958.

40. *Congressional Record*, 85th Cong., 2nd sess., 1958, 104, app.: A3493.

41. *Congressional Record*, 86th Cong., 1st sess., 1959, 105, pt. 1:1524–26.

42. Russell Press Release, January 15, 1960, box 457, Senate Armed Services Committee Papers, RG46, National Archives.

43. Bipartisan Briefing of Congressional Leaders, November 17, 1954, box 1, Legislative Meetings Series, Whitman Files, Eisenhower Papers, Dwight D. Eisenhower Library; *Congressional Record*, 85th Cong., 2nd sess., 1958, 104, pt. 9:11940.

44. *Congressional Record*, 88th Cong., 1st sess., 1963, 109, pt. 13:17154; Bipartisan Briefing of Congressional Leaders, November 17, 1954, box 1, Legislative Meetings Series, Whitman Files, Eisenhower Papers, Dwight D. Eisenhower Library.

45. *Congressional Record*, 86th Cong., 2nd sess., 1960, 106, pt. 12:16090–16108.

46. *Congressional Record*, 86th Cong., 2nd sess., 1960, 106, pt. 12:16095.

47. Richard Reeves, *Profile of Power* (New York: Simon & Schuster, 1993), 550.

48. *Congressional Record*, 88th Cong., 1st sess., 1963, 109, pt. 13:17154–67.

49. "If H-Bombs Fly . . . a Secret Debate," *U.S. News & World Report* 65 (December 2, 1968): 13; *Congressional Record*, 90th Cong., 2nd sess., 1968, 114, pt. 14:18398–18400; Fite, *Russell*, 459–60.

50. "New View on Missiles: Russell Has Compromise Plan," *U.S. News & World Report* 62 (April 3, 1967): 15; *Congressional Record*, 90th Cong., 2nd sess., 1968, 114, pt. 14:18398–18402.

51. *Congressional Record*, 90th Cong., 2nd sess., 1968, 114, pt. 14:18398–18402 and pt. 19:24665; Fite, *Russell*, 459–60.

52. Logue and Freshley, *Speeches of Richard B. Russell*, 67–68, 74–75, 82–83.

53. Logue and Freshley, *Speeches of Richard B. Russell*, 298–304.

4

Two Worlds

As executive policy leaders' respect for Richard Russell's power grew, their regard for his worldview declined. By the early 1960s, administration policy makers considered Russell's global vision passé. Liberal internationalists at the helm of the nation's ship viewed the world through a modernist lens that refracted interconnections at all geographic points and optimism for an international democratic peace. Their world was full of people who shared a common humanity and a hope for liberty, justice, and property. It was a world where American power could be used as a positive, progressive force in ensuring those shared values. Russell saw global realities through older panes. His was a world still fundamentally separated by barriers of space, time, and race. It was full of people yet to take responsibility for their liberty, justice, and property. It was a world where American power was limited and best massed in the defense of its narrow interests.

This contrast between the executive branch liberal internationalists and the conservative protectionism of Russell and his ilk was apparent in their debates on Latin America and Africa. Russell's was a two-world view of American policy that separated American interests in terms of proximate and distant threats and similar and dissimilar cultures. That threats geographically closer to the United States were also in part a concern of liberal internationalists meant that the senator's recommendations on Latin America gained significant consideration by White House officials. But because liberal internationalists chafed at Russell's racist notions about the pace of democratic change among dissimilar cultures, the senator's challenges concerning policy in Africa were largely ignored.

By 1962, Richard Russell vigorously supported using the Monroe Doctrine to contain Communism in Latin America. He advocated the use of force to destroy Soviet nuclear capabilities in Cuba that fall. Two years later, he strongly opposed any move to relinquish U.S. power over the Panama Canal when riots threatened the status quo there. And he unequivocally endorsed President Johnson's decision to send troops to the Dominican Republic in 1965. Russell, though, had shown little overt interest in Latin America before 1960. He always kept up with world affairs, but like most Americans, his focus was mostly on Europe as the front line of World War II and then the Cold War. Like President Eisenhower, he registered no significant public or private response to Fidel Castro's victory in Cuba. Fulgencio Batista was a corrupt, inefficient dictator, and not until the spring and summer of 1960 did Castro declare his allegiance to Marxism and alliance with the Soviet Union. Even more important for Russell, that spring he and other Southerners were consumed with a filibuster of the latest civil rights bill.[1]

Russell's concerns about federally imposed racial change in the South had grown dramatically since the battles over the FEPC. After the 1954 *Brown v. Board of Education* decision calling for the desegregation of public schools, he helped draft the Southern Manifesto pledging the signers to the "use of all lawful means" to reverse the Supreme Court ruling and "to prevent the use of force in its implementation." According to Russell, the desegregation efforts that resulted from *Brown* amounted to an attack on Southern culture and "the reserved rights of the States and the people."[2] In 1957, he again rallied the Southern legislators in defense of the region's putative honor and segregation. Taking the floor against the 1957 Civil Rights Act, Russell declared that federal enforcement of black civil rights in the South was worse than anything proposed by Thaddeus Stevens or Charles Sumner. Like carpetbaggers one hundred years before, "outside agitators" backed by the "naked power" of the federal government were threatening "immediate and revolutionary" changes in the region.[3] Russell's arguments helped to dilute the 1957 act's strength. In 1960, the senator once more railed against the civil rights legislation as a "force bill," and against federal efforts as reminiscent of the "carpetbagger regimes" during Reconstruction. The filibuster he organized and led against the act again weakened the final legislation.[4]

Preoccupied with civil rights, Russell made only a few passing references to potential hemispheric problems. In February 1960, he questioned George Smathers (D-FL) in the Senate about his recent trip to Latin America and the arrests of people alleged to be conspiring against the Dominican and Cuban governments. He ventured to suggest that the aggressive repression of dissent by Dominican dictator Raphael Trujillo and Cuban leader Fidel Castro was excusable. Though Russell admitted that Trujillo limited democracy to "Hitlerian" elections, the dictator was of the desirable type that raised the standard of living and maintained internal security.[5] A month later, the senator's concern grew ever so slightly. When a constituent sent a letter to Russell in March 1960 about money owed to his business from Cuba after Castro had begun to seize the nation's assets for the state, Russell sent the letter on to the secretary of state, who informed Russell and his constituent that the situation was not encouraging.[6]

Russell remained tight-lipped about Cuba through the summer, fall, and winter of 1960, even as Castro publicly embraced Khrushchev and Communism. The civil rights fight and the presidential election demanded his attention. It is reasonable to conclude, however, that Russell's silence also had something to do with his probable knowledge of the plans then being mounted for the Bay of Pigs operations. Long a trustee of CIA information, he was surely aware of the operation by the time the invasion became something of an open secret during the winter of 1960 and 1961. His revulsion against leaks of national security information was well known, and his low profile on Cuba may have resulted from that concern. After the election, his silence was also surely political. He did not want to pressure the new president, a member of his own party who was then working with him to increase defense spending, by suggesting that Kennedy was soft on Communism in Cuba.

Russell's silence continued for many of the same reasons even after the American-trained Cuban Exile Brigade landed at the Bay of Pigs on April 17, 1961. There was much to comment on. The fight had gone well until the brigade ran short of ammunition. Miscalculations by the CIA and Joint Chiefs, and the reluctance of the president to grant any overt American support for the invasion, contributed decisively to the operation's failure. A day after the invasion began, the would-be liberators were either dead, imprisoned, or hiding in a swamp. That evening, President Kennedy hosted a White House reception for the cabinet and Congress. Shortly before midnight, a group of top advisers and congressional leaders, including Russell in white tie and tails, were briefed on the Bay of Pigs failure.[7] Russell again demurred from commenting publicly or privately on the failed invasion.

Some of his likely sentiments at the time can be deduced from later statements. After the Bay of Pigs, President Kennedy appointed retired general Maxwell Taylor to investigate the failed Cuban invasion.

Taylor reported confusion, a lack of coordination, and inadequate planning. He put much of the blame on the CIA for misinterpreting intelligence suggesting the possibility of a popular uprising. One result of the report was President Kennedy's dismissal of the director of central intelligence, Allen Dulles, and the CIA deputy director for planning, Richard Bissell. When the president chose the former chair of the Atomic Energy Commission, John McCone, to replace Dulles, the Intelligence Subcommittee chair, Richard Russell, participated in discussions on McCone's nomination. Russell suggested that the president was entitled to have a man of his choice in the office and that McCone was imminently qualified. He then subtly added that criticisms of McCone by some were based on the misconception that the director of central intelligence (DCI) made foreign and defense policy. The DCI, he reminded the subcommittee and the CIA, served the commander in chief directly, who always had the last word in foreign and defense matters. To debate McCone's views on foreign and defense policy was irrelevant, he suggested, while discussion of current CIA operations would only endanger those involved.[8] Russell clearly was chastising the CIA while protecting it. He was also protecting the president's choice while suggesting that the blame be put squarely on the president for decisions in matters like the Bay of Pigs.

Russell's only other comment on the failed invasion came briefly in 1963 when Senator Barry Goldwater demanded that the Senate investigate the U.S. role in the invasion. Russell, again protecting Kennedy and the CIA, said that the investigation would serve no "useful purpose," even though the administration's coordination of the invasion deserved criticism. He stated that from conversations he had with Allen Dulles and Maxwell Taylor as well as testimony before the subcommittee on the CIA, he had concluded that there was little "doubt that the people who made the invasion thought they had air cover arranged for." Whether the CIA, Joint Chiefs, or the president were most to blame in reneging on the promise, Russell did not say.[9]

While Russell remained essentially silent on the Bay of Pigs, the incident surely awakened the senator's concern about Communism in the Western Hemisphere. By the time the general alarm was sounded over Soviet missiles in Cuba, Russell had embraced the Monroe Doctrine as a means of protecting the hemisphere from Sino-Soviet imperialism and/or Communist subversion. His first significant statements on American policy in the hemisphere came in September 1962, when a joint committee of the Senate Armed Services and Senate Foreign Relations Committees met to consider the Soviet threat in Cuba. Russell presided over the secret hearings. On September 19, the joint committee adopted a resolution on the problem of the "intrusion of international communism into Cuba" that quickly passed both houses of Congress. Written separately in different committees, it was Russell who synthesized the material into a final draft, reviewed it with the committee, and expertly managed a consensus. The document reached the president's desk on October 3.[10]

The resolution cited the Monroe Doctrine's assertion that any attempt by outside powers to extend their influence in the Western Hemisphere would be considered "dangerous to our peace and safety." It supported the Organization of American States' (OAS) conclusion in early 1962 that Cuba had become a Marxist-Leninist state that was accepting military assistance from the Soviet Union, and it reiterated the tenets of the Rio Treaty of 1947 that declared that "an armed attack by any State against an American State shall be considered as an attack against all the American States." The resolution thus declared Congress's intention to prevent by whatever means necessary the extension of Communism in the hemisphere, to support Cuban self-determination, and to "prevent in Cuba the creation or use of an externally supported military capability endangering the security of the United States."[11]

The resolution resulted in part from Russell's and the other joint committee members' mounting concern over aggressive Soviet actions in Cuba. Over the summer, Soviet general secretary Nikita Khrushchev, at the request of Fidel Castro, began pumping military and economic aid into the island. We now know that the decision to do this was based in large part on the assumption of Castro and Khrushchev that the United States planned to invade Cuba, an assumption inspired by the continued covert raids by the United States against Cuba carried out under Operation Mongoose. Only secondarily, the Soviets hoped to balance the placement of U.S. Jupiter missiles in Turkey in 1961.

More immediately, the resolution was a response to a speech delivered by the president on September 13 declaring that while he saw no immediate danger, if Cuba threatened U.S. interests directly or became "an offensive military base of significant capacity for the Soviet Union," the United States would do whatever was necessary to protect its security and that of its allies. To persuade the joint committee of the potential of such a development, the secretary of state and Department of Defense provided the members with secret intelligence supporting the president's concerns.[12]

The speech and the resolution were also designed to counter Republican moves to make Cuba and the Bay of Pigs disaster the dominant issue in the fall political campaign. On August 31, Republican senator Kenneth Keating from New York had declared that he possessed evidence of the presence of 1,200 Russian troops and the beginnings of a Soviet missile base in Cuba. If that proved true, the Republican charge that Kennedy had neglected to secure the nation against Soviet aggression in Cuba might turn the midterm elections against the Democrats. Thus the resolution was a show of unity in behalf of the administration for both domestic and foreign consumption.

Russell, in fact, sought to broaden presidential power as much as possible in the days leading up to the Cuban Missile Crisis. He led the joint committee, for example, in offering Kennedy the authority to call up 150,000 reservists in reaction to the Communist buildup. Russell personally spearheaded the resolution in Congress, calling it a "shotgun behind the door" in case something were to happen while Congress was out of session during the forthcoming election season. It was, according to the Georgian, "another reminder to those hostile to us that we are united, and are determined to protect our interests, and that the president will be fully supported in the actions he takes as our leader."[13] Russell's words certainly protected Kennedy's political flank but could have also added to Khrushchev's and Castro's paranoia and pushed the president into more aggressive action in Cuba.[14]

Russell privately worried that the administration might not take a hard enough line against the Soviets in Cuba. As he prepared the joint committee resolutions, he probed the administration's intentions with the unusual help of a seventh grade social studies class at the Elm Street School in Rome, Georgia. Russell, submitting a sheaf of letters from the students, asked the State Department to answer the class's concerns about the situation in Cuba. Assistant Secretary Frederick Dutton wrote back declaring that "United States policy is to get rid of the Castro regime and Soviet Communist influence in Cuba." While "unilateral military intervention on the part of the United States cannot currently be required or justified . . . if at any time the Communist buildup in Cuba endangers or threatens our security in any way, we will do whatever must be done to protect our own security." To date, there was no significant offensive capability in Cuba, Dutton said; therefore, the country had nothing to fear.[15] Seventh graders in Rome must have felt both justified and terrified three weeks later when the existence of offensive weapons capabilities was verified in Cuba.

On October 15, American U-2 spy planes recorded evidence of the construction of Soviet medium-range ballistic missile sites in Cuba. A day later, the president first met with ExComm, the name given to the executive committee of the National Security Council that included, among other advisers, National Security Advisor McGeorge Bundy, Secretary of State Dean Rusk, Defense Secretary Robert McNamara, Attorney General Robert Kennedy, Vice President Lyndon Johnson, CIA Director John McCone, and Chairman of the Joint Chiefs of Staff Maxwell Taylor. At the meeting, most of the participants, including the president, favored an immediate air strike on the surface-to-air and long-range missile installations. Others suggested an all-out invasion. But after days of debate and the realization that an attack might lead to the launch of Cuba's missiles and/or significant damage to U.S. prestige in the region, a consensus began to build around a blockade of supplies coming from the Soviet Union to Cuba, or what administration officials referred to as a "defensive quarantine," a term designed not to run afoul of international law. After seven days of discussion, ExComm and Kennedy settled on Monday, October 22, at 7:00 P.M. as the time the president would announce on television the country's intention to quarantine Cuba.

Two hours before the speech, after meeting with the full National Security Council and his cabinet, the president, Rusk, McNamara, McCone, CIA nuclear weapons expert Arthur Lundahl, and U.S. ambassador to the Soviet Union Llewellyn Thompson briefed some twenty congressional leaders, including Russell. Unlike his colleagues, Russell already knew about the U-2 findings and the administration's intentions. Before going home to Georgia for the fall election recess, he had asked the White House for a report on Cuba. National Security Advisor McGeorge Bundy warned the president that it would not do for Russell to go home with an incomplete picture when the senator had directly requested an update. Kennedy had Vice President Johnson confide the secret to his old friend during an automobile ride along the Potomac. At the full briefing, then, Russell had an advantage over his colleagues. Like the administration officials in attendance, he had had some time to consider the options and form an outline of his remarks. They would be some of the most telling of his career.[16]

As he concluded his prepared statement, President Kennedy called for questions. Russell, in a series of calm, cool, and expert inquiries, established the specifics of currently operational weapons in Cuba. Administration members revealed that while they were unsure of the status of nuclear warheads, the advisers believed that the surface-to-air sites were fully operational and that two to three of the medium-range ballistic missile sites had sixteen launchers ready to fire. The exchange confirmed for others in the room that the threat was significant if not imminent. Russell effectively laid the foundation for his position that aggressive, military action needed to be taken.

The discussion quickly turned to Soviet intentions. Ambassador Thompson said he believed that Khrushchev was seeking leverage for a showdown on Berlin. Secretary Rusk added that he had seen a shift in Soviet policy in the last few months toward greater toughness. With hard-liners ascendant, the Kremlin had decided to take the big risk of placing missiles in Cuba. Russell seized the opportunity: "Mr. Secretary, do you see any off chance that it'll get any better? That they'll keep on establishing new bases and dividing our space. How can we gain by waiting?" Rusk replied that he was not suggesting that conditions would get better. Anticipating Russell, the president chimed in. He explained that confirmation of the intelligence on Cuba was only a few days old and that any military response could ignite retaliation in Berlin. Kennedy explained that the administration had decided after days of deliberation that doing nothing was a mistake but that an invasion and air strike might not hit all of the mobile targets and could result in a possible nuclear attack on the United States. The middle ground, they had determined, was to announce that evening that the administration would blockade the shipment of further offensive weapons to Cuba.

The president was reluctant to predict how Khrushchev would respond but added that it could mean war; therefore, preparations were being made for that possibility. Russell's handwritten notes from the meeting suggest that the senator was more certain of the Soviet leader's thinking: "Khrushchev believes what he says—we are afraid."[17] The senator deemed the Soviet general secretary likely to call the president's bluff and run the blockade. When Rusk explained that the blockade was designed to give the Soviets time to pause and reflect on their actions, providing them a last chance to pull back, Russell again chimed in. "It seems to me that we are at a crossroads. We're either a first-class power or we're not. You have warned these people time and again, in the most eloquent speeches I have read since Woodrow Wilson, that's what would happen if there was an offensive capability created in Cuba. . . . The Secretary of State says: 'Give them time to pause and think.' They'll use that time to pause and think, to get better prepared." If offensive nuclear missiles were installed in Cuba, Russell continued, the Cubans could "stop transit . . . in the Windward Passage and the Leeward Passage. . . . They could blow Guantanamo off the map. And you have told them not to do this thing. They've done it. And I think that we should assemble as speedily as possible an adequate force and clean out that situation."

What followed was one of the most astonishing statements of his career. "The time is going to come," Russell declared, "when we're going to have to take this step in Berlin and Korea and Washington, D.C., and Winder, Georgia, for the nuclear war. I don't know whether Khrushchev will launch a nuclear war over Cuba or not. I don't believe he will. But I think that the more that we temporize, the more surely he is to convince himself that we are afraid to make any real movement and to really fight."

Winder, Russell knew full well, was in range of the already operational medium-range missiles. The senator was, in effect, risking his home and family on the correctness of his reading of Khrushchev. That reading had in part to do with a strategic comparison. Russell saw the Soviet's calculus in Cuba as no different than the U.S. calculus had been in Hungary. Neither would take such an enormous risk in a nuclear confrontation over territory clearly in the other's backyard, where there was an overwhelming military disadvantage.[18] But it also came down to schoolyard politics. Khrushchev was a bully. Punch him in the nose, Russell suggested, and he would back down and be less willing to risk a confrontation in the future. Back down, and he would pick on the United States again and again.

The president was not as willing to take the risk as Russell. Kennedy was less sure of Khrushchev's response, less sure of first air-strike success, and less sure that a nuclear response after an American air strike was worth the assumed guarantee of long-term security. The president clearly wanted the ball in Khrushchev's court. It was a different assessment of schoolyard politics. Draw the line and let the bully cross it. Stare Khrushchev down, and maybe he will back away without a fight. In any case, the president could not let Russell dominate the discussion. He cut the Georgian off and suggested that a statement from Secretary McNamara might clarify things. The defense chief duly described the sea and air support for the quarantine, the reinforcement of Guantanamo, and the Strategic Air Command's readiness.

Russell refused to be diverted. In his infuriatingly calm, passive-aggressive style, the senator said that he did not want to make a "nuisance" of himself but would like to complete his statement. He reiterated his view that the Soviets had been warned, that Khrushchev had never given any indication that he would fight over Cuba, and that to appease him at this point would be to invite confrontation in the future, a confrontation in which "we'll lose a great many more men than we would right now." Kennedy replied, "But, senator, we can't invade Cuba. . . . We're not in a position to invade in the next 24 to 48 hours." It may come to that eventually, he assured Russell, but he and the secretary of defense had agreed that they would need some seven days to move an invasion force of ninety thousand men into place and mount an estimated two thousand bombing sorties to soften up the island.

Russell knew better. The Armed Services Committee chairman had learned that the military had already fortified Guantanamo; it had brought the first armored division from Ft. Hood, Texas, to Ft. Stewart, Georgia, and had gathered amphibious vehicles ready to transport them; it had moved some thirty thousand marines into position on the coast, and it could mobilize two thousand aircraft from fields in North Carolina to the Florida Keys if needed.[19] While perhaps not yet ideal, preparations were sufficient, and if a conventional war in Cuba ensued, as Russell thought it probably would, the element of surprise was more important than having the full force in place. A blockade, he repeated, would just "put them on alert." The time for action had come. Fail, and the Soviets would be emboldened to take action in other areas, forcing the United States to divide its forces further and weaken it "around the whole periphery of the free world." Berlin would always be a hostage, and the United States would lose its position as a great power, Russell concluded, until it was willing "to take a chance somewhere, sometime."

President Kennedy, inwardly agitated but outwardly calm, replied that the administration had considered air strikes but had decided against them for reasons beyond local considerations. If the United States attacked, American bases in Turkey or Italy could receive a second strike in response that would compel commanders on the scene to unleash their own nuclear weapons at Russia. An all-out nuclear war would result.

Russell let the president have the last word. His primary purpose had been to present his reasoning to those at the meeting in an effort to sway or hone the final decision. In the end, he knew that it was the president who would make the call. Russell was at once expressing his conviction, playing the devil's advocate, and protecting himself politically if the whole thing went wrong. Kennedy sensed that the latter was more the case than either of the former.

It would have ended at that, but amazingly, and much to the Georgian's surprise, the Senate Foreign Relations Committee chairman, J. William Fulbright (D-AR), jumped on the bandwagon. Fulbright argued that the blockade was a more direct act of war against the Soviet Union than an air strike or invasion of Cuba and agreed with Russell that invading Cuba was the better move.[20] It was the worst scenario the administration could have faced in the meeting. Two Democrats, the chairmen of the Senate Foreign Relations and Senate Armed Services committees, opposed the administration's plan. Kennedy certainly had not expected opposition from Fulbright, who had just months before been such a staunch critic of the Bay of Pigs invasion. Incredulous, Kennedy asked the Arkansan to clarify: "What are you in favor of, Bill?" Now the executive's Brutus, Fulbright answered, "an invasion, and an all-out one, and as quickly as possible." Kennedy felt second-guessed after having carefully planned his strategy over four excruciating days of intense deliberation. He also felt as if he alone were being left politically liable for any mistakes that might result from his decision. Later, Kennedy suggested that Russell had swayed Fulbright and the others at the meeting. When Russell spoke, he said, the others fell in line. As the meeting ended, and just before going on television to announce the quarantine, the president whispered to Theodore Sorensen, "If they want this job, fuck 'em. They can have it. It's no great joy to me."[21]

Kennedy overreacted. Russell knew that once the decision of the president had been made, he and the others in Congress would be compelled to support it, even if they disagreed. Most of the legislators at the briefing understood that they were being informed rather than consulted. It was the way things happened in discussions of Cold War foreign and defense policy; Congress being presented the fait accompli was the norm. Still, Russell felt it was his job to disagree. If real advice in advance of the decision was not sought, Congress had to assert its power of consent. Russell had done so, respectfully and appropriately in private.

Russell's views on the Cuban Missile Crisis revealed much about his thinking on the global Cold War struggle. His responses suggested that he viewed conflicts on the periphery of the Communist and non-Communist world as inevitable. Khrushchev and the Soviets would continue to seek advantage through "wars of national liberation." In picking where to confront the Soviets, Russell adopted a two-world concept not unlike John Quincy Adams's when he penned the Monroe Doctrine. For Russell, the Western Hemisphere and Western Europe had to be aggressively defended against the Communists while American efforts in behalf of Eastern Europe, Africa, and Asia had to be limited. The reason was proximity. The threat of attack, if only in terms of nuclear missile range and accuracy, was greater closer to home and closer to America's principal allies.

Thus American military operations ninety miles off the coast of Florida, for Russell, were fully justified, while operations halfway around the world in Vietnam were not. Russell also understood that actions taken in the Western world might have an impact elsewhere. An effective military strike against Cuba could deter Communist aggression in other areas. The war on the periphery might be won without a fight. For Russell, Cuba was a crucial missed opportunity.

Despite his vigorous dissent behind closed doors, in public Russell supported the president's actions. He refused to talk directly to the press about the meeting but urged Americans to get behind the commander in chief. Rowland Evans nevertheless published an article in the *Herald Tribune* claiming that Russell had suggested that an invasion would be launched within days. Some suspected that Russell had taken his dissent to the public through a leak. At a second administration meeting with congressional leaders on October 24, after the Russian ships carrying offensive weapons to Cuba had turned around in the mid-Atlantic, Russell denied the accusation. He said that Evans had indeed called him, but he had refused to talk. He then offered a fig leaf. He announced to those in attendance that "inasmuch as I've been devil's advocate, Mr. President, I've been at times harshly critical of the State Department, I would like to take this opportunity to heartily congratulate the Secretary of State on what I regard as a magnificent triumph in the Organization of American States yesterday." The OAS had denounced the attempt to put offensive weapons in Cuba and had tacitly approved armed action to protect the hemisphere. Russell further praised the secretary of defense's statement outlining the limits of the quarantine.[22]

Russell, however, was only willing to keep his dissent silent for as long as he felt that his statements might hurt the president's ability to negotiate terms with the Russians or might hurt his party's election chances. After the crisis had diminished and midterm elections were completed, all bets were off. Playing to his Georgia constituents, he publicly criticized the administration's handling of the crisis and its immediate aftermath. In December, he told an Atlanta television station, "Three months ago we were pledged to see that Castroism in this Hemisphere was destroyed. We have now been euchred into the position of babysitting for Castro and guaranteeing the integrity of the Communist regime in Cuba." "We don't know," he added, "for a positive fact that the missiles and bombers have been removed." The administration had not followed up on its demands for "on-the-spot inspection." Moreover, it had not used the lifting of the quarantine as leverage to bring about those inspections. Until Castro was eliminated, he concluded, there would be no "peace in this Hemisphere."[23] In the years that followed, Russell would claim that the president's decision not to take out Castro encouraged Communists to test American resolve in other conflicts around the world, including most significantly Vietnam.[24]

Through the final months of the Kennedy administration, Russell grew increasingly more concerned about the Monroe Doctrine and hemispheric solidarity against Communist expansion. Once a professed believer in self-determination and noninterventionism, Russell altered his outlook following the situation in Cuba. After October 1962, he consistently argued for the right of the United States to assert its full power and influence to stop Marxist revolutionaries in Latin America.

In 1964, for example, Russell advised a tough line as the United States helped force a vote in the Organization of American States to sever relations with the Castro regime over reported aggressions against Venezuela. When Mexico, since 1960 a frequent defender of Castro's Cuba, became the only nation not to break with that nation in the OAS, President Lyndon Johnson called Russell to ask him how he should approach the subject with newly elected Mexican president Diaz Ordaz. Russell responded, "I'd just tell him that you judged it as being very unfortunate, and that it was a great burden on a good neighbor policy." The United States had been a good friend to Mexico, Russell said, but given the public sentiment against Cuba, it would be difficult for the administration to "go all out there for him." And, he added, you should tell him "very frankly *you* couldn't understand their attitude either."[25]

Russell had also advised strong action earlier in the year. When Havana cut off water supplies to the American naval base at Guantanamo over a dispute about Cuban fishing boats in U.S. waters, the senator urged the president to make a statement that would come across loud and clear to Moscow as well as Havana. While it should not be for "bloodshed and warfare," the United States could not take a "cringing position." He agreed with the president that the United States should supply its own water to the base and replace civilian jobs held by Cubans with Americans. According to Russell, it was most important to make it clear to Khrushchev in the stated U.S. response that Castro was "irrational and there will be a limit to our patience. That if he keeps on we'll have no alternative but to take some very affirmative steps there, and that it would be very tragic if he were to support a man who would be doing things to us that he would not tolerate himself under the same conditions. So I hope they make that perfectly clear to him. Remind him a little of Hungary while they're talking to him."[26]

President Johnson generally agreed with Russell's approach to U.S.–Latin American relations. The main objective was to convince the Soviets that the new administration was a firm defender of U.S. interests and would not respond passively to any Communist aggression in the Western Hemisphere. To this end, in December 1963, Johnson appointed Kennedy's Alliance for Progress director, Thomas C. Mann, to be his special assistant and to be assistant secretary of state for inter-American affairs. Johnson liked Mann because he was a tireless negotiator, a superb diplomatic technician, and could be counted on to carry out orders. Johnson also liked him because he was a Texan and a tough guy who would stand up for American interests. Johnson emphasized the latter in conversations with Russell. "Now they tell me that everybody in Latin America are scared of this fella Mann," he told the senator. "They highly regard him because he is a tough guy." Russell replied, "Well I hope he his. He's much tougher than the one's we've had. He has a velvet glove, but I hope he has these little iron fingers under it." "I think he does," Johnson said; "I'm counting on that."[27]

Because they shared his opinions about a bold hemispheric anti-Communism, Russell and Mann became Johnson's closest advisers on Latin America. Johnson's solicitation of Russell's advice in this area also had much to do with the desire to mend personal and political fences. In late 1963 and early 1964, Johnson was looking for a way to keep Russell close. The Georgian had been Johnson's mentor in the Senate, and the president genuinely wanted and respected his advice. Russell was also a crutch at times for Johnson's fragile ego, propping up the president when he was unsure of himself. But a serious political rift had developed between the two over the winter. Civil rights and Great Society reforms placed the two at opposite ends of the debate. Johnson needed an issue, like Latin America, on which they could share common cause. Even more than J. Edgar Hoover, Johnson needed Russell "inside the tent pissing out" rather than "outside the tent pissing in."

The Panamanian crisis marked the high point of this effort. Johnson literally exhausted Russell on Panama issues trying to bring him into the inner circle of advisers. He made the senator his first consultant in Washington while Mann took care of things in Panama City. Johnson called Russell every few days in the spring of 1964 with an update and, paying deference to the senator's legal skills, had him review every draft of every statement he issued concerning the crisis.

The effort kept Russell close and soothed Johnson's need for affirmation in the early days of his administration. And, as a bonus, like Johnson's appointment of the Georgian to the Warren Commission investigating President Kennedy's assassination, it kept Russell busy so that he had less time to fight the civil rights bill and Great Society legislation in general.

The Panamanian crisis erupted on January 9, 1964, when "zonians"—U.S. citizens working and living in Panama—clashed with Panamanian students over efforts to fly the Panamanian flag alongside the American flag over U.S. territory within the canal zone. The conflict reflected long-standing popular irritation in Panama over the provision in the 1903 treaty that gave U.S. control of the canal zone "in perpetuity." Three days of riots and disorder cost twenty-four Panamanian and four American lives, persuading Panamanian president Roberto Chiari to break diplomatic relations with the United States.

Johnson sent Mann to lead a group of advisers in talks with the Chiari government in mid-January. As Mann and his colleagues were taking off, the president called Russell. He explained that he had been on the phone with Chiari and had established the basic position of the administration: first, "that the enemies of both of us were exploiting this thing," and, second, that revisions of treaties or any other agreements could not be automatically agreed to until a full investigation was concluded. The president assured Russell that he would not give in to the demands of violent protesters and was "cold and hard and tough as hell" with Chiari. Russell applauded him. "I'm so pleased. Now that's a great president. That's a man that will go down in history."[28]

Johnson and Russell never admitted to exchanging quid pro quo favors directly, but they certainly traded courtesies and bonded during the crisis. For example, to keep pressure on the Panamanians, Russell agreed to make a statement suggesting that the United States was pursuing the building of an alternative canal route. Both men understood that realistically the alternative canal would never be built, but they hoped the suggestion would moderate Panamanian demands. In other words, "Uncle Dick" agreed to act the "bad cop." Johnson, in the same conversation, asked Russell if he had anybody in Georgia who could help out in the State Department or as an ambassador. Russell mentioned Tap Bennett, the son of an old friend from Georgia who was a young consul in Greece. Five days later, Johnson told Russell he was naming Bennett U.S. ambassador to the Dominican Republic.[29]

Russell encouraged Johnson to be "tough" at every step. What "tough" meant to Johnson was holding the line against Panamanian calls for treaty revisions that compromised U.S. control of the canal zone. When the Panamanians declared, in Johnson's paraphrase, that they would not "pee a drop until you revise the treaty," Mann hammered out the framework for talks with an Organization of American States peace committee. In a conversation with Russell, Johnson blasted Mann for giving in and appearing weak. The president insisted that the word "negotiate" be stricken and replaced with "discuss." He told Russell, "we're not going to do it by implication or innuendo or connotation that this means that we are in the wrong or that there is something wrong with the treaties." Johnson said that the peace committee agreed to the changes, and he believed that "being firm with them caused them to cave." "No question about it," Russell replied, "and we just had to do it."[30]

Johnson, however, felt increasing domestic and foreign pressure to reverse his refusal to "negotiate" revisions to the 1903 treaty and quickly settle the situation in Panama. He feared that the *New York Times* and the *Washington Post* would take the side of the Panamanians and portray the United States as exploiters and imperialists. Secretary of State Rusk also pressed him to treat the Panamanians fairly. Finally, the United Nations and the Organization of American States insisted that Washington agree to settle the issue before it escalated and that it act with their good offices. Russell made the counterargument. When Johnson told his friend that he intended to move the discussion along by making a statement acknowledging past wrongs and that the United States was open to discussing matters that marred the relations between the two countries, Russell advised him not to give in. He told Johnson that he agreed with British newspapers, which were suggesting that the United States "ought to have learned by one mistake in Cuba and not to make another now by surrendering here in Panama." Johnson insisted he was not surrendering. "I'm not about to get on my knees and go crawling to him and say I want to apologize to you for you shooting my soldiers," he told his mentor. "I wasn't raised in that school." But, he said, there were a number of "chicken things" he could do to settle the issue, like reforming the board overseeing the canal and replacing the governor in the zone. Russell suggested that Johnson make no statement. Let Chiari "sweat," Russell told the president. "You've got all the cards," he insisted, and could afford to wait. The American people are behind you, he told the president, and that was what counted. "You just go on and do what's in this country's interest," he advised, "and tell Rusk and these other fellas to jump in

the lake, and it will stay that way. The American people have been crying for somebody that had some of the elements of 'Old Hickory'
Jackson in him. . . . You know this government. You know the
world."[31]

Johnson, as he often did, relented to the greater pressure.
Compared to the State Department and the American press, Russell
was no match. In the end, the president was forced to tell the
Georgian that he could no longer wait and had to settle on talks to
avoid a crisis. Johnson reached a settlement with Chiari in April that
committed both sides "to review every issue which now divides us."
Eight months later, Panama and the United States began negotiations
on a new treaty.[32] Russell grudgingly consented. "I just get tired of us
feeling like having a guilt complex about every damn thing on earth,"
he said. "We've done more for Panama than anybody else. They were
the most primitive people in all of Latin America and we built a canal.
Now they've got the highest per capita income." But in consulting
Russell so extensively and in taking a firm stand initially, the president had partially placated his friend.[33]

Although not completely satisfied with the president's settlement
of the Panamanian crisis, Russell thought that the administration's
attempts to make firm stances there, at Guantanamo, and in Mexico
were small steps in the right direction. The big step, however, one to
finally make up for the missed opportunity in October 1962, had yet
to be taken. That step would come in the spring of 1965.

On April 24, 1965, a coup in the Dominican Republic provoked the
display of American military might in the hemisphere that Russell had
desired. The groundwork for the coup had been laid four years before
when Rafael Trujillo, the brutal thirty-year military dictator of the
Dominican Republic, was assassinated. In elections held in December
1962 to determine a successor, the Dominicans chose a liberal intellectual named Juan Bosch to be the president. The Bosch regime lasted
only seven months. An anti-Communist coup brought to power a military junta under Donald Reid Cabral, a pro-American businessman.
Thomas Mann and new Dominican ambassador Tap Bennett found
Cabral easy to work with, but they knew that his power over the country was weak. Bosch, then in exile in Puerto Rico, was still a popular
figure in the country. If he were restored to power, Bennett and Mann
feared, the leftist Bosch might establish a Communist regime in the
Dominican Republic. To bolster the Cabral government, the
Americans arranged for $100 million in guaranteed loans to the
Dominican Republic. Still, unemployment, strikes, and rebel activity
continued to plague the island, culminating in April 1965 when the

Dominican Revolutionary Party (PRD), in the name of Juan Bosch and aided by some military officials, led a general uprising.

The Johnson administration at first waited, hoping the rebels would be crushed. Over the ensuing three days, it became clear that this was a "countercoup" aimed at possibly restoring the presidency of Juan Bosch. Bennett and Mann saw those developments as conflicting directly with U.S. interests and encouraged the Cabral government to hold out against Bosch and what they identified as "Castroite" influences in the PRD. The government appeared to take the upper hand as attacks on April 27 threatened to overwhelm the rebels. When the rebels asked for mediation to end to crisis, the government refused, citing the Communist danger posed by the PRD. A day later, in a remarkable turnaround, the rebels regained the initiative. Bennett cabled the State Department that morning saying that "Castro-type" elements had moved in. To prevent the takeover, Bennett urged the administration to land U.S. marines on the island to protect American lives.

President Johnson had been kept abreast of the situation. Besides Bennett, the Central Intelligence Agency was his main source of information. CIA briefs confirmed the ambassador's reports that left-wing groups sought to establish a "Castro-type government." They also confirmed reports of anarchy and violence that could threaten American lives on the island. And then there was Russell's advice to make a strong stand in Latin America that would make up for the lost chance in Cuba. After obtaining virtually unanimous approval from his advisers, Johnson authorized Bennett's request for marines.

Two hours after his order to mobilize the marines, the president met with congressional leaders and stressed that the threat to American lives was the principal basis of action. When Everett Dirksen and John McCormack asked about the Communist threat, Johnson cryptically replied that all responsible officials recommended action without delay. Russell could not attend the meeting. He was at home in Georgia recovering from severe cases of bronchitis and emphysema that had necessitated a tracheotomy in early February. But the president had called him to confirm his approval. Russell, like those at the meeting, asked immediately about Communist influence. Johnson told him directly that there was little doubt that there were Communists among the rebel forces. Russell advised him that he had no alternative but to send armed forces to Santo Domingo "to avoid another Cuba."[34]

While the number of marines in the Dominican Republic would grow from four hundred to twenty-four thousand, the immediate crisis was resolved relatively quickly. The competing factions, under OAS and U.S. pressure, signed a cease-fire agreement in early May. Over the summer, the Dominicans negotiated with an OAS committee to hammer out conditions for a provisional government and free elections.

The political fallout in the United States from the intervention, however, gained steam just as the crisis in the Dominican Republic waned. Over the summer, it became evident to many that the president had exaggerated the threat to American lives and had overstated the evidence of Communist subversion in justifying U.S. intervention. Critics in the media, universities, and Congress launched investigations. Foremost among them was J. William Fulbright, chairman of the Senate Foreign Relations Committee. From mid-July through mid-August, his committee questioned Mann, Bennett, and other administration officials directly involved in the decision to intervene. Based on the evidence, Fulbright concluded that the administration had greatly exaggerated the threat of a Communist takeover and had overreacted to the danger to American lives. The marines had really been landed to prevent Bosch's return to power. Rejecting pleas from the administration and members of the committee who urged Fulbright to keep his conclusions to himself, the Arkansas senator prepared a Senate speech on the Dominican intervention.

On September 14, the president received word from McGeorge Bundy that Fulbright would speak the next day, indicting the administration for mishandling the Dominican affair and placing most of the blame on Tap Bennett. Johnson immediately called Russell. "This damned idiot of a Fulbright has got to come out and denounce our own ambassador and denounce his own country and denounce his own government." Fulbright, Johnson said, was specifically after Bennett, "the very best we got in the state department," in an effort "to destroy his career." Russell replied that he doubted he could convince Fulbright not to give the speech, but he would "go up there and talk to him."[35]

Russell called the president back a short time later. While he could not persuade Fulbright to forego the speech, he had gained the Arkansas senator's assurance that he would not mention Bennett by name. Johnson expressed relief, but Russell added that Fulbright considered Mann most responsible for the misguided intervention. "Well that's a damn lie," the president replied. "Mann wasn't even in on the meeting. We called Mann. The man responsible for it was Johnson, McNamara and Rusk, Bundy and Bill Moyers." Russell told the president to add his name as well. "You called me for the first part of it. I

Senator Russell visits with Ambassador Tapley Bennett and Brigadier General Linvill in the Dominican Republic, fall 1965. Courtesy of the Richard B. Russell Library for Political Research and Studies, Athens, Georgia.

never would have advised sending the paratroopers down there, but I don't think that . . . I strongly support everything you did. You may have overdone it just a little bit, but that's a good thing in the long run. Show them that you're not going to tolerate any . . ." Johnson urged Russell to say as much in the Senate.[36]

Russell did. A week after Fulbright delivered his address condemning U.S. intervention in the Dominican Republic, Russell spoke in its defense. He called the president's actions "prudent, patriotic, and forthright." "I do not know," he answered the administration's critics, "how it would be possible to measure in exact numbers how many Communists must be involved in an operation of this kind before it becomes dangerous to a republican form of government." It only took a "mere handful" in Cuba and Czechoslovakia, and, he implied, it could have taken far fewer in the Dominican Republic. The speech was also designed to give public cover to his old friend's son and fellow Georgian, Tap Bennett. Bennett was "an experienced and distinguished career diplomat," Russell declared, who neither panicked nor gave the president faulty advice. To the contrary, he was confident that the administration had set a course of action that would "establish a permanent republican form of government in Santo Domingo."[37]

For Russell, the ends justified Johnson's means in the Dominican affair. The goal was to establish a stable, anti-Communist government and deliver a warning to all Communist insurgents in the Western Hemisphere that the United States would protect its interests, almost regardless of cost. Unlike Fulbright, Russell had little regard for the Good Neighbor Policy, OAS cooperation, or America's reputation in Latin America. Those considerations paled in compared to the risk of "even remotely having another Castro anywhere in this hemisphere." Russell had even suggested that he was willing to forego the truth for action. When Fulbright told his colleague from Georgia, "We ought to at least wait until we know [about the extent of Communist subversion in the Dominican Republic]," Russell replied, "If we wait till we know, it's too damn long. We'll have to kill a whole lot of people to reestablish things."[38] Russell was even willing to tolerate dictatorship and violent anti-Communist purges. "Had our foresight been as good as our hindsight," he later told Johnson, "we'd a left old Trujillo alone. . . . Good God old Trujillo killed everybody who even claimed he knew a Communist."[39] However the president did it, Russell observed approvingly, the point was that "we do not have today another Castroite dictatorship in the Caribbean."[40]

Russell had become a ruthless hemispheric anti-Communist in the wake of Castro's rise to power in Cuba. Aggressive protection of national security interests, for Russell, was appropriate and necessary that close to home. The senator justified military incursions in the Western Hemisphere so long as they deterred Communist expansion. When it came to the non-Western world, Russell was much more restrained. In Africa, for example, Russell was among the most cautious of noninterventionists.

The senator's tendency to take a hard line in Latin America but not in places like Africa had much to do with the realist's concern for proximate threats. Successful attacks on the United States were simply much easier to launch from Cuba than they were from the Congo. Russell's two-world thinking also had much to do with his understanding of race, culture, and the limits of American power. The senator considered nonwhite Africans, whose blood and history had left them impoverished, technologically backward, and culturally retarded, to be less of a direct danger to the United States and less worthy of U.S. investment. Because he believed that nonwhite Africans were not yet capable of assimilating democratic institutions, Africa was a poor place to compete with the Communists. The United States, he assumed, could not spread democracy and stability to Africa. Indeed, he considered such efforts dangerous. As he told one constituent, "Our six percent of the world's population will not be able to lift the others, but it will be comparatively easy for us to pull down our own standards."[41]

By the early 1960s, Russell believed that American "standards" had already been eroded beyond recognition. The Supreme Court and the civil rights movement had begun to dismantle segregation, a system the Southern exceptionalist considered a bulwark for democracy in that it maintained peaceful race relations and preserved the primacy of local and states' rights. Almost as frightening, the international Communist movement had made greater the need for executive power, which upset the critical balance between the government's three branches. Linking these trends was the rising popularity of liberalism and modernism, which Russell believed had begun to undermine respect for traditional American, and what he considered Southern, values, including most importantly local political control and established racial norms.

Russell apprehended that these trends increasingly affected American military and foreign policy during the Kennedy and Johnson administrations. He was taken aback in July 1962, for example, when soldiers joined desegregation demonstrations. His questions about the events helped convince Secretary of Defense Robert McNamara to issue a memo to the military departments effectively banning military personnel from participating in civil rights demonstrations.[42] Russell again expressed his concern for creeping liberalism at the conjunction of the Cold War and the black civil rights struggle two years later. When President Johnson told Russell that he intended to name Carl Rowan, a black man, to head the United States Information Agency, the senator warned the president that if Rowan used the position to be a "spokesman for all the Negroes by denouncing the South before the world," there would be a heated reaction by the Southern bloc, and it would be bad for America's image abroad.[43]

Russell's demand that the American image abroad reflect Southern conservative values underlay his policy views in Africa. When, for example, the State Department ordered the crew of the U.S. aircraft carrier *Franklin D. Roosevelt* not to go ashore in Cape Town, South Africa, for fear of showing American support for the apartheid regime, Russell complained that the decision was "discourteous" to the white South African government.[44] He also vigorously opposed U.S. support for a British-led effort in the UN to impose sanctions on the minority white regime in Rhodesia for failing to grant full political rights to the dissimilar black African majority.[45] Russell simply did not agree that it was in the interest of the United States to support black self-rule in Africa, especially if it meant alienating white segregationist and anti-Communist governments like those ruling South Africa and Rhodesia.

At no point was this more apparent than when Russell became a leading critic of the Kennedy administration's policies in the Congo. In June 1960, Belgium abruptly acceded to Congolese independence, leaving the country with no foundation for self-rule. Only a handful of Congolese had been educated under the colonial order, leaving few with the skills to rebuild the abandoned political and economic infrastructure. Making matters worse, Katanga province, the Congo's main economic engine, seceded, with white Belgian nationals still in control of the lucrative mining industry. Political and civil chaos quickly swept over the region. The Congolese army, resentful that Belgian troops still remained, robbed, raped, and murdered white settlers. When Belgium flew in paratroopers to restore order, the Congo's new premier, Patrice Lumumba, denounced the move as an attempt to reimpose colonial rule. The UN sent twenty thousand troops to maintain a fragile peace just as Kennedy was coming into office.

Three factions competed for power in the Congo. Lumumba and Antoine Gizenga controlled the most radical of the three. The Lumumba-Gizenga faction had accepted Soviet equipment and technicians after the return of Belgian paratroopers. Colonel Joseph Mobutu and Congolese president Joseph Kasavubu controlled the second. Reportedly with CIA and Belgian assistance and the blessings of Kasavubu, Mobutu had led a coup against the premier, placing Lumumba under house arrest and expelling the Soviet advisers. Conservative Moise Tshombe, the pro-Belgian provincial president of Katanga, led the third faction.

Kennedy sought to end the power struggle through a greater UN presence and a coalition government. The result, the president hoped, would be a stable, democratic regime that could resist Soviet inroads in central Africa. Kennedy also understood that his efforts would be seen as a test of his commitment to African nationalism. The president thus decided to include the popular, though Communist-tainted, Lumumba-Gizenga faction in the coalition government while denouncing Katanga's secession. Conservatives like Russell were disturbed. Lumumba had accepted aid from the Soviets and might do so again in order to gain control of the Congo. U.S. support of Tshombe and a separate Katanga, on the other hand, would ensure that a pro-Western, anti-Communist, white-friendly government controlled the principal economic resources of the region. Moreover, an increased UN presence could mean an unnecessary additional commitment of American soldiers as well as an unsavory cooperation with Communist governments in the general assembly.

Russell, like most Southerners and conservatives, had become increasingly frustrated with the UN over the years. Since its creation, the organization had grown to double its original size and promised to grow even further as the nonwhite former subjects of European colonization gained independence. According to Russell, the additional members diluted U.S. power in that body, despite U.S. veto power in the Security Council. Each nation had a single vote in the general assembly, regardless of population. Thus, countries like Gabon and Iceland exercised power hundreds of times greater per representative than did the United States. Blocs of the new member nations could pit the superpowers against one another, demanding a proportionally larger contribution of money and men to their causes. A leading cause that the emerging nonwhite majority supported with the backing of the Soviet Union, Russell lamented, was the elimination of the vestiges of racist imperialism in places like the Congo.

Events in February 1961 served to bring the Soviets and African nationalists even closer together. That month, the world learned that Katangan authorities, with probable CIA involvement, had assassinated Patrice Lumumba. The Soviets and African nationalists immediately issued harsh protests in the United Nations. The UN responded with a resolution condemning the murder and promised a renewed commitment to bringing the remaining factions together.

Russell, like most Americans, had devoted relatively little attention to Africa. That, combined with the honeymoon period that he and others had granted the new president, kept Russell from commenting on the situation in the Congo. Things changed following the Bay of Pigs fiasco. The humiliation of the United States there shook the senator's faith in Kennedy. The time had come to offer leadership in guiding the nation's foreign policy. Russell first registered concerns about UN actions in the Congo in May 1961, when the Congolese government held Moise Tshombe for treason while the pro-Belgian Katangan president attended a UN-sponsored peace conference. Tshombe, Russell told his Senate colleagues, had been detained while under a UN pledge of safe conduct. If a protest were not launched that matched the resolution against Lumumba's assassination, he suggested, the UN would have created a "double standard of morality" and destroyed its usefulness as a fair mediator between states.[46]

For Russell and other conservatives, Tshombe and Katanga came to represent the paragon of African capitalism, anti-Communism, and civilization, while the UN increasingly represented the voice of nonwhite nationalist revolution and Communism. When later that year a new Congolese government under Cyrille Adoula requested UN and

U.S. support for the reintegration of Katanga, Russell again vigorously protested. He wrote the president and Secretary of State Rusk passionate dissenting letters in early December 1961: "I most earnestly protest the employment of any American servicemen, equipment or tax dollars in the present ill-advised drive by the armed forces of the United Nations, launched on the command of the Russian delegate, to destroy the only organized anti-Communist force in the Congo." Russell's letters, together with public criticism from other leading conservatives and the need for European support during the Berlin crisis, convinced Kennedy not to add American troops to those fighting against Katanga. The president gambled correctly that UN forces would end Katanga's independence without direct U.S. military aid. When Belgian foreign minister Paul-Henri Spaak surprisingly accepted UN plans to crush the Katangan secession, Tshombe's independent rule came to an end. On Christmas Eve, Indian-led forces backed by Swedish air strikes overwhelmed Katanga's military.[47]

That Kennedy had resisted direct military intervention in the Congo satisfied Russell, but the president's consistent opposition to Katangan independence and his willingness to accept Soviet-initiated UN policies left the Georgian dubious of the administration's Africa policy. When administration supporters in Congress led an effort to purchase UN bonds that would help finance an advance reserve for UN military ventures like the one in the Congo, Russell quickly moved to block the measure. The Senate Armed Services Committee chairman proposed a substitute amendment that forgave UN debt to the United States incurred from operations in the Congo and the Middle East but restricted the administration's ability to give equipment, materiel, or men in support of UN military actions in the future. Such aid, under the Russell amendment, would require a joint resolution of Congress. Russell's amendment ultimately gained only twenty-one votes from his most conservative colleagues, but the senator never gave up his efforts to limit U.S. involvement in Africa.[48]

In defending his amendment, Russell delivered a revealing speech. He declared that he did not, as some had suggested, seek the abolition of the UN, but that body had committed an "unnecessary act of aggression" against a nation with "Christian institutions of government" and that was "strongly opposed to communism." In doing so, the UN had undermined its own ability to fulfill its original purpose: to peacefully mediate the settlement of disputes between nations. It had also acted contrary to American interests. To support reserve funds for undetermined efforts in the future, he argued, would be tantamount to giving the UN partial control of U.S. foreign policy. Congress, as the only branch of government constitutionally empowered to declare war, should be the only body to approve such measures. The anti–League of Nations argument had resurfaced.

While defending these conclusions, Russell outlined his fundamental positions concerning revolution, colonialism, and the emerging Third World. The United States, he declared, must find a consistent policy concerning revolutionary independence movements. "Despite our expressed dedication to the cause of revolution, and freedom of choice for people everywhere as to the kind of government they should have," he argued, "we have made an exception in the case of Katanga." Instead of supporting a stable anti-Communist government, the United States had given in to the demands of suspect African nationalists like the Gizenga faction and its ally from Ghana, Kwame Nkrumah, while making a devil's pact with the Soviets, the "rapists" of Hungary and Poland. In doing so, the United States had spread to Katanga "the chaos, the confusion, and the barbarism" that characterized the other areas of the Congo. At the core of the matter was U.S. acquiescence to "anticolonialism, without regard to the probable effect of destroying established government, even though colonial, and granting independence to people *who are not ready for it* [emphasis added]." While the history of colonialism was "sordid" and marked by "exploitation and imposition," the colonial powers "in this enlightened age" have sought to prepare the people for independence. But time and again, the demand for emancipation had accelerated the process to an unwise pace; thus, the Belgians had left "before the natives were really ready." The Congo, he was convinced, was "going back into the jungle and to the primitive civilization that existed before the Belgians came in." The administration, in short, had mistakenly sought the favor of uncivilized, fickle African nationalists who were easily manipulated by Communists. It had sought democracy where Russell believed it was unlikely to blossom. In doing so, Kennedy had undermined the last stable anti-Communist government in central Africa.[49]

U.S. involvement in the Congo continued into the Johnson administration. With Katanga back in the fold by early 1963, the U.S. objective shifted to protecting a moderate government and preventing Gizenga or any other prominent Lumumbist from coming to power. The Kennedy and Johnson administrations both backed the Adoula government, but, understanding the need to back a leader with stronger popular support and an effective power base, they provided aid—vehicles, communications equipment, training, and CIA support—to Mobutu's military forces in the capital, Leopoldville. By

October 1963, the remaining Lumumbist factions dispersed. A year later, with the departure of UN forces, Mobutu took control of the government in Leopoldville and moved to bring rebellious factions around Stanleyville in line. His control was not yet total, however, as the United States and Belgium prevailed upon Mobutu to accept former Katangan leader Moise Tshombe as prime minister.

Lumumbists gained resurgent popular support from those inside and outside the country who still considered Tshombe a traitor. A group of them organized as the Conseil National de Liberation (CNL) seized Stanleyville and proclaimed a people's republic in late 1964. When CNL-allied insurgents took hostages that included American missionaries and consulate staff to use as bargaining chips to keep Mobutu from attacking Stanleyville, President Johnson authorized the use of American transport planes to carry Belgian paratroopers ordered to rescue and evacuate the hostages. Tshombe's power withered as the rebellions continued into the next year. Mobutu seized the advantage and led a coup d'etat that left him the sole head of state. An American client, supported by Belgium and white mercenaries, Mobutu had little popular support, but his dictatorial rule, Washington believed, ensured stability and the safeguarding of American interests.

During the November 1964 hostage crisis, Russell contacted the president and privately protested against the military assistance given to Mobutu and the use of American planes in the rescue operation. At the time, the senator refrained from publicly denouncing the Johnson administration's policies, but he was not so restrained in the summer of 1967. Over the ensuing two years, Russell had increasingly become an open critic of Johnson's policies in Vietnam. Fearing that the Congo could become another quagmire, the senator felt more and more compelled to speak out. But the immediate factor in spurring Russell's comments was another U.S. move against insurgent forces in Katanga.

In June, the administration decided to supply three U.S. C-130 cargo planes and 150 support personnel to buttress the airlift capacity of Mobutu's forces in their campaign against mutinying mercenary and former Katanga gendarme units. On July 8, just before the planes took off, Secretary of State Rusk called Russell and Senate Foreign Relations head J. William Fulbright to inform them of the situation. Rusk left the impression that the expedition was necessary to rescue Americans in the area. The following day, however, the secretary called again conceding that the planes would be used primarily to move Mobutu's troops.

Russell was upset at the news and told Rusk as much. The senator had taken to heart earlier statements President Johnson had made concerning the Congo. The president had informed Mobutu that the United States would avoid any direct involvement in the Congolese fighting. He also told the dictator that he would look askance at any aggressive act against the now exiled Moise Tshombe. Russell felt that he and the American public had been lied to.[50]

On July 10, in the midst of urban rioting in the United States, Russell took the floor of the Senate to register his "earnest protest against the action of our Government in sending planes and troops into the Congo." What some termed a rebellion, Russell considered an internal disturbance that had nothing to do with "the question of communism." It was just one of many "local," "tribal" wars in Africa where the United States had "no stake and where we have no legal or moral commitment to intervene." Intervention would only provoke the Soviets and Chinese to action. Once again, he declared, the administration had disregarded his private objections and compelled him to speak out.[51]

As had been the case in 1962 and was now the case in both the Congo and Vietnam, the principal issue for Russell was unchecked executive control over military affairs in a pattern where repeated interventions seemed to be the administration's solution to all problems around the world. Although he disagreed with Russell on many foreign policy issues, including American strategy in Vietnam, Senator Fulbright shared the Georgian's distress. During a long lunch in the Senate dining room, the two discussed Fulbright's resolution that would require legislative approval for any national commitment by the United States to a foreign power. The Congo proved sufficient to drive Russell into Fulbright's camp, and he subsequently voted for the national commitments resolution. Russell and Fulbright together joined with many other congressmen in a long struggle against the imperial presidency, a struggle that as one historian put it, would ultimately "flower into the Hatfield-McGovern and Cooper-Church resolutions as well as the War Powers Act."[52]

An already prickly relationship between Russell and the administration grew even more pointed over the Congo intervention. Particularly disturbing to the administration was the alliance between Fulbright and Russell. In an effort to patch things up with Russell, Secretary Rusk hurried to Capitol Hill with a promise of an early withdrawal of the planes and men. He also announced the rejection of a similar aid request from Nigeria.[53] Later that year, the president himself made a further effort to reassure his friend about the "carefully limited" nature of the action. In December, he wrote to Russell that the U.S. transport aircraft dispatched to the Congo in July had completed their mission and safely returned without casualties or damage. The mission, Johnson argued, was a success.[54]

Russell disagreed. The senator answered that while he was "happy over the safe return of our men and planes from this mission, I must regretfully advise that I still do not believe in the United States moving into situations of this kind unilaterally." While he had disagreed with U.S. backing of UN intervention in the Congo in 1962, at least the United States had not acted alone. In this instance, as the senator understood it, the United States had acted directly on the request of Mobutu. "I cannot subscribe to any policy," he wrote Johnson, "predicated on the assumption that the United States alone has an obligation to avoid domestic strife in Africa or elsewhere." He added that, "despite any great advancement that may have been made in Africa in recent years, from what I have been able to learn, tribal loyalties are still superior to any feeling of nationalism and we are likely to have tribal rebellions and wars for some time to come." He opposed all U.S. interventions in such conflicts. Despite a follow-up letter from Secretary Rusk reassuring Russell that the action was not exactly unilateral and that the results were positive, the senator was never convinced that the favorable outcome justified the risk to American lives.[55]

Race and cultural history were, in the end, crucial factors in Russell's foreign policy formulations concerning the non-Western periphery. In fact, they would be the deciding factors in his perspective on emerging nations from the Congo to Vietnam. In 1964, Russell claimed that it would be nothing less than a "tragedy for us to go and get involved in the Congo as we are in Vietnam."[56] According to the senator, both areas of the world lacked strategic importance as well as the racial and cultural makeup that fostered democracy. His suggestions amounted to a kind of racial containment. Where the United States did not have vital strategic or economic interests at stake, and where Anglo-Saxon rule was not entrenched, Washington should avoid involvement. For Russell, the only apparent exception to this rule applied when the Western Hemisphere was threatened, as it had been in Cuba and the Dominican Republic.[57]

Russell was keenly aware that his record on race in the United States compromised the advice he gave to Kennedy and Johnson on Africa. When suggesting that racial issues were driving UN involvement in the Congo in 1962, he understood that the statement "would have been more impressive" coming from some other senator "than it is coming from me."[58] He also knew well that the Kennedy and Johnson administrations were announcing to the world their support for black African nationalists over white mercenaries and European clients.[59] Due in equal parts to racism and Realpolitik, such a statement, for Russell, his Southern constituents, and many Americans, was not worth the risk to American soldiers and friendly relations with European allies.

During the 1960s, Richard Russell had developed a two-world view of American interests based principally on geography and race. Threats to direct military and economic interests closer to home demanded an aggressive response, even intervention, regardless of race. Russell showed no real concern for racial issues in his responses to the Cuban Missile Crisis, the Panamanian crisis, or Dominican intervention. But farther away from home, where direct military and economic interests were not at stake, race and cultural history determined Russell's opinions on American action. In the Congo, Russell either supported European and colonial powers racially and culturally similar to white America, or he wrote off any connection to Africa as unwise. The senator's views on Vietnam derived primarily from the same set of considerations.

Notes

1. See *Congressional Record*, 86th Cong., 2nd sess., 1960, 106, pt. 6:7052–53; pt. 7:8603–4.
2. "Declaration of Constitutional Principles," March 12, 1956, box 27, series 3, Russell Papers, Richard B. Russell Memorial Library.
3. *Congressional Record*, 85th Cong., 1st sess., 1957, 103, pt. 8:10771–75; "Declaration of Constitutional Principles," March 17, 1956, box 27, series 3, Russell Papers, Richard B. Russell Memorial Library.
4. Gilbert C. Fite, *Richard B. Russell, Jr., Senator from Georgia* (Chapel Hill: University of North Carolina Press, 1991), 347.
5. *Congressional Record*, 86th Cong., 2nd sess., 1960, 106, pt. 3:3442–44.
6. Jolley to Russell, March 11, 1960, and Russell to Macomber, March 22, 1960, box 17, series 16, Russell Papers, Richard Russell Memorial Library.
7. Randall Woods, *Fulbright: A Biography* (New York: Cambridge University Press, 1995), 269.
8. *Congressional Record*, 87th Cong., 2nd sess., 1962, 108, pt. 1:1322–24.
9. "Fulton Lewis Jr. Memo, January 23, 1963," in CREST [database] (College Park, MD: National Archives, 2005 [cited June 23, 2005]); E. W. Kenworthy, "Goldwater Asks Senate Inquiry into U.S. Role in Cuba Invasion," *New York Times*, January 24, 1963, 1.
10. Executive Session Relating to Cuba and the Monroe Doctrine, September 19, 1962, box 50, Executive and Unpublished, Senate Armed Services Committee Papers, RG 46, National Archives.
11. S.J. Res. 230, Calendar no. 2077, September 19,1962, box 50, Executive and Unpublished, Senate Armed Services Committee Papers, RG 46, National Archives.

12. Report to Accompany S.J. Res. 230, Calendar no. 2077, September 19, 1962, box 50, Executive and Unpublished, Senate Armed Services Committee Papers, RG 46, National Archives.

13. *Congressional Record*, 87th Cong., 2nd sess., 1962, 108, pt. 14:19349–51.

14. James Giglio, *The Presidency of John F. Kennedy* (Lawrence: University of Kansas Press, 1991), 191–93.

15. Dutton to Russell, October 2, 1962, box 15, series 16, Russell Papers, Richard Russell Memorial Library.

16. Michael Beschloss, *The Crisis Years: Kennedy and Khrushchev, 1960–1963* (New York: Edward Burlingame Books, 1991), 480; *Richard Russell, Georgia Giant*, Documentary Script Number 3, 1970, box 1, Russell Personal Papers, Lyndon Baines Johnson Library.

17. Beschloss, *The Crisis Years*, 480.

18. "What It Will Take to Win in Vietnam," *U.S. News & World Report*, September 6, 1965, 56–60; *Richard Russell, Georgia Giant*, Documentary Script Number 3, 1970, box 1, Russell Personal Papers, Lyndon Baines Johnson Library.

19. *Richard Russell, Georgia Giant*, Documentary Script Number 3, 1970, box 1, Russell Personal Papers, Lyndon Baines Johnson Library.

20. Ernest R. May and Philip D. Zelikow, eds., *The Kennedy Tapes: Inside the White House During the Cuban Missile Crisis* (Cambridge: Belknap Press, 1997), 245–76.

21. Beschloss, *The Crisis Years*, 481.

22. May and Zelikow, *The Kennedy Tapes*, 367–81.

23. "Russell's View: We Must 'Get Rid of Castro,'" *U.S. News & World Report* 53 (December 17, 1962).

24. "What It Will Take to Win in Vietnam," *U.S. News & World Report*, September 6, 1965, 56–60; *Richard Russell, Georgia Giant*, Documentary Script Number 3, 1970, box 1, Russell Personal Papers, Lyndon Baines Johnson Library.

25. Johnson Tapes, WH6411.18, PNO6–7, 11/12/64, 8:55A, 6340, Lyndon Baines Johnson Library.

26. Johnson Tapes, WH6402.08, PNO5, 2/7/64, 11:17A, 1919, Lyndon Baines Johnson Library.

27. Johnson Tapes, WH6401.11, PNO2, 1/10/64, 1:25A, 1305, Lyndon Baines Johnson Library.

28. Johnson Tapes, WH6401.11, PNO2, 1/10/64, 1:25A, 1305, Lyndon Baines Johnson Library.

29. Johnson Tapes, WH6401.14, PNO4, 1/15/64, 4:30A, 1364, Lyndon Baines Johnson Library; Johnson Tapes, WH6401.17, PNO12–13, 1/20/64, 7:20P, 1437–38, Lyndon Baines Johnson Library.

30. Johnson Tapes, WH6401.14, PNO4, 1/15/64, 4:30A, 1364, Lyndon Baines Johnson Library; Mann unpublished memoir, 213–26.

31. Johnson Tapes, WH6401.19, PNO2, 1/22/64, 6:55P, 1477, Lyndon Baines Johnson Library; Johnson Tapes, WH6401.21, PNO12, 1/25/64, 2:30P, 1545, Lyndon Baines Johnson Library.

32. Robert Dallek, *Flawed Giant: Lyndon Johnson and His Times, 1961–1973* (New York: Oxford University Press, 1998), 93–96.

33. Johnson Tapes, WH6401.21, PNO12, 1/25/64, 2:30P, 1545, Lyndon Baines Johnson Library. See also Johnson Tapes, WH6401.24, PNO9, 1/29/64, 10:30P, 1612, Lyndon Baines Johnson Library; Johnson Tapes, WH6402.22, PNO4, 2/26/64, 12:10P, 2205, Lyndon Baines Johnson Library; Johnson Tapes, WH6403.07, PNO5, 3/9/64, 9:45P, 2441, Lyndon Baines Johnson Library; Johnson Tapes, WH6403.13, PNO6–7, 3/21/64, 1:32P, 2587–88, Lyndon Baines Johnson Library.

34. *Congressional Record*, 89th Cong., 1st sess., 1965, 111, pt. 18:24557–58; Johnson Tapes, WH6509.04, PNO7–8, 9/14/65, 8:00P, 8865–66, Lyndon Baines Johnson Library.

35. Johnson Tapes, WH6509.04, PNO1, 9/14/65, 6:35P, 8859, Lyndon Baines Johnson Library.

36. Johnson Tapes, WH6509.04, PNO7–8, 9/14/65, 8:00P, 8865–66, Lyndon Baines Johnson Library.

37. *Congressional Record*, 89th Cong., 1st sess., 1965, 111, pt. 18:24557–60.

38. Johnson Tapes, WH6509.04, PNO7–8, 9/14/65, 8:00P, 8865–66, Lyndon Baines Johnson Library.

39. Johnson Tapes, WH6509.04, PNO1, 9/14/65, 6:35P, 8859, Lyndon Baines Johnson Library.

40. *Congressional Record*, 89th Cong., 1st sess., 1965, 111, pt. 18:24557–60.

41. Russell to Mrs. Roger Johnson, August 30, 1961, box 1, series 9, Russell Papers, Richard Russell Memorial Library.

42. Russell to McNamara, July 11, 1963; Long to LeMay, July 16, 1963; and McNamara to Russell, July 16, 1963, Russell Papers, box 3, series 10, Richard Russell Memorial Library.

43. Johnson Tapes, WH6401.17, PNO12–13, 1/20/64, 7:20P, 1437–38, Lyndon Baines Johnson Library.

44. Russell to Parker, March 7, 1967; Jackson to Russell, March 2, 1967; McArthur to Russell, February 28, 1967; Russell to Parker, February 17, 1967; Parker to Russell, February 9, 1967; Russell Papers, box 24, series 16 B, Richard Russell Memorial Library.

45. "Senator Russell on Vietnam: 'Go in and Win—or Get Out,'" *U.S. News & World Report*, May 2, 1966, 56; Russell to Key, January 11, 1967; Russell to Stephens, November 2, 1967; Russell to Lott, June 5, 1968; box 24, series 16 B, Richard Russell Memorial Library.

46. *Congressional Record*, 87th Cong., 1st sess., 1961, 107, pt. 6–7:7484–85, 8711–12.

47. Russell to Kennedy, December 7, 1961; Russell to Kennedy, December 8, 1961; Russell to Kennedy, December 12, 1961, Russell Papers, series 16, box 12, Richard Russell Memorial Library.

48. *Congressional Record*, 87th Cong., 2nd sess., 1962, 108, pt. 5:6070.

49. *Congressional Record*, 87th Cong., 2nd sess., 1962, 108, pt. 3, 5:5106, 5886–97.

50. Felix Belair Jr., "Senators Assail U.S. Aid to Congo," *New York Times*, July 10, 1967; Don Oberdorfer, "Noninterventionism, 1967 Style," *New York Times Magazine*, September 17, 1967.

51. *Congressional Record*, 90th Cong., 1st sess., 1967, 18093–97. Indeed, the Congo had ceased being a major supplier of uranium to the United States by 1960. Still, many were convinced that unrest in central Africa would lead to the possible overthrow of anti-Communist allies like South Africa. Editorial Note, *Foreign Relations of the United States: Africa*, July 28, 1960, 353; Thomas J. Noer, *Cold War and Black Liberation* (Columbia: University of Missouri Press, 1985), 57–58, 253–55.

52. Woods, *Fulbright*, 456–57.

53. Don Oberdorfer, "Noninterventionism, 1967 Style," *New York Times Magazine*, September 17, 1967.

54. Johnson to Russell, December 16, 1967, box 344, Name File Russell, White House Central File, Lyndon Baines Johnson Library.

55. Russell to Johnson, December 21, 1967; Rusk to Russell, January 29, 1968, 15, box EE, Letters to Save, Lyndon B. Johnson, Russell Papers, Richard B. Russell Memorial Library.

56. "Russell Says Senate Group Will Weigh U.S. Saigon Role," *New York Times*, December 31, 1964, 2.

57. "Russell Endorses Dominican Action; Wary on Vietnam," *New York Times*, May 6, 1965, 16.

58. *Congressional Record*, 87th Cong., 2nd sess., 1962, 108, pt. 5:5891.

59. Dean Rusk, *As I Saw It* (New York: W. W. Norton, 1990), 280–81.

5

Dove's Lost Cause

Lyndon Johnson and Richard Russell spoke the same language. They could talk about hunting, football, the weather, honor, manhood, politics, and even race in an idiosyncratic "Southern" way.[1] They were also close friends, confidants as well as colleagues. Russell spent as much time with the Johnson family as he did with anyone. The Johnson girls called him "Uncle Dick," and Lady Bird doted on the aging bachelor. But Russell's closeness with Lyndon Johnson and his family did not mean they always or even frequently agreed on policy. When asked about his relationship with Johnson, Russell admitted they were close but was quick to add, "He doesn't always take my advice."[2]

While Richard Russell was never completely successful in selling his overall vision of U.S. defense and foreign policy, he was able to strengthen the military and limit American commitments abroad during the Truman, Eisenhower, and Kennedy administrations. When his closest friend in the Senate became president, many expected Russell to wield even more influence. It was an ironic testament to both their quirky relationship and the strength of the liberal internationalists' influence over the president that Russell was less able to guide policy in the Johnson administration than in any other after World War II. Indeed, on the most pressing foreign and defense issue since the world war, Vietnam, the president chose at almost every point to ignore his mentor's advice.

Looking back, Russell believed the conflict in Vietnam had been lost in 1954 when the United States made its first commitment to preventing the spread of Communism in South Vietnam. Once American prestige was on the line, Russell knew that it would be next to impossible to withdraw.

But the truth was that he had many opportunities to restrict, and even reverse, the commitment in Vietnam in subsequent years. Russell was among the first people President Johnson called to gain advice on the Gulf of Tonkin Resolution and military escalation in the winter and spring of 1965. His advice fell on nearly deaf ears. As historian David Halberstam suggested, Russell had been to some degree written off by the White House as a conservative isolationist who did not care about "colored people."[3]

It was largely because of his views on "colored people" and his intimate knowledge of lost causes that the senator saw the situation in Vietnam as more complicated and dangerous than any of the Cold War administrations would admit. Richard Russell believed that the United States could not help those who would not help themselves. His understanding of race and democratic evolution limited the list of those who would help themselves to an enlightened, mostly white, few. At times, Russell's racism was blatant. In private, he referred to the Chinese as "coolies" and the Laotians as "rats," and he frequently alluded to the common American stereotype that Asians had over-bred themselves into a yellow horde that threatened to overwhelm the world. Even more significant in his thinking was the conviction that he had held since his visit to Asia during World War II, that Asians were unwilling to take responsibility for their own destiny and were unlikely to join the fold of democratic nations. Of the Vietnamese specifically, he contended that it was "all just through generations or even centuries, they've just thought about the individual and glorified the individual, and that's the only utilization of power—just to glorify the individual. . . . They just can't shed themselves of that complex." Russell felt that Asians, like Africans, had not yet developed a spirit of individual liberty; thus any American attempts to spread democracy in these regions were doomed to fail.[4]

Racism permeated Russell's worldview, but the Georgian's peculiarly Southern way of thinking about history and nationalism also influenced his outlook. He recognized that the Vietnamese, like many Southerners, were less interested in building an abstract nation than in focusing on their immediate needs for security and livelihood. The land provided. And in times of need, so did a charismatic patron. It was Russell's understanding of the familial and social relationships in the American South that led him to conclude that the term "uncle" that the Vietnamese used to refer to Ho Chi Minh was one of great respect for a protector and benefactor, one who would care for his kith and kin in times of flood, famine, and drought. Nationalism in Vietnam, as in the South, Russell concluded, was about tangible things like blood, soil, and tradition, not abstractions like progress, human rights, and civil liberties.

His two-world understanding of strategic interests finally played a role in the senator's views on Vietnam. Maintaining prestige and holding the line against Communism, he argued, could be done closer to home, in Cuba, where the effort would yield immediate and certain results. Military action in the Western Hemisphere was as likely to stop dominoes falling in Burma and Thailand as action in Vietnam, Cambodia, and Laos. Russell, again like George Kennan, saw no direct strategic benefit, no legitimate American interest protected, by joining the conflict in Vietnam.

From the end of World War II, Russell advised against any American involvement in Southeast Asia. Between 1946 and 1954, he rejected every call to send financial aid to Vietnam, but his pleas were drowned out by the calls for an ever more vigorous confrontation against Communism. At the Potsdam conference in the summer of 1945, the Truman administration had committed the United States to helping return Indochina to France. When Communist insurgents threatened to overrun the French in 1950, the president authorized the first military aid to fight the Cold War in Southeast Asia. Truman's National Security Council, to Russell's dismay, viewed the expansion of Communism in China, along with its possible extension into Indochina, as a direct threat to non-Communist allies in the region, such as Thailand and Burma. President Eisenhower succumbed to the same logic when he took office in 1953. All told, the United States would commit $2 billion in economic and military aid to France and South Vietnam between 1946 and 1954, constituting some 78 percent of the cost of the French-Indochina War. After a CIA briefing in 1953, Russell summed up his opinion of that course: "You are pouring [money] down a rathole: the worst mess we ever got into this Vietnam. . . . We are in for something that is going to be one of the worst things this country ever got into."[5]

Russell had ample opportunity to express his dissent to Eisenhower, but the timing was never more important than in 1954. Early that year, the president authorized another large military aid package—some $385 million in arms—for the French effort against Communist forces in Indochina. In February, he again upped the stakes by suggesting the transfer of a fleet of B-26 bombers along with two hundred technicians to help the French. When the president briefed congressional leaders on the plan, Russell voiced his opposition, arguing that the move would constitute the first steps toward America's direct involvement in the war.

A month later, the Communist-led Vietminh surrounded twelve thousand French troops at a remote outpost called Dien Bien Phu. Desperate, the French requested U.S. air strikes in support of the besieged garrison. Eisenhower hoped to stop Communist advances in Asia but understood that the air strikes were not guaranteed to work. He, too, feared American involvement in a ground war if the conflict escalated. So, on April 3, the president asked that Russell and other congressional leaders meet with Secretary of State Dulles and Admiral Arthur Radford, chairman of the Joint Chiefs of Staff and the strongest advocate for the American air strikes. Dulles requested congressional authorization to use carrier-based U.S. air strikes against the Vietminh in the hills around Dien Bien Phu.

Russell pressed Dulles and Radford to define the limits of American involvement, to clarify the degree to which other U.S. allies would participate, and to declare whether all of the Joint Chiefs were in agreement on this course of action. Russell knew full well that the military was not agreed, that allies had not been brought on board, and that the limits of involvement had been left open-ended. He and others in the meeting insisted that the administration at least solicit allied assistance and form a more definite strategy before Congress approved the mission. When allied support did not materialize, Dulles was forced to drop the plan. The French forces at Dien Bien Phu surrendered on May 7, 1954.

Russell's victory in forcing the administration to adopt a united action policy that limited American involvement in Indochina was short lived. Events quickly turned against the Georgian when the Supreme Court laid waste to his beloved segregation in the *Brown v. Board of Education* decision on May 17 and the Geneva Conference opened on May 18. Preoccupied with *Brown* and out of the loop when it came to the administration-led negotiations, Russell could do little as American involvement in Southeast Asia increased dramatically as a result of the meeting in Geneva. The administration had hoped to persuade the French to continue to fight, but Paris was tired and ready for a negotiated settlement. On July 21, the Geneva Accords established Cambodia and Laos as independent nations and temporarily divided Vietnam at the 17th parallel in preparation for national elections to be held in 1956. The Vietminh forces remained in the North, while American-backed anti-Communist forces took control of the South. The administration immediately began angling to establish the area south of the 17th parallel as an independent, anti-Communist state under the protection of the Southeast Asia Treaty Organization. Eisenhower also committed economic aid and military advisers to the new Bao Dai/Ngo Dinh Diem regime. By February 1955, U.S. forces were in Southeast Asia training the South Vietnamese army.

Russell was disappointed but was resigned to the president's decision. Later, he would regret having not lodged a stronger protest against American support of the South Vietnamese, but in 1955 he trusted the administration's assurances that it had no intention of assuming a direct combat role in Vietnam. He also had little choice. Like so many foreign policy decisions, the commitment of American military advisers to Vietnam was presented to Russell as a fait accompli. Nevertheless, Russell could and did protest in private. When Assistant Secretary of State Thruston Morton was sent to tell Russell that the White House would be sending an estimated 200 men to South Vietnam along with further funding, Russell told Morton it was a mistake. What was then two hundred, he predicted, would become twenty thousand and even two hundred thousand. "I think you are opening up a trail today," he told Morton, "that will be costly in blood and treasure to the country. . . . I could not be more opposed to it." Morton concluded the meeting by telling Russell that the president and secretary of state would be going ahead without the senator's approval. "I know," Russell replied; "he [Eisenhower] mentioned that he might do it. Tell him, then, that I think it is a terrible mistake but that if he does it I will never raise my voice." Once troops had been committed, Russell had to fall in line or risk his power and reputation as leader of the Armed Services Committee. He fell in line.[6]

The pace of change had once again exceeded Russell's comfort level. He deemed both the new U.S. commitment in Vietnam and the dramatic ruling in *Brown* hasty and unwise. Those decisions had set courses that the country could not reverse. He would do what he could to stop and reverse them, but he understood, perhaps better than anyone at the time, that his would be another lost cause.

The hundreds of military advisers that Russell predicted became thousands under Eisenhower. They then became tens of thousands under Kennedy. Russell was in part complicit in this buildup. On the heels of the Bay of Pigs disaster, Russell committed his full support to training and maintaining special counterguerrilla forces. In a memo to President Kennedy and Vice President Johnson dated April 20, 1961, Russell advised, among other things, that "the president's suggested program for specialized training in ranger or counterguerrilla operations for certain units of the Army and Marine Corps should be prosecuted with relentless vigor." What Russell had not considered was that they would be field tested in Vietnam.[7]

President Kennedy's interest in expanding American influence in Southeast Asia in general and in Vietnam in particular grew out of an emerging crisis in Laos. The United States and France had supported the Laotian government against a Communist insurgency in the 1950s. When Soviet-backed troops of the Pathet Lao threatened to overrun the Phoumi government in early 1961, President Kennedy committed the United States to its protection. A consensus in support of military intervention quickly faded following the shock and embarrassment of the Bay of Pigs fiasco. Suspicious of the Joint Chiefs and CIA, Kennedy rejected a series of proposals to put troops in Laos to stave off the defeat of the government. Congressional leaders and administration officials agreed that escalation in Laos was ill advised. Senate majority leader Mike Mansfield (D-MT), for example, warned that intervention in landlocked Laos "would be worse than Korea, would cost a great deal more and would very likely bring us into conflict with the Communist Chinese."[8] Ambassador to India John Kenneth Galbraith added that as a "military ally, the entire Laos nation is clearly inferior to a battalion of conscientious objectors from World War I."[9] It was also quite clear to Kennedy supporters that it would be exceedingly difficult to explain to the American people and to powerful senators like Richard Russell why he sent troops to Laos but had refused to send them to Cuba.

Russell, not surprisingly, had been among the chorus opposing military intervention in Laos. In February 1961, Kennedy, Johnson, and Rusk met with Russell and Mansfield to discuss possible military action in that tiny, landlocked country. Russell argued that resources would be better used in more secure, stable areas like Thailand and Burma. In another meeting in April, the Georgian bluntly declared, "We should get our people out and write the country off."[10] Russell's and the others' advice helped confirm the president's instincts to take a different course. Kennedy decided to move for a negotiated settlement in April 1961. The United States subsequently met with the belligerents at a peace conference in Geneva that summer.

That decision led Kennedy to look more carefully at Vietnam. Because he had not committed troops to Cuba or Laos, the pressure to take a firm stand elsewhere was mounting. And because negotiations in Laos were uncertain, the administration needed a fallback in Southeast Asia. Administration officials agreed that Vietnam was strategically a more auspicious place to make a stand. Russell, of course, dissented. In November, the senator advised Kennedy not to commit troops to Vietnam or Laos. American forces would be spread too thin. But if the United States must be there, Russell suggested the use of Special Forces who could infiltrate enemy cells as they had in Greece in the late 1940s.[11]

Russell's thinking on the situation in Laos came down to a familiar formula: the United States should not, indeed could not, fight to defend a people against Communism who were unwilling to fight for themselves. Russell told Kennedy as much on February 21, 1962, when the president and congressional leaders met again in Laos after resumed fighting threatened to disrupt the Geneva talks. Russell would repeat this mantra again and again during the Kennedy and Johnson administrations. When in 1964 President Johnson told Russell over the phone that Vietnam was "wobbly" and that Laos was ready to crumble, Russell summed up his feelings:

> Laos Laos Laos. Hell it ain't worth a damn. They've been talking about all these battles down there and I've tried to get the best information I could from the CIA and from Defense both on all this fierce fighting on the Plain of Jars and all, and the highest estimate on the casualties is a hundred and fifty. That Laotian thing is absolutely impossible. It's a whole lot worse than Vietnam. There are some of these Vietnamese who after they beat them over the head that will go in there and fight, but Laos is an impossible situation. That's just a rat hole there.[12]

Despite a negotiated settlement in Geneva during the summer of 1962, open hostilities in Southeast Asia continued. Russell had helped prevent a full military intervention in Laos but had also inadvertently contributed to the gradual escalation of the conflict in Vietnam. The Southern senator was still, however, a relatively minor player. The two men who had the greatest control over American policy in Southeast Asia at this juncture were not Americans. Ho Chi Minh and Ngo Dinh Diem, as much as anyone, would determine the course of American policy in Southeast Asia.

Russell thought he understood both men and their place in the political dynamic of Vietnam. While the senator recognized Ho Chi Minh as a ruthless Communist, he also argued that Ho was "the ablest of all the Communist leaders" and, more importantly, was "almost worshipped by his people." That popularity came less from his association with Communism than from a charismatic nationalism, according to Russell. Ho, the Georgian suggested, was better known for driving the French out of Indochina than for his particular take on Marxist doctrine. "The people there [South Vietnam] don't have much sense of nationalism to start with," he would tell television and radio audiences in 1965. "And no cause can ever win that hasn't got a champion that the people admire. Whenever the people go to calling their leader 'Uncle' you had better look out, Uncle Ho, Uncle Mao Tse-tung, and all these others all through history. When they have a man in whom they have implicit confidence, [as the North had in Ho] you are dealing with a very dangerous enemy."[13]

Diem, Russell recognized, had no such hold on the South. The thoughtless, ruthless, and oppressive tactics Diem employed in an attempt to consolidate his power had backfired, making him increasingly ineffectual as a leader. But he was Western educated, a Christian, and a committed anti-Communist, and, as Russell argued, he could be controlled. When Diem was assassinated in November 1963, Russell knew that the United States had been in some way complicit. Later, he told President Johnson directly that he did not have "any doubt" that Vietnamese ambassador Henry Cabot Lodge Jr. "had old Diem killed out there." According to Russell, it had been a "bad mistake." Diem, for all his faults, was America's man and was certainly better able to fight the Communist insurgency than some untested, unrecognizable figure who was likely to replace him.[14]

Once Diem had been assassinated and Ho was seemingly at the height of his power, conditions in Vietnam once again changed. Russell realized that the best the United States could hope for was stability and a continued effort by the South Vietnamese to fight the Communists without further American involvement. Then suddenly President Kennedy was felled by a sniper's bullet, and Russell's protégé and closest friend, Lyndon Johnson, became president.

Johnson immediately looked to Russell as an adviser on foreign and defense matters, especially concerning Latin America and Vietnam. The president wanted the senator in on meetings, hammering out policy with the key administrators like Secretary of State Dean Rusk, Secretary of Defense Robert McNamara, and National Security Advisor McGeorge Bundy. Indeed, early on, Russell offered the main counterpoints to those who wanted to escalate in Southeast Asia. The already powerful senator became an insider's insider. Yet, for all his influence, during one of the most crucial periods of the war, the spring and summer of 1964, the White House ultimately rejected Richard Russell's suggestion that the United States withdraw from Vietnam.

The aging Georgian was keenly aware that time was passing him by, a sense that was reinforced by his friend's ascendancy to the presidency. Russell was frequently sick, was battling emphysema derived from a lifetime of cigarette smoking, and was exhausted from the mountain of work that kept him busy every waking hour. His committee duties and leadership of the Southern bloc in the then fierce fight over what would become the Civil Rights Act of 1964 were never more time consuming. Also, Russell had to contend with the president's Great Society legislation. Just as with certain aspects of the New Deal, the Georgian feared that the Great Society would diminish states' rights, increase federal power, and threaten the racial and political status quo in the South. In addition, Johnson had appointed and had then forced the senator to join the Warren Commission investigating the assassination of President Kennedy. Johnson, moreover, badgered Russell for advice at all hours on military and foreign policy issues. Over the winter and spring, as the Panamanian Crisis mounted, the president nearly worked his mentor to death.

But it was not Johnson's demands that really oppressed the senator. It was the overall pace of change that he felt had recklessly jostled the world along since World War II. Russell considered the revolutionary changes in civil rights, social and economic security, and Vietnam to be of a piece. For the Georgian, they were all examples of peoples forced to deal with accelerated change beyond their ability or will to comprehend and adjust. Such changes, he believed, were doomed to bring disorder, destruction, and tyranny.

This historical perception weighed heavily on Russell in the spring and summer of 1964. He had just finished reading historian Bruce Catton's *Terrible Swift Sword*, the second in a three-volume centennial history of the Civil War.[15] Russell certainly recognized the cautionary current running through the book's climatic pages as President Abraham Lincoln pushed for emancipation on the heels of

President Lyndon Johnson meets with Senator Richard Russell in the White House Cabinet Room, December 1963. Photograph by Yoichi R. Okamato, courtesy of the Lyndon B. Johnson Presidential Library.

the Battle of Antietam. According to Catton, Lincoln struggled with the idea of loosing uneducated, poor blacks into a society that would only resent them. The increasingly violent war, Lincoln reasoned, necessitated a greater justification for the struggle. Emancipation would deliver that, but the price, the president was fully aware, was a "remorseless revolutionary struggle." Emancipation could mean massacre and utter destruction, but there seemed no alternative. Catton offered Lincoln's words in conclusion: "We—even we here— hold the power, and bear the responsibility. In giving freedom to the slave, we assure freedom to the free—honorable alike in what we give and what we preserve. We shall nobly save, or meanly lose, the last, best hope of the earth."[16]

Heady stuff for a Southerner who was then struggling with both the landmark 1964 Civil Rights Act and the crises leading to American escalation in Vietnam. What was the proper course for those seeking liberty and a stable democratic world, he wondered. On both civil rights and Vietnam, Russell concluded that caution was the best policy. He understood fully that Jim Crow was on his last legs. Russell could not prevent integration, but as leader of the Southern bloc, he might slow the process and through his opposition allow for a more gradual and peaceful transition. He also understood that the nation was on a path to even greater intervention in Vietnam. He might not be able to prevent it, but his relationship with the president, a Southerner who could identify with his view of history, combined with the Georgian's leverage as head of the Senate Armed Services Committee, might allow him to limit the escalation.

Meanwhile, the situation in Vietnam continued to deteriorate. On January 29, 1964, the military junta that overthrew Diem was itself overthrown by a group of young officers led by General Nguyen Khanh. During the spring, Khanh had little success in quelling the growing Communist insurgency in the South. Defense Secretary Robert McNamara told Johnson and Secretary of State Rusk after returning from a trip to Saigon in March that the situation was bleak. The Vietcong controlled 50 percent or more of the land in twenty-two of the forty-four provinces. There were widespread signs of apathy and indifference among the South Vietnamese, and desertion rates in the army were on the rise. Khanh, in addition, lacked any significant political support and showed no sign of being able to consolidate in those parts of the country that Saigon claimed to control. McNamara suggested a wait-and-see approach, neither reducing nor escalating American participation in the conflict. Johnson agreed. Hold the line at least until the election was over in the fall.

The writing, though, was on the wall. To keep the insurgency from consuming the Khanh government, further U.S. support would likely be necessary. The administration prepared for that eventuality by drafting a congressional resolution authorizing military intervention. Johnson knew that if any of his domestic or foreign policy initiatives were to succeed, he would need Congress on his side. He did not want to repeat Truman's mistake of not securing legislative approval before going into Korea. "By God, I'm going to be damn sure those guys are with me when we begin this thing," McNamara remembered Johnson saying, because "they may try to desert me once we get in there."[17]

Johnson, Rusk, and Ball met with Senate leaders throughout late May, June, and July. Russell and John Stennis (D-MS) represented the Armed Services Committee in the meetings, while Mike Mansfield and J. William Fulbright (D-AR) were there for the Foreign Relations Committee. Minority leader Everett Dirksen (R-IL) also attended. The administration attempted to set the senators on the idea that Vietnam was legitimately within the sphere of U.S. influence and interest, but assured them that the administration was not thinking about widening the war. The proposed resolution authorizing the president to use force was designed merely to demonstrate American unity to Hanoi and deter the Communists from overrunning South Vietnam and Laos. Russell never conceded a point in any of the meetings. To the contrary, he insisted that Southeast Asia had no military, strategic, or economic value to the United States. Direct U.S. involvement could not be justified, "even if it [Vietnam] were to fall into the hands of the Chinese or the Russians."[18]

Throughout the spring of 1964, Russell seized several public and private opportunities to reexpress his long-held opposition to American involvement in Southeast Asia.[19] The most revealing and candid of these declarations came on May 27, 1964, when a somber Lyndon Johnson called Russell for advice. Johnson, in truly atypical fashion, just let Russell talk. "It's the damn worst mess I ever saw," Russell told Johnson as he laid out his general views of the South Vietnamese condition: "It appears that our situation is deteriorating, and it looks like the more we try to do for them, the less they're willing to do for themselves. It's just a sad situation. There's no sense of responsibility there, on the part of any of their leaders apparently. . . . It's a hell of a situation. It's a mess. And it's going to get worse." The military outlook was bleak, Russell added. "The French lost 250 thousand men and spent a couple of billion of their money and two billion of ours down there and just got the hell whipped out of em." On top of that, he argued, the American people were not ready for the United States to send regular troops into Vietnam, especially if it meant a ground war with China. But perhaps most important, Russell emphasized, Vietnam served no strategic interest for the United States except in terms of prestige.[20] The best solution, he urged, was to find a way to get out.

But the way out proved elusive. When President Johnson asked for a solution, Russell suggested that the White House find a South Vietnamese leader who would ask the United States to leave. But even if that were possible, Johnson asked, "wouldn't that pretty well fix us in the eyes of the world . . . and make us look mighty bad?" Russell replied with a laugh, "We don't look too good right now. And of course you'd look pretty good I guess going in there with all the troops and sending them all in there, but I tell you it will be the most expensive venture this country ever went into."[21]

Russell was well known for his political empathy, his ability to place himself in the shoes of those facing a tough situation. He fully understood Johnson's dilemma. American prestige was on the line just as the Republican right was beginning its campaign to challenge Johnson for the presidency that fall. The administration's Great Society programs were also in jeopardy. But, by Russell's reckoning, the American people would not abandon the president. Johnson asked him directly, "Well they'd impeach a president though that [would] run out [of Vietnam] wouldn't they?" Russell answered, "I don't think that they would." Despite public opinion polls suggesting that the United States should do whatever was necessary to prevent Communism from spreading in Vietnam, Russell understood and Johnson admitted that most Americans knew very little about Vietnam and cared even less. The Georgian sensed that if the United States were asked to leave, or if a negotiated settlement could be hammered out, the troops could withdraw without the White House losing face. When pressed by the president, though, Russell could not explain how exactly to bring those conditions about. Over and over throughout the conversation, and most of their conversations on Vietnam, the senator had to admit, "I wish I could help," but "I don't know what to do."[22]

Even without a concrete solution, Russell's arguments had found a sympathetic ear. Johnson, too, found it difficult to justify the sacrifice of American lives for so little gain. "I've got a little old sergeant that works for me over at the house," he said, "and he's got six children, and I just put him up as the United States Army and Air Force and Navy every time I think about making this decision. And I think about sending the father of those six kids in there and what the hell we gonna get out of his doing it. And it just makes the chills run up my back. . . . I haven't got the nerve to do it, and I don't see any other way out of it." Their talk ended with that sad sense of unresolved frustration. "I love you," Johnson told Russell, "and I'll be calling you."[23]

Johnson did not tell McGeorge Bundy, Robert McNamara, or Dean Rusk that he loved them, but it was their advice that Johnson ultimately took over Russell's. Johnson agreed with Russell on several points: escalation in Vietnam might develop into a broader conflict with China, an antiguerrilla campaign would be a strategic nightmare, and the long-term costs of the war might threaten the Great Society even more than right-wing criticism for not fighting it would. Ultimately the president concluded that the greater good would be served by reinforcing the anti-Communist regime in the South. The needs to contain Communism, uphold treaty obligations, protect American prestige, win the election, and preserve the Great Society were certainly part of his calculus, but it was just as important that Johnson ultimately was not as pessimistic about the course of human progress as Russell. That difference, in the end, led Johnson to escalate rather than take Russell's advice to withdraw.

Johnson's motivation for helping those seeking liberty in South Vietnam was the same as his motivation for supporting the Great Society and civil rights for African Americans.[24] If a better world could be made for the poor, the disaffected, and the oppressed, it was the moral obligation of the United States to come to their aid, even if the possibility for failure was great. As one student of the Johnson administration put it, the president, and white middle-class Americans in general, were in the 1960s "undergoing a catharsis in which they were being forced to reconcile their Judeo-Christian principles with the evils of racial discrimination. Given the logic of the Second Reconstruction, that no believing person could deny equal opportunity and political freedom to another human being, how could the new America and its Texas prophet, trading in the angst of Kennedy, a fallen martyr, fail to come to the rescue of the non-white people of Vietnam in their struggle to resist communist totalitarianism?"[25] Johnson, unlike Russell, put his faith in the power and duty of the United States government to promote liberty and democracy at home and abroad. It was that faith in making things better that was necessary for Johnson to commit his paternal sergeant to combat in Southeast Asia.

Ironically, for Johnson and his other adviser from Georgia, Dean Rusk, this conclusion was in part a "Southern" thing. The burden of

Southern history, "the historical suffering of the South and its endemic problems," taught them that intervention in Vietnam was worth the risk.[26] Believers in a new historiography, they understood that the Southern experience in the Civil War and Reconstruction, however terrible, had generated long-term benefits for the region. Emancipation and northern investment had rebuilt the South on a more solid footing. The Southern economy had diversified, and liberal democratic institutions had taken root. Johnson's take on liberal internationalism was derived in part from that conclusion. He was optimistic that people could change, even needed to change, according to a modern, industrial sense of time that valued linear progress. Even after their gloomy conversation on May 27, Johnson found reason to be confident about his "province program" in Vietnam. "We've been doing better in the last few weeks," he said, "because the folks think they have some little something to hope for and live for. We [are] doing a little with a school and a hospital here and there, and they [are] getting a little better. And we haven't done bad."[27]

Russell identified with an older South, one more pessimistic about change, especially change imposed from the outside. He remained convinced that Reconstruction and the Civil War had destroyed the South and forced an alien way of life on a resisting people that had not changed. Russell, unlike the president, believed that human society best evolved slowly, according to a traditional, agricultural sense of time that valued cyclical consistency. Russell believed that this was as true in Vietnam as in Mississippi. "I don't know these Asian people," he would observe, "but they tell me they worship their ancestors, and so I wouldn't play with their land if I were you. You know, whenever the Corps of Engineers has some dam to dedicate in Georgia, I make a point of being out of state, because those people don't like economic improvement as much as they dislike being moved off their land." Neither Old Southerners nor the Vietnamese, Russell suggested, would necessarily "share American enthusiasm for 'progress' and political modernization."[28]

It was ironic, then, that despite his record of advice and his deep-rooted conviction that American efforts to intervene in and reform Vietnam were in vain, Russell became one of the administration's leading allies in support of the Gulf of Tonkin Resolution. During the first half of 1964, pressure on South Vietnam had increased as the North Vietnamese redoubled their support of the insurgency and made roads of the footpaths on the Ho Chi Minh Trail. To protect against possible retaliatory air strikes from the South Vietnamese or their American allies, Hanoi asked Russia to install modern antiaircraft missiles and radar stations around the main cities in North Vietnam and along the coastline of the Tonkin Gulf.

In early June, American reconnaissance planes were shot down over Laos. When Johnson called Russell for advice, the senator agreed to the need to retaliate against the antiaircraft batteries but warned the president that a counterstrike launched from South Vietnam would invite direct retaliation against U.S. facilities, drawing the nation further into the conflict. The senator suggested that the strike come from nearby aircraft carriers instead. Johnson insisted that his military advisers thought it best to send up air force rather than navy aircraft to conduct the mission. Russell conceded, knowing that the president would choose the military command's tactical procedure over his own, but it was an agonizing step. The war was escalating beyond his, the president's, or anyone's control.[29]

As tensions increased over the summer, the administration developed contingency plans for a blockade, a bombardment, and even an invasion of North Vietnam. Intelligence gathered from U-2 flights and other surveillance resources in the Gulf of Tonkin would be needed to complete the plans. The mapping of coastal installations turned out to be a problem. High-altitude photography could not penetrate the jungle canopy, and low-altitude reconnaissance aircraft could be easily shot down. The solution was to send South Vietnamese commandos in to harass coastal installations. North Vietnamese radar transmissions and chatter in response could then be picked up and their locations charted by American electronic surveillance vessels in the Tonkin Gulf. These were the so-called DeSoto missions. They supported the administration's contingency plans while a sister operation carried out by a State Department/CIA task force called "OPLAN-34" harassed the North with covert South Vietnamese operatives.

The U.S. destroyer *Maddox* was participating in DeSoto patrols off the North Vietnamese coast on August 2 when three North Vietnamese patrol boats launched a torpedo attack. The torpedoes missed, and the *Maddox* returned fire with air support from the nearby U.S. aircraft carrier *Ticonderoga*. The Americans sank one of the hostile craft and crippled the other two. With no casualties, President Johnson preferred not to antagonize the situation further; he chose not to retaliate, but he did order an additional destroyer, the *C. Turner Joy*, into the Tonkin Gulf and gave orders to American vessels to attack if attacked.

That night, President Johnson had Russell to Sunday dinner. They no doubt discussed the incident, but Russell, along with other members of the Senate Armed Services and Foreign Relations Committees, received a formal briefing the next morning from secretaries McNamara and Rusk. Senator Wayne Morse (D-OR) came away convinced that the administration was determined to go to war with the North. J. William Fulbright later said that the meeting helped convince him that Johnson had learned from the August 2 attack that he might use another such incident to bring the United States more directly into the war. Russell, though, took from the meeting that the president did not want full U.S. participation in the war. The Georgian understood that the presence and participation of American forces there would lead to more attacks and would naturally escalate the conflict. He, unlike the others, still trusted Johnson to limit that escalation.

Two days later, the country took another step toward increased participation in the conflict. On August 4, a stormy night in the Gulf of Tonkin, the *Maddox* intercepted reports seeming to indicate that patrol boats were preparing for another assault. When sonar equipment picked up multiple blips, the American destroyers started firing in all directions and taking evasive action to avoid North Vietnamese torpedoes. Officers reported the sinking of two or three Communist craft. Johnson monitored all of this from the Situation Room in the White House. Although the information was sketchy, the president decided to recall the congressional leadership to the White House that morning. He advised the leaders, including Russell, that a second unprovoked, deliberate attack on the *Maddox* and *C. Turner Joy* had occurred. He said that the United States had no choice but to retaliate, and he intended to ask Congress for a resolution in support of his action. Majority Leader Mike Mansfield and others opposed such a step, but Russell, still trusting his friend, argued that limited retaliation was in principle the right thing to do. He only questioned whether the United States had enough manpower and equipment in the area to do the job. Fulbright, at the time, agreed, suggesting that no response from the United States might even provoke further attacks. The Republicans sided with the Southerners and the administration. It was no time to tuck tail and run.

In part, the administration used the meeting to gauge the political consequences of retaliation. Russell and Fulbright helped make it clear that the president risked losing Southerners and strengthening the Republicans and their presidential candidate Senator Barry Goldwater (R-AZ) if he did not respond. It also helped make any reaction short of a counterstrike less feasible, even as the captain of the *Maddox* began expressing second thoughts about the attack. Freak weather and jumpy sonar operators may have created an imaginary incident. But when naval intelligence confirmed that the North Vietnamese had ordered patrol boats into action, there was no turning back. Johnson called Russell again that afternoon, presumably to confirm his course of action. No record of that conversation exists. If Russell expressed any reservations or altered his prior support, Johnson was not convinced to change directions. As National Security Advisor McGeorge Bundy suggested, the decision had been made before Johnson talked to Russell. Johnson, Bundy recalled, had "made a political decision, confirmed it with Senator Russell, and the last thing he wanted to do was reexamine that."[30] Late that afternoon, the president authorized retaliatory air strikes against North Vietnamese torpedo boat bases and nearby oil dumps. The strikes damaged twenty-five patrol boats and 90 percent of the oil storage facilities.

The next day, the administration resumed work on a congressional resolution endorsing Johnson's actions. While the president did not deem the resolution legally necessary, he observed that it was "a lot better to have it in the light of what we did in Korea."[31] Johnson reported to a national television audience that the "unprovoked attack" against U.S. forces had taken place, and the nation's military had responded appropriately. Immediately afterward, he invited Senator Fulbright back to the White House to manage the congressional resolution on the hill. There is no evidence that Fulbright had any knowledge of the DeSoto patrols or of the reports from *Maddox* captain John Herrick suggesting that the attacks had not occurred, and, perhaps more importantly, he, like Russell, did not think he was being asked to support a resolution that would be used to widen the war. Russell likely knew more. Given his relationship with the president, the Defense Department, and the CIA, he in all likelihood knew of the DeSoto missions and OPLAN-34, yet he continued to support the resolution. His trust would endure longer than Fulbright's.

On August 6, Undersecretary of State George Ball met with Majority Leader Mansfield, Fulbright, Russell, Republican senators Leverett Saltonstall (R-MA) and George Aiken (R-VT), and Senate committee staffers. The group determined that Fulbright would introduce the resolution as soon as possible, with Russell, Saltonstall, and Senator Bourke Hickenlooper (R-IA) cosponsoring. The Foreign Relations and Armed Services committees would hold perfunctory hearings, and passage should come easily that afternoon. Defense Secretary McNamara appeared before joint hearings the same day. Pat Holt, the head staff person for the Senate Foreign Relations Committee, recalled that McNamara arrived early and talked informally with several senators, including Fulbright and Russell. The secretary told them that if the question came up as to why U.S. ships were operating in the Gulf of Tonkin and Senator Wayne Morse (D-OR) was in the room, he would not answer. Whatever their prior knowledge of the operations in the Gulf, they must have deduced by this point that the attacks were not completely unprovoked.[32] In the meeting, McNamara stuck to the administration line that the attacks were deliberate and unanticipated. When Morse, who had information leaked to him about the DeSoto operations, confronted the secretary with the idea that the American patrols in the Gulf were not routine, McNamara denied it.

The same afternoon, the joint committee introduced the Gulf of Tonkin Resolution to the full Congress for debate. It authorized the president to take "all necessary measures to repel any armed attacks against the forces of the United States and to prevent further aggression."[33] When confronted by senators opposed to the grant of authority to the president, Russell joined Fulbright in arguing that the president's response was justified, and unity and resolve against the attackers was necessary. Russell admitted that the American presence was annoying to the North Vietnamese, but it did not justify the attack. The U.S. ships were in international waters. The resolution, furthermore, was no different from the Formosa, Middle East, and Cuban resolutions that Congress had passed in recent years. Specifically in Formosa, he argued, the resolution had "prevented much more serious and much broader military action." He assured his colleagues that the Gulf of Tonkin Resolution would "achieve the same purpose and avoid any broadening of war, or any escalation of danger." He reminded the senators that he had opposed the original decision to go into Vietnam, but now at stake was "our national honor." "We cannot and we will not shrink from defending it," he said. "No sovereign nation would be entitled to the respect of other nations, or, indeed, could maintain its self respect, if it accepted the acts that have been committed against us without undertaking some sort of response. . . . I firmly believe there is much more danger in ignoring aggressive acts than there is in pursuing a course of calculated retaliation that shows we are prepared to defend our rights."[34]

For Russell, the Gulf of Tonkin Resolution was clearly about preventing a wider war, not escalating it. He trusted that the president would do what he could to keep American involvement to a minimum. But Russell also fully understood that this was a turning point in the conflict. Americans would increasingly be put in harm's way, drawing further need for retaliation. Russell, like Johnson, saw no immediate way out. He told the president in a solemn conversation on the evening of August 7 that further strikes in North Vietnam might be necessary as the American force grew larger in the Gulf. Clearly saddened, he added, "I just don't know anything else to do. They put our hands to the plow now."[35]

Russell's trust that the administration would remain committed to only limited, retaliatory strikes only went so far. He was willing to give his friend in the White House the benefit of the doubt, but he also knew that there would be mounting pressure on him to intensify the war effort. Before sending the Gulf of Tonkin Resolution to the full Senate for consideration, Russell attached an amendment that empowered Congress, at any time and for any reason, to terminate the extraordinary presidential powers and, through a concurrent resolution that would be veto proof, to annul the Gulf of Tonkin Resolution. The amendment, Russell hoped, for his own benefit and for the president's, would, if the situation in Vietnam accelerated out of control, force the administration to ask for further congressional consent before undertaking a full-scale military operation.

Debate on the Gulf of Tonkin Resolution lasted fewer than ten hours. The final vote in the Senate was 88 to 2. Only Democrats Wayne Morse of Oregon and Ernest Gruening of Alaska voted against it. The House took a mere forty minutes to pass the measure on August 7. Russell's support of the resolution was crucial. Johnson ceremonially gave his friend the pen used to sign it into law. Later, critics would suggest that Johnson made Russell an accomplice in an escalation that he wanted no part of, but Russell's support of the resolution was neither naive nor coerced. He saw the mandate given by Congress as limited and took precautions to make it so. For Russell, the resolution was not as Johnson once described it: "grandma's nightshirt." It did not simply cover everything.

Hoping to capitalize on the American use of force against the North, the Khanh government in South Vietnam assumed near-dictatorial powers and moved to suppress internal dissent. An angry mob took to the streets of Saigon, forcing the resignation of the general and ending another untenable government. The administration at first resisted escalation but remained ready to respond to North Vietnamese attacks on a "tit for tat basis." By late November, a new administration consensus envisioned an orchestrated bombing attack against the North, easing the growing pressure on the South. From that point on, it was only a matter of waiting for the right opportunity.

Russell said little publicly about the administration's decision to begin a bombing campaign in the North. As he stated before, he was simply not sure what course would keep the United States from escalating the conflict. He made sure, however, that the administration remained aware of possible long-term consequences. In mid-January 1965, Russell commented on the situation after an Armed Services Committee briefing given by CIA director John McCone. Until "a more stable government" was established, he reminded those present, the situation in Vietnam would continue to compel U.S. involvement. As it stood, the situation was "at best a stalemate that promises to be prolonged endlessly."[36]

Ostensible justifications for a bombing campaign occurred weekly, but it was not until February 6, when the Vietcong attacked a U.S. Army barracks at Pleiku and a nearby helicopter base that killed nine Americans and destroyed five aircraft, that President Johnson retaliated with air strikes against the North Vietnamese just across the 17th parallel. A day later, Johnson met with congressional leaders. He cited the Gulf of Tonkin Resolution and the constitutional powers of the president to justify his actions.

Further strikes and retaliations followed through the spring as the military mounted Operation Rolling Thunder. Publicly, the administration refused to justify its actions, claiming only that the air assaults were measured responses to attacks against American forces, but behind the scenes, plans were being made to significantly escalate the war. In early March, the president committed troops to support the air base at Danang. And in April, he dispatched another forty thousand soldiers to protect other American military installations. General William Westmoreland, the commander of American forces in Vietnam, submitted plans calling for an eventual buildup to three hundred thousand troops.

Russell remained silent through the crucial months of the buildup. In February, he fell ill and convalesced away from Washington until May. Just before he became sick, he urged that the American position in Vietnam be reevaluated, but he could offer no viable solution. There is no indication that the administration would have reversed its course on Russell's advice had he been able to remain in Washington. Increasingly, the president and his advisers were writing Russell off as a racist isolationist.[37] The president's March 6 telephone call to Russell at the hospital where he was recuperating revealed as much. When Johnson asked what the senator thought of his decision to send in troops to protect Danang, Russell meekly replied, "Well I don't know. We've gone so damn far it scares the life out of me but I don't know how to back up now. It looked to me like we just got no way out and we just get pushed forward and forward and forward."

In this conversation, the president explained that the navy planned to lower its entry standards to accommodate poorer, uneducated people. Both men knew that for Russell that meant blacks. Johnson said, "It seems to me that you're paying a mighty big price on an Anglo Saxon white man to make his boy go and fight in Vietnam but none of the others can because they don't have the exact I.Q. that the missile operator . . ." Russell was irritated. The dilemma he had faced in World War II had returned. Defense needs were again securing the cause of integration, but as an Armed Services Chairman committed to a strong defense and universal military training, he could not easily withhold support for overall troop increases. Even more irritating was the fact that the lowering of standards was designed to build a military force for a war he opposed. Russell could only reply, "You've got the authority to change it . . . [though] I held up the whole thing for years." Johnson said, "Well I think we can make them [poor blacks] where they're smarter and improve them."[38]

However ill at ease Russell felt about the president's support of racial integration and troop deployment in Vietnam, he empathized with the larger problems facing the administration. Withdrawal meant losing Vietnam to Communism, political suicide for the Democrats at home, and a loss of faith in containment abroad. Escalation meant losing American lives, draining the nation's resources, and enduring international condemnation. Johnson and Russell shared this frustration in their March telephone conversation. "Dick the trouble is a man can fight if he can see daylight down the road somewhere, but there ain't no daylight in Vietnam." "That's right," Russell replied; "there's just no end to the road. . . . We gonna wind up with the people mad as hell with us that we're saving by being in there. It's just awful. The Australians, everybody else, is going to be madder than hell. It's the biggest mess I ever saw in my life. You couldn't have inherited a worse mess." Johnson glimpsed the future: "If they say I inherited it, I'd be lucky, but they'll all say I created it. You get well."[39]

Notes

1. Kent Germany, "'I'm Not Lying about That One': Manhood, LBJ, and the Politics of Speaking Southern," *Miller Center Report* 18 (summer 2002).

2. *Congressional Record*, 89th Cong., 1st sess., 1965, 111, pt. 14:19673–76.

3. David Halberstam, *The Best and the Brightest* (New York: Penguin Books, 1983), 641.

4. Johnson Tapes, WH6405.10, PNO3–5, 5/27/64, 10:55A, 3519–21, Lyndon Baines Johnson Library; see also *Congressional Record*, 88th Cong., 2nd sess., 1964, 110, pt. 5:6630.

5. Quoted in Caroline Ziemke, "Senator Richard B. Russell and the 'Lost Cause' in Vietnam, 1954–68," *Georgia Historical Quarterly* 72 (Spring 1988): 42.

6. Halberstam, *The Best and the Brightest*, 181; Ziemke, "Senator Richard B. Russell and the 'Lost Cause' in Vietnam," 44; Gilbert Fite, *Richard B. Russell, Jr., Senator from Georgia* (Chapel Hill: University of North Carolina Press, 1991), 359.

7. Quoted in William Conrad Gibbons, *The U.S. Government and the Vietnam War: Executive and Legislative Roles and Relationships, Part II: 1961–1964* (Princeton, NJ: Princeton University Press, 1986), 34.

8. Quoted in James Giglio, *The Presidency of John F. Kennedy* (Lawrence: University of Kansas Press, 1991), 65.

9. Quoted in George Herring, *America's Longest War: The United States and Vietnam, 1950–1975* (New York: Knopf, 1979), 77.

10. Quoted in Ziemke, "Senator Richard B. Russell and the 'Lost Cause' in Vietnam," 45.

11. Kennedy-Russell Conversation, November 9, 1961, series 16, Russell Papers, Russell Memorial Library.

12. Johnson Tapes, WH6405.10, PNO3–5, 5/27/64, 10:55A, 3519–21, Lyndon Baines Johnson Library.

13. *Congressional Record*, 89th Cong., 1st sess., 1965, 111, pt. 14:19673–76; Russell to Lyon, November 22, 1965, box 40, and Russell to Jordan, May 8, 1967, box 35, series 16, Russell Papers, Richard Russell Memorial Library.

14. Johnson Tapes, WH6405.10, PNO3–5, 5/27/64, 1055A, 3519–21, Lyndon Baines Johnson Library.

15. "Senator Russell of Georgia: Does He Speak for the Whole South?" *Newsweek* 62 (August 14, 1963). Also found in *Congressional Record*, 88th Cong., 1st sess., 1963, 109, pt. 11:14864–66.

16. Bruce Catton, *Terrible Swift Sword* (Garden City, NY: Doubleday, 1963), 480.

17. Quoted in Randall Woods, *Fulbright: A Biography* (New York: Cambridge University Press, 1995), 347.

18. *Richard Russell, Georgia Giant*, Documentary Script Number 3, 1970, box 1, Russell Personal Papers, Lyndon Baines Johnson Library.

19. Fite, *Russell*, 417, 437.

20. See also *Congressional Record*, 88th Cong., 2nd sess., 1964, 110, pt. 5:6630.

21. Johnson Tapes, WH6405.10, PNO3–5, 5/27/64, 10:55A, 3519–21.

22. Johnson Tapes, WH6405.10, PNO3–5, 5/27/64, 10:55A, 3519–21.

23. Johnson Tapes, WH6405.10, PNO3–5, 5/27/64, 10:55A, 3519–21, Lyndon Baines Johnson Library; Robert Dallek, *Flawed Giant: Lyndon Johnson and His Times, 1961–1973* (New York: Oxford University Press, 1998), 144–45.

24. Randall B. Woods, "Dixie's Dove: J. William Fulbright, the Vietnam War, and the American South," *Vietnam and the American Political Tradition* (New York: Cambridge University Press, 2003), 152–53.

25. Interview with Randall Woods, May 25, 2004.

26. See C. Vann Woodward, *The Burden of Southern History*, rev. ed., (Baton Rouge: Louisiana State University Press, 1968); and Woods, "Dixie's Dove."

27. Johnson Tapes, WH6406.05, PNO17–18, 6/11/64, 1226P, 3680–81, Lyndon Baines Johnson Library.

28. Joseph A. Fry, *Dixie Looks Abroad: The South and U.S. Foreign Relations, 1789–1973* (Baton Rouge: Louisiana State University Press, 2002), 283–84.

29. Johnson Tapes, WH6406.03, PNO9, 6/8/64, 435P, 3639, Lyndon Baines Johnson Library.

30. Dallek, *Flawed Giant*, 155.

31. Dallek, *Flawed Giant*, 153.

32. Gibbons, *The U.S. Government and the Vietnam War, Part II*, 310.

33. Quoted in Herring, *America's Longest War*, 122.

34. *Congressional Record*, 88th Cong., 2nd sess., 1964, 110, pt. 14:18411.

35. Johnson Tapes, WH6408.09, PNO15, 8/7/64, 807P, 4788, Lyndon Baines Johnson Library.

36. *New York Times* (January 12, 1965); Gibbons, *The U.S. Government and the Vietnam War, Part II*, 398.

37. Halberstam, *The Best and the Brightest*, 641. Also in Leslie Gelb and Richard Betts, The Irony of Vietnam: The System Worked (Washington: Brookings Institution, 1979).

38. Johnson Tapes, WH6503.03, PNO1–2, 3/6/65, 1205P, 7026–27, Lyndon Baines Johnson Library.

39. Johnson Tapes, WH6503.03, PNO1–2, 3/6/65, 1205P, 7026–27, Lyndon Baines Johnson Library.

6

Hawk's Lost Cause

The "mess" in South Vietnam continued as Russell returned to work in May 1965. The government that came to power that month headed by Nguyen Cao Ky and Wguyen Van Thieu held no more control over the country than its predecessors. Military officials, meanwhile, anticipated that the Vietcong would launch a summer offensive that could defeat the latest Southern regime. General Westmoreland and the Joint Chiefs pushed for intensified air war and ground support. That dictated an additional 179,000 U.S. troops by the end of July.

The increase helped create a fault line in Congress. "Doves" argued that American interests in Vietnam were nowhere near worth the cost to the United States. Most significantly in the Senate, the leading proponent of this argument was Foreign Relations Committee Chairman J. William Fulbright (D-AR). Fulbright, the driving force behind the Gulf of Tonkin Resolution, increasingly felt that the administration had betrayed its promise not to escalate. America's policy, he now argued, should be "one of determination to end the war at the earliest possible time by a negotiated settlement involving major concessions by both sides." In opposition were congressional "hawks," who argued that the United States must pay whatever price necessary to win the war. Russell, though most often associated with the hawks, was perhaps better placed in what historians Leslie Gelb and Richard Betts awkwardly referred to as the "investment trap-sunk costs rationale" camp. The leaders of this group suggested that the government must support the nation's troops now that they had been committed. They also reasoned that to renege on the U.S. investment in preventing Communism from spreading in Vietnam would undermine the country's credibility and hurt its ability to continue to contain Soviet imperialism. The strategic endgame was still dovish—withdraw from the conflict in Vietnam as soon as possible. But the tactical means to that end were hawkish—fight to force a negotiated settlement with the nation's prestige in tact.[1]

Russell's revised position on Vietnam began to solidify in June as he was brought back into the president's inner circle of advisers. On June 10, Johnson met for two hours with all of the top policy makers on Vietnam, including Maxwell Taylor, Dean Rusk, McGeorge Bundy, and Robert McNamara, to consider General Westmoreland's most recent request for troops. The meeting was deliberately tailored to answer Russell's concerns. President Johnson worried that Russell, like Fulbright, might pose problems as a critic of the troop increases. For the senator's benefit, the president asked his advisers to state their respective positions. McNamara and Rusk agreed with the decision to raise the total number of U.S. troops to one hundred thousand. The president then turned to General Taylor: "Why must we do it [send more troops]?" Taylor replied, "If we don't, we may lose some territory." "Don't you think it will be read as land war in Asia?" the president asked. Taylor answered, "We have to explain this is not a Korean war." CIA officials in the meeting agreed that a buildup was necessary, and the faster the better. Several officials then confirmed the president's legal authority to increase the troop strength as commander in chief and under the Gulf of Tonkin Resolution.

All were shots across Russell's bow, but the senator waited until the discussion turned to the endgame. The administration was clearly divided. Some suggested that the goal of the war was to defeat the Vietcong by exerting pressure on the North and stabilizing the South. Others argued that the goal was self-determination, and still others argued that democratic government was inadequate and unattainable under the present circumstances. The leading critic of escalation within the administration, Undersecretary of State George Ball, argued that the real intent was just to hold on through the monsoon season, which would end around the first of October. Russell entered the conversation near its conclusion and only briefly. "Driblets," Russell said, "were not the answer." He had searched for a way out, but he did not see a path that would allow the United States to keep its promise to stop the spread of Communism. If the United States was bound to the fight, though the cause might be lost, it must wage war as aggressively and honorably as it could.[2]

Three days later, Richard Russell accepted the Georgian of the Year Award from the state Association of Broadcasters. In what was otherwise to be a light talk on broadcast journalism, Russell felt compelled "to strike a somber note." He directly addressed the administration's divided strategic objectives and tactical gradualism:

> I can see why many Americans have difficulty understanding how our national interest is being served by the growing commitment of U.S. money, munitions, and men in Vietnam. . . . I have never been able to see any strategic, political, or economic advantage to be gained by our involvement. Most of the military leaders whose knowledge and advice I most respect have warned repeatedly that it would be an incredible mistake for the U.S. to engage in a full-scale land war on the Asian mainland.

However, when it came down to American boys then fighting in Southeast Asia, Russell expressed his undying support. "They are fighting—and some of them are dying—in a mean and dirty war," he said. "Whether or not the initial decision was a mistake is now moot. The United States does have a commitment in South Vietnam. The flag is there. U.S. honor and prestige are there. And U.S. soldiers are there."[3]

Unable to offer a clear solution himself, but also unwilling to let the administration off the hook for its ill-conceived strategy and gradualist tactics, Russell resorted to the only solution he could muster: support the troops. As he told the United Daughters of the Confederacy thirty-five years before, it was in the soldiers of the lost cause that the true "heritage of honor, chivalry, and devotion to ideals" could be found. "Poor is that country which has no heroes," he recalled the cliché, "but beggard that country which having them forgets." Russell had not forgotten. In confronting inevitable failure in Vietnam, he still hoped to preserve the nation's honor with a vigorous commitment to the cause.[4]

Robert McNamara's trip to Saigon in early July convinced the defense secretary that a more vigorous commitment was needed as well. McNamara suggested, and President Johnson approved, fifty thousand additional soldiers and increased bombing. Johnson also privately committed to another fifty thousand by the end of the year. Johnson would neither ask Congress nor the American people for their consent. These decisions were, as historian George Herring put it, "the closest thing to a formal decision for war in Vietnam." Johnson, though, accepted them as a compromise between withdrawal and total war. In the president's words, they would accomplish "what will be enough, but not too much."[5] The question of what was enough but not too much, he failed to realize, was an inherently public matter.

Requests for more troops meant deficit spending and supplemental funding bills. They also meant gaining legislative authority to call up reserves and extend tours of duty. Among those most opposed to reserve call-ups and tour extensions was Armed Services Committee member and Russell protégé, John Stennis of Mississippi. The president sent Deputy Secretary of Defense Cyrus Vance to talk to Russell about Stennis. Russell agreed to try to get Stennis to support a one-year call-up of reserves and National Guard forces, but, he added, an extension of the draft would better suit the nation's needs. Russell was now complicit in the troop increase.

The Georgian had not completely abandoned alternatives to the escalation of ground forces. Around the same time, he began suggesting that an all-out bombing campaign against the North was a reasonable substitute for increased troop deployments and a possible way to quickly end the war. He also had not lost sight of the preferred endgame: rapid withdrawal. In July, Russell met in Mike Mansfield's (D-MT) office with a group of doves and hawks including John Sparkman (D-AL), George Aiken (R-VT), John Sherman Cooper (R-KY), and J. William Fulbright (D-AR). They agreed that despite their differences, "insofar as Viet Nam is concerned we are deeply enmeshed in a place where we ought not to be; that the situation is rapidly going out of control; and that every effort should be made to extricate ourselves." Russell and the other senators penned a letter embodying their shared views and sent it to Johnson. The American people, the senators reminded him, were backing him because he was the commander in chief, not because they sympathized with his policies. The morning after, Johnson called the dissidents to the White House. He again outlined the deteriorating military and political situation in Vietnam and said there was no turning back even though the war might last six or seven years. The troop increases would go forward.[6]

At noon on July 28, President Johnson finally announced publicly his decision to escalate. He said that he would raise the total number of U.S. troops in Vietnam from 75,000 to 125,000. He added that additional forces would be needed later and would be sent as requested. For the time being, he would not call up the reserves but would increase the draft from 17,000 to 35,000 a month. The president insisted, incredibly, that these moves did not constitute a change in policy.

Russell responded to the president's announcement on August 1 when he agreed to appear on CBS's television program *Face the Nation*. He played the good soldier and said the administration's announced decision was "about right for the conditions as we find them today," and the troop numbers the president mentioned were "about as many as we can send and support over there at this time." The draft, he added, rather than a reserve call-up would better distribute "the responsibility for defending this country around as widely as possible." But Russell could not avoid the strategic problem that still loomed large. Among the nation's many mistakes in Vietnam, the greatest "was overemphasizing the military and not putting sufficient emphasis on the civilian side." The truth was that the South Vietnamese "would vote in a plebiscite to place themselves under Ho Chi Minh rather than any one of those that are in control now." Nevertheless, it was necessary "to show the world that when the United States pledges its honor and its word in any written document, even if we are mistaken in signing it, that we will do it." Both the United States and the South Vietnamese must recommit to the cause.[7]

From that summer on, Russell increasingly focused on the tactical concerns of providing troops with the support and material they needed rather than grand strategy. As he did, the hawk in Russell emerged full blown. Just a month after his appearance on *Face the Nation*, and under some rather harsh criticism for his suggestion that Ho Chi Minh could win a fair election in Vietnam, *U.S. News & World Report* published an interview with Russell that brought his tactical vision into sharper relief. The senator now justified in detail the massive buildup of ground troops. He argued that ferreting out the Vietcong was difficult given the tunnels that stretched five to six miles between villages. The United States did not need ten-to-one superiority, but it did need an estimated 250,000 to 300,000 men. The administration, he added, should also invest a great deal more in the air war than it had previously. Bombers should take out the surface-to-air missile sites near Hanoi and "render ineffective the shipping facilities of Haiphong harbor." Reversing his earlier statements, Russell further argued that this escalation was unlikely to bring the Russians and Chinese into the conflict. The United States needed to display its resolve, including cutting back on Great Society programs in order to fund the war. The proposed $1.7 billion supplemental appropriation was "just earnest money" on the following year's operations. More was needed, especially as the draft expanded. If this was to be a war fought responsibly and honorably, he implied, every citizen must sacrifice. Only when they did would the United States be in a position to force a settlement and bring the troops home.[8]

Russell felt the sacrifice personally in late 1965, when Walter Russell Jr., his nephew and a lieutenant colonel serving in Vietnam, was shot and nearly killed. The incident shook Richard Russell but did not alter his course. In fact, it further spurred his commitment to support the fighting men.

The administration gained a powerful supporter of escalation in Russell. The Georgian remained openly critical of the White House's overall strategy, but he was now complicit in providing them with the funding and authority to fight the war. Russell therefore remained an insider, unlike J. William Fulbright and the doves. When Fulbright began criticizing American actions in the Dominican Republic as well as Vietnam, the president had cut off the Arkansan's access to the White House.[9] "Fulbright's awful mean and awful narrow," Johnson told Russell.[10] The doves had pushed for a good-faith reduction of hostilities to prompt a settlement, a course the president knew he could not take and still remain politically viable. Johnson was convinced that the doves would lead the administration down Truman's path, rendering the Democratic Party continuously vulnerable to the charge that it was "soft on Communism." Russell the hawk filled the administration's needs and protected the president's political flank from right-wing attacks.

The Georgian provided much-needed political cover for the president that fall, ushering through the supplemental defense appropriation, publicly supporting the president's troop increase, and expressing his contempt for antiwar protests that he said would "prolong the war in Vietnam" and "certainly increase the casualty lists of American boys."[11] Johnson rewarded Russell's loyalty by appeasing the doves. On Christmas Eve 1965, American and South Vietnamese bombing of the North Vietnamese Army between the 17th and 20th parallel, which had been going on since May, suddenly stopped. The hawks grumbled, but the president explained to them that the move was a final attempt at diplomacy that would likely fail, setting up a huge two-year military escalation that McNamara estimated would bring American troop numbers in Vietnam past the five hundred thousand mark. Russell took the bombing pause as evidence of Johnson's weakened resolve to stand up to the doves and commit to the fight.

The pause did not change conditions on the diplomatic front. The North remained unwilling to back off its pressure on the South, and the Soviets and Chinese were unable to change Hanoi's mind. The Johnson administration did not help matters by locking out of the negotiations insurgent groups in the South that it considered pawns of the North. Convinced that no settlement would be forthcoming, in late January the administration recommenced the bombing.

Russell was among the hawks, including Minority Leader Everett Dirksen (R-IL) and the Republican leadership, who urged the president to resume and expand the bombing in a late January meeting. "For God's sake, don't start the bombing halfway," Russell said. "Let them know they are in a war. We killed civilians in World War II and nobody opposed. I'd rather kill them than have American boys die. Please, Mr. President, don't get one foot back in it. Go all the way." The leading doves, Fulbright and Mansfield, pushed for a continued lull, since the "best chance of getting to [the] peace table is to minimize our military action." Johnson worried about both sides. Fulbright's course meant sure defeat. Russell's course meant a possible war with China or the Soviets, and maybe even nuclear conflict. The president settled on the middle ground of measured escalation. That course gradually shattered Russell's faith in Johnson.[12]

Russell's thinking was not nearly as radically militaristic as his rhetoric sometimes suggested. He was not for using nuclear weapons or invading the North with ground troops. His call was more about rallying the public to the cause; getting them to accept the real costs of war; showing Hanoi, Beijing, and Moscow America's resolve to fight; and pressuring the president to commit. Johnson, in principle, agreed with this but politically felt like he could not completely abandon the doves.

Russell must have understood. The Georgian was not immune from political pressure from the doves himself. When bombing began again on January 31, 1966, J. William Fulbright appeared on national television declaring the war to be morally wrong and counterproductive to U.S. interests. He added that it had been a mistake to endorse the Gulf of Tonkin Resolution. Wayne Morse (D-OR) and Ernest Gruening (D-AK), the two Democratic senators who had refused to vote for the Gulf of Tonkin Resolution, then moved to invoke the Russell Amendment allowing Congress to rescind the Gulf Resolution. The administration was their target, but Russell suffered the collateral damage. Russell was forced to support his own measure despite his concern that the doves were effectively weakening the military effort in Vietnam by rescinding the Gulf Resolution. Predicting political disaster for the Democrats if the effort succeeded, Mike Mansfield rescued Russell by blocking the measure.

In the weeks that followed, Fulbright's Foreign Relations Committee proceeded with public hearings on Vietnam as Russell's Armed Services Committee reported out a $12 billion supplemental aid bill for the war. A direct showdown had finally come between Fulbright and Russell. In televised hearings, Fulbright's committee elicited testimony from the nation's best-respected critics of the war, including containment policy originator George F. Kennan. The hearings also featured prominent defenders of the administration, culminating with a dramatic confrontation between Fulbright and Secretary of State Dean Rusk.[13] Russell certainly recognized the Senate Foreign Relations Committee's right to consider and criticize American foreign policy, but he lamented that the hearings were so public. The televised proceedings, he feared, would threaten the appropriation that American troops desperately needed to carry on the fight.

In speaking for the supplemental defense appropriation, Russell indirectly addressed Fulbright's hearings. Congress, he declared, "could not properly be considered as determining foreign policy, as ratifying decisions made in the past, or as endorsing new commitments." Playing the strict constitutionalist, he argued that the executive branch alone determined whether American troops would be committed to battle. Congress could only "influence how many members of the Armed Forces the president has to command, and determine the nature of the equipment with which they will be provided, and how they will be cared for and protected." The appropriation should not be used as a poll on congressional approval of foreign policy. To do so might deny vital equipment to the troops who were only in harm's way because they were following the orders of the commander in chief.[14]

As the debate carried on into late February, Russell suspected that Fulbright and the doves were ignoring his pleas and were holding the appropriation up as a show of legislative power. Russell decided to confront Fulbright directly on the Senate floor on February 28: "We have the amazing spectacle of one major committee delaying action or filibustering, or whatever one might call it, on the floor of the Senate so that they can conduct televised hearings on the same subject that another committee has reported legislation on." Fulbright insisted that there was no need for urgency in acting on the supplemental appropriation and criticized Russell for attempting to cut off debate.[15]

The confrontation ended with the weekend recess. During the break, Russell's frustration morphed into a measured, even poetic explanation delivered a few days later. "By instinct and inclination, I must confess that I am an isolationist," he said. "I do not believe that the might and power of the United States can bring about the millennium. I do not believe that any number of treaties, however solemnly drafted, however well-intentioned, will absolutely clear up all the strife among the peoples of the world, of different nationalities, different races, and different creeds. There is nothing in all history to suggest that they will." "But," he went on, "I am in favor of striving for peace, because this is indeed a laudable aim to work for. Nevertheless, as a realist, I am not in favor of contributing American money and American blood in unlimited quantities for a goal that I do not believe is attainable." But the time for discussing "possibilities and theories and contingencies" had passed. "We are confronted with a condition where more than 300,000 of the flower of the young manhood of this nation are 9,000 miles away from home, on foreign soils and waters." The United States was like a man trapped in quicksand: "He has slowly sunk until only his eyes can be seen. Along comes his brother with a rope under his arm. The unfortunate man says, 'Brother, please help me out of the quicksand.' The brother asks, 'How did you get in the quicksand? What did you want to walk over there for? You ought to have had more sense. When are you going to get out of the quicksand?'" Russell said, "I am not going to go through all of that. I am going to throw the rope." Russell's appropriation passed the same day by a vote of 93 to 2, with Fulbright and all of the members of the Foreign Relations Committee on board. Only Gruening and Morse voted against it.[16]

Russell had no illusions about the United States winning the war in Vietnam. The hawks' path was merely a means to force a negotiated settlement and an honorable withdrawal. A May 2, 1966, *U.S. News & World Report* interview with Russell revealed his grasp of the situation. To force the Communist insurgency to stop would require a "great cost of life" and "tremendous expense in dollars," he declared. "We would have to take the whole countryside, and practically make hostages of the South Vietnamese." Even then, the victory would only last so long as the American presence remained. Withdrawal would eventually be the only option.

Russell had never before been able to conceive of a solution that would allow that withdrawal, but in this interview, he finally suggested one. First, "a very careful survey should be made in South Vietnam as to what people in the cities really think," he said. "If that survey shows that the majority of them are anti-American, I think we should withdraw now, because we can't possibly win if we are fighting an enemy in front of us while the people we are supposed to be helping are against us and want us out of their country." The senator knew perfectly well what the outcome of such a survey would be, given popular support for the insurgency. But the South's rejection of the United States, he hoped, would provide Washington an excuse to leave based on a democratic vote. The United States could then hold the line in Thailand and Burma, nations, Russell argued, that had "an entirely different set of ethics and tradition" and promised to be more helpful in keeping Communism from expanding. The United States need not worry about the effect on its allies, Russell maintained.

Korea and the Philippines had both recently been reluctant to send support to the South, and Great Britain continued to trade with North Vietnam. The UN, he added, while a useful forum where men could talk rather than fight, "as a military factor is about as weak a reed as you could find to lean on." Second, adequate pressure could be delivered on the North by the United States without allies and without putting more troops in harm's way. With "absolute command of the seas and the air, we could accomplish a withdrawal without great loss." The idea was to "apply greater force to the regime in North Vietnam . . . the source of all our trouble." That meant closing the harbor at Haiphong and other ports by blockading the coast and "bombing the iron works in Hanoi, the fuel dumps, and any other resource that they have that can be utilized to any degree by them to kill American boys." The United States could also "see that the two railroad lines from China into North Vietnam cannot function on the North Vietnamese side of the border." These things should be done so "that those people like civilized beings, would come to a conference table and settle this thing"; otherwise it might take "eight or 10 years" to pacify the South.[17]

The contradictions that riddled Russell's plan revealed his increasing desperation. Why would Hanoi agree to a negotiated settlement when Russell admitted that the American cause was likely lost? Why also would the United States risk bringing the Chinese and Soviets into the war if Communism would take over in Vietnam anyway? Russell knew that his bombing strategy was inherently flawed. In 1964, he had even warned the president that bombing North Vietnam would be as expensive and ineffective as it had been in Korea. In Korea, U.S. B-29s "knocked out the roads at night," he told Johnson, "and in the morning the damn people'd be driving over it. . . . We never could actually interdict all their lines of communications in Korea even though we had absolute control of the seas and the air. . . . And you ain't going to stop these people [the North Vietnamese] either."[18] Russell nevertheless committed to the bombing campaign as a show of American resolve, unity, and honor.

However flawed, Russell's plan did have the political advantage of escalating the fight while decreasing the number of American soldiers put in harm's way. It risked confrontation with the Soviets and Chinese, but it offered a decisive step in changing the conflict in a way that might bring about a conclusion. It also gave the terminal patient a way to fight for life en route to a dignified death. Convinced of this course, Russell repeatedly called for the bombing of Haiphong and for increased air pressure on the North over the next two years.[19]

Refusing to heed these calls, President Johnson continued down a path between the hawks and the doves, a path that the senator believed only risked more lives, sunk the nation further into the quagmire, and promised a certain, dishonorable withdrawal. The president resisted the aggressive air campaign that Russell and others, including the Joint Chiefs, argued would resuscitate South Vietnam, but the good doctor kept the country on life support by gradually increasing air strikes against strategic targets in the North. The damage from the strikes was ultimately great. They destroyed most major targets by the end of 1967, but they still did not have the desired effect on the war. Gradualism did not work. Russell and the hawks would never find out whether a more rapid increase in the air war would have changed the diplomatic calculus for Hanoi.[20]

In the fall of 1966, Johnson worked diligently to try to convince his friend, and himself, that victory was still possible under his plan. Having just returned from a trip to Vietnam, the president reported to Russell that the power base in the South was strong and showing progress. He also reported a pervasive sense of gratitude toward the United States for its military support and its help in building democratic institutions. Southeast Asia, he argued, was moving to shoulder the burden of democracy.[21]

Russell remained pessimistic. He had already written off South Vietnam and was convinced that the administration's vacillation in carrying the war to the North was a mistake. Another cease-fire over the Christmas holiday only intensified his frustration. Russell suspected that in his choice of priorities, the president was playing politics with American lives. The president had denied the fighting men in Vietnam the nation's full financial support by continuing to spend money on the Great Society and by focusing on a ground strategy rather than an air strategy. Russell hoped to pressure the White House with this criticism indirectly through John Stennis's Armed Services Preparedness Investigating Subcommittee's scrutiny of the administration's failed air war.[22]

Johnson continued to tolerate Russell's sniping, mainly because of the consistent help he provided the administration in financing the war effort. The Senate point man on Defense Appropriations, Russell guided through another $12.2 billion supplemental bill in February 1967. It was a heavy cost for the nation to bear, according to the senator, but not "so dear as the loss of life" to American soldiers that would result if funding were withheld. The money, he argued, should be used to continue bombing the North, but of course that ultimately was the president's decision. A month later, Russell also guided a $21 billion defense authorization bill through the Senate, taking the total 1968 defense appropriation to $75 billion. Defense amounted to more than half of the total $144 billion budget for fiscal year 1968.[23]

Russell, somewhat ironically, also continued to be the administration's strongest ally in support of the draft and executive control of troop deployments. While he pushed for a reduction of the ground war in favor of an increased air campaign, his longtime support for maintaining adequate manpower in confronting Communists worldwide continued. Russell explained as he ushered through basic revisions to the nation's draft laws in May and June 1967 that the responsibility for the war should encompass a broad and equitable selection of men. Too few, he had long believed, had born the burden of defending democracy for the many. He thus limited deferments and held off those pushing for an all-volunteer army. Russell also blocked attempts to provide congressional limits on the president's authority to use troops. When Fulbright attempted to amend the defense appropriation by requiring a declaration of war before any additional troops could be sent to Vietnam, Russell declared the amendment inappropriate. While he agreed that the growing power of the executive was a concern, the president needed the full right to commit American troops where he saw fit.[24]

(Clockwise from top) General William Westmoreland, Senator Richard Russell, Secretary of State Dean Rusk, and President Lyndon Johnson in the White House Cabinet Room, October 1968. Photograph by Yoichi R. Okamato, courtesy of the Lyndon B. Johnson Presidential Library.

Russell was even willing to relent on racial considerations if it meant maintaining overall troop strength. While he held out for the priority of local draft board decisions, he acknowledged the need to eliminate discrimination based on sex, religion, and race in the military. Most importantly, he acquiesced to Project 100,000, a Department of Defense project to recruit volunteers who could not meet the standard mental or physical requirements. The program offered recruits remedial education and health programs to get them up to standard. The administration geared the project toward blacks who had been denied opportunities in other walks of life. Russell doubted the usefulness of the program but agreed that it should be tried. Times had certainly changed. Russell defended the administration against charges by, among others, Robert Kennedy that local draft boards discriminated against blacks and that blacks were enduring an unfair burden of combat and combat casualties. Russell even cited the testimony of Burke Marshall, who was then working with the civil rights section of the Justice Department. Marshall declared that black reenlistment rates were higher due to a lack of opportunity outside the military. It was a significant step for the man who had considered black soldiers in World War II to be worthless. Russell even went so far as to admit that blacks had fought well in Vietnam and deserved better opportunities inside the military and outside. The arch-segregationist had actually become complicit in support of a program designed to offer opportunities to blacks. None of this meant that Russell had changed his racial views. He still considered blacks inferior. But he also strongly believed in individual opportunity and that inherent traits could be overcome with time. As Russell told his colleagues of the changes in racial norms, "People have been trying to adapt themselves and comply with the new order and conform, whether they believe in it or not."[25]

It was becoming increasingly difficult for Russell to conform to the new order in American foreign relations. Victory in Vietnam remained elusive in 1967. The administration's middle way had brought neither a quick victory nor movement in negotiations. The problem, as Russell saw it, boiled down to a crisis of will. Liberal internationalist moralizing and the administration's myopic concern for social progress had compromised its resolution in conducting the war. Russell looked to the American commitment in World War II as a guide. Japanese and German civilian deaths in that war had been considered an acceptable price of victory, yet large numbers of civilian deaths that would result from the bombing of North Vietnam now seemed unthinkable. The fire bombing of Tokyo resulted in "an inferno of fire and terror," he said, that killed 100,000. Allied bombing left some 250,000 dead in Germany. That Japan and Germany represented tyrannies of the right rather than the tyranny of the left in North Vietnam seemed the only difference. The wringing of hands by doves in Congress and gradualists in the administration, he charged, was politically rather than morally motivated. War could not be "governed by the same kind of rules that apply to an athletic contest." The United States needed to bomb the North because the North threatened American soldiers. Bombing the North saved American lives. It was immoral, according to Russell, for the United States to stop the aerial assault.[26] The Georgian directly repeated this plea to President Johnson on May 12, 1967. He did not want a ground war with the Chinese or a nuclear conflict with the Soviets, but the time had come to take a chance or give up. "We've just got to finish it soon," Russell said, "because time is working against you both here and there." Johnson refused; he concluded that the risk of a broader confrontation was too great.[27]

Just as Russell was arguing for a decisive commitment, further cracks had begun to appear in the public's support for the war. Antiwar rallies had increased markedly during 1966 and 1967, including a protest at the Pentagon in October 1967 that drew fifty thousand people. Americans became acutely aware of the costs in tax money and lives. Taxes went up over the summer, the draft reached thirty thousand men per month, and the death toll of American soldiers in Vietnam reached thirteen thousand. For the first time, polls indicated that a majority of Americans thought that the nation's original involvement in the war had been a mistake. Approval ratings for the administration's handling of the war reached a new low of 28 percent.

And then there was the credibility gap. While General Westmoreland and the Joint Chiefs continued to insist that the war was progressing satisfactorily and that victory was in sight, civilian advisers were changing their minds. Bill Moyers and George Ball, for example, became highly critical of the war effort within the administration's inner circle but felt helpless to change things. Others simply jumped ship. Robert McNamara began questioning the war effort in 1966 as Vietnam drew more and more resources from the global security effort. By the spring of 1967, he admitted that escalation had not produced the results he had wanted or anticipated. Suddenly, he began advocating bombing restrictions and caps on ground forces. President Johnson was confused and embittered by his secretary's reversal, and their relationship soured. When the top job opened at the World Bank in November, McNamara jumped at the opportunity.

The secretary of defense's resignation clearly showed that something was amiss in the nation's war plans.[28]

Russell's relationship with McNamara had been complicated. Russell would call McNamara one of the most "remarkable" men he had ever met and one of the "greatest cabinet members of history."[29] But he also had his suspicions about the defense secretary, especially when it had come to Vietnam. In 1964, the senator had told President Johnson that McNamara might not be "as objective as he ought to be in surveying the conditions out there [in Vietnam]. He feels like he, it's all up to him presently to see that the thing goes through, and he's a can do fella, but I'm not too sure he understands the history and background of those people out there as fully as he should." McNamara was smart, Russell said, but "he is opinionated as hell." In the months before escalation, Russell felt that the secretary had made up his mind too hastily on committing more troops to the conflict in Vietnam.[30] Russell's suspicions about McNamara's limitations and priorities increased in 1967 when the secretary restricted the air campaign. In response, the senator cosponsored the Mansfield Troop Reduction Bill. The bill would have reduced U.S. troop commitments to Europe by 13 percent and would have denied further increases in military manpower until the United States either pursued a winning strategy in Vietnam or withdrew. Russell also helped block Defense Department requests for fast deployment logistics (FDL) ships that would speed American forces to crisis areas. "If it is easy for us to go anywhere and do anything," Russell declared, "we will always be going somewhere and doing something." McNamara all but burned the bridge to the Georgian when he attempted to tie the FDL request to airlift capabilities requiring the Lockheed C-5A Galaxies. Lockheed was a major Georgia corporation that had a very close relationship with Russell. The senator managed to salvage some of the airlift appropriation while blocking the ship purchase. Russell's distrust of McNamara reached a new high, and the secretary's departure from office no doubt had something to do with his frustration at having to operate without the cooperation of the Armed Services Committee chairman.[31]

As the administration moved to shore up public support for the war in the wake of McNamara's resignation, the Tet Offensive in January 1968 proved to Americans that despite administration promises to the contrary, the war was nowhere close to an end. That month, Richard Russell began his thirty-fifth year in the Senate to much fanfare and praise. As it had during the crucial early days of 1965, his health would again keep him from service in the crucial early days of 1968. But, prepared as always, he did play a role.

Russell knew better than perhaps anyone in the country that the war in Vietnam was nowhere close to a conclusion. Just days before Tet, on January 26, 1968, he wrote to a constituent that he did not find recent North Vietnamese offers to negotiate in exchange for the cessation of American bombing to be sincere. He noted, "We have stopped bombing on several occasions, once for thirty-seven days, and rather than negotiating, the North Vietnamese used the time to replenish their supplies and regroup their forces for renewed assaults on our forces. This cost us hundreds of American lives and untold dollars in equipment destroyed. I am very frankly not willing to risk additional lives by stopping bombing again until the North Vietnamese have indicated a willingness to sit down at the conference table without first placing enumerable [*sic*] conditions on their appearance."[32] Russell correctly sensed what was in truth a North Vietnamese ploy. The Democratic Republic of Vietnam and the National Liberation Front were hoping to use the negotiation offer to drive a wedge between the United States and the Thieu government in the South and undermine Saigon by establishing a "popular front" of neutralists. The diplomatic ruse was coupled with attacks on U.S. armed forces outside of Saigon, just across the Laotian border, in the Central Highlands, and in particular at Khe Sanh, just South of the demilitarized zone. The overall plan was to prepare the way for Tet. The military engagement would draw Americans away from the cities so that the Tet Offensive could strike urban areas, the heart of Thieu's support. Meanwhile, the diplomatic effort would offer temporary relief from the bombing and/or destabilize the government in Saigon to the point that it would crumble under the weight of the military offensive in the cities. On the same day that Russell sent his prescient letter, he was again admitted to Walter Reed Hospital.

Four days later, on January 30, 1968, as the South Vietnamese relaxed for the Tet holiday, the lunar New Year during which both sides had throughout the war observed a cease-fire, the North Vietnamese army and the Vietcong launched a huge offensive. They struck in thirty-six of the forty-four provincial capitals and in five of the six major urban hubs. The North Vietnamese and Vietcong even took control of the ancient Citadel at Hue, a strong point the American and South Vietnamese forces fought three weeks to regain. But generally the Americans and South Vietnamese regrouped quickly and delivered what amounted to a significant military victory. All attacks were eventually repelled, and Communist forces took heavy losses; nevertheless, the military victory turned out to be a psychological defeat. Clearly the administration's promises that the war would be quickly won were wrong.

Russell did not go back to work until the middle of February. During his convalescence and even after he returned, he had strikingly little to say about Tet. In part, his illness had kept him absent at the height of the fracas, but more importantly, Tet had changed nothing for Russell. He remained convinced that the United States must continue to display its resolve and intensify the bombing of the North. Months later, even after talks between the belligerents had begun in Paris in June 1968, he informed an airman that the United States should continue the bombing pressure on the North to force acceptable negotiating terms. "Nothing," he wrote, "has happened recently to cause me to change my mind, and I must add that the recent Saigon offensive gives us very little reason for hope about the intentions of the North Vietnamese."[33]

The administration's position had again changed. Since McNamara's departure, the White House had been trying to find avenues through which talks with Hanoi could be opened. Neither these efforts nor administration attempts to rally public opinion ceased with Tet. Stressing the U.S. military reward, these attempts had some early effect. Public support for the war effort actually rose in February. But by mid-March, public opinion was again slipping rapidly. The most recognized representative of the media, Walter Cronkite, declared in late February that the situation in Vietnam was deadlocked and that continued fighting would accomplish nothing. President Johnson reportedly responded, "If I've lost Cronkite, I've lost Middle America." Pessimism set in. Polls began indicating that Americans were doubtful that military success would come anytime soon. Presidential approval ratings plummeted as Johnson vowed to hold the line, whatever the cost.

In March, the Joint Chiefs and General Westmoreland requested a call-up of reserves that would provide an additional one hundred thousand troops in Vietnam. That month, the new defense secretary, Clark Clifford, sounded out Congress on the idea. Russell and other top-ranking Democrats on the Armed Services Committee responded that calling up the reserves was a bad idea. For Russell, it would just put more soldiers in harm's way for no real purpose. Clifford advised the president to grant no more than a token increase in troops. Johnson ultimately agreed to only a slight increase in support personnel.

In part, Johnson's decision was based on improving conditions in South Vietnam. Stability had been restored in the cities, and the South

Vietnamese Army gained another 135,000 troops under new draft provisions. Secretary of State Rusk suggested the cessation of bombing north of the 20th parallel in an effort to bring the North to the negotiating table. Russell, consistent with his previous recommendations, vigorously opposed a unilateral cessation. The United States, he told Johnson, needed to secure a guarantee of reciprocity from the North before bombing could be curtailed. When Defense Secretary Clark Clifford, former secretary of state Dean Acheson, and the group of so-called Wise Men backed Rusk's call for a reduction of the bombing, Johnson took their advice over Russell's.

The friendship between the senator and the president had, as always, continued despite their differences, but the pressure on the relationship had grown intense. On March 12, 1968, when Russell was given the Veterans of Foreign Wars Congressional Award for Service, President Johnson made a surprise visit, introducing Russell and praising him for friendship and leadership. But in accepting the award, Russell took the occasion to criticize the president's policies. He again questioned the resolve of the administration in Vietnam. Only a resolute commitment to victory—a term he insisted was not outmoded—would return the soldiers home in an honorable way, in the shortest amount of time, and at the lowest cost. The United States could not stay "submerged in a strategy of self-imposed restrictions with the rising casualties and the unending need for additional troops which accompany this strategy." He would send no more troops to Vietnam unless "the entire civilian population and total wealth of our country—all that we have and all that we are—is to bear a commensurate responsibility in affording him the fullest support and protection of which we are capable." It was irresponsible, indeed a "moral weakness," to sacrifice ground troops when other methods might be used to take the war to the enemy with fewer casualties.[34]

Johnson had lost McNamara, Cronkite, Middle America, and Richard Russell. Though it shocked many at the time, Johnson's decision not to run again for the presidency in 1968 was understandable. Russell received the March 31 news that the president would withdraw from the race fifteen minutes before the televised speech that announced his intention to the nation. Johnson's decision apparently had not come up before. Russell had discussed with him the portions of the speech concerning the reduction of bombing north of the 20th parallel in Vietnam, but the president had not mentioned his political future. Russell at the time thought Johnson's decision not to run was directly tied to Vietnam. Just after the speech, the senator called it "a very noble individual sacrifice in an effort to secure peace. . . . I hope it will succeed, but I would be less than frank if I did not say I have very grave doubts that Hanoi will change its policy."[35]

The relationship between Russell and Johnson had been strained by their different views on Vietnam as well as the pressing racial issues of the day, but it had endured. Indeed, it was part of their bond that they could disagree on policy while remaining personally close. Russell could call the president's policies immoral on the same day that Johnson welcomed him to an informal private dinner at the White House. And Russell almost always accepted, even though Johnson mercilessly badgered him. By late 1967, though, the emotional strain on the two men was noticeable. Russell remembered that Johnson would sometimes break out crying and could not stand to be alone, even in the White House. Russell at the same time was in and out of the hospital, lonely, and overworked.

The relationship famously disintegrated in the late spring and summer of 1968. When a vacancy in the U.S. District Court for the Southern District of Georgia came open, Russell exercised his prerogative and nominated Alexander Lawrence, a Savannah attorney and Russell family friend. The president delayed taking action on the

Senator Richard Russell and President Lyndon Johnson, October 1967. Courtesy of the Richard B. Russell Library for Political Research and Studies, Athens, Georgia.

nomination. The spring was filled with one crisis after another: Tet, the decision not to run, and then Martin Luther King's assassination on April 4. In response to the assassination, Washington, D.C., erupted in riots. Russell watched the burning buildings from his office, had a drink, took two pistols out of his desk, and drove home, determined not to have his life disrupted by the mob. Johnson called Russell that night and asked him to be at the White House the next morning for a talk on Vietnam. Russell agreed but needled the president about not being able to keep law and order. The next morning, the senator jumped the president. He suggested that Johnson was not doing all that he could in response to the violence. "Why don't you arrest Stokley Carmichael?" Russell asked. Johnson indicated that the attorney general's office feared a backlash if he did. Russell left fuming. The president was again vacillating in the face of danger. The Georgian stopped as he normally did at the Capitol for breakfast, and on a whim he asked a guard there if he could see one of the rounds for the new M-16 he was carrying. The guard told him it was not loaded. The senator angrily called the president and told him to allow the soldiers to protect the Capitol. By summer, the Lawrence nomination had still not cleared the White House. When the senator asked the president why, Johnson indicated that the attorney general was concerned about anti–civil rights statements that Lawrence had made in the past. Russell also suspected that the nomination was being held up to keep the senator in line on the president's recent nomination of Abe Fortas to replace Chief Justice Earl Warren who had announced his retirement in June. On July 1, Russell sent an angry letter to Johnson, accusing him of as much. Johnson denied it and finally sent the Lawrence nomination up, but the bad blood between the two remained. For the rest of Johnson's term, Russell remained out of the White House loop.[36]

Richard Russell continued to be a major player in defense policy, but it was at a greater distance than he had enjoyed for the previous four years. In the fall, he helped usher through the largest defense procurement in the nation's history—$71.8 billion—and joined in initiating funding of the anti–ballistic missile program. His views on Vietnam changed very little. He continued to argue that North Vietnam's participation in peace talks was a cover for ongoing military aggression. The "North Vietnamese accepted the invitation [to the Paris Peace Conference] . . . to recoup, rearm, and restore the hopes and confidence of their people." Bombing, he said, must continue. He also continued to doubt that the South Vietnamese had the manpower or the will to defend itself against Communist intrusion.

"Anyone who thinks that the South Vietnamese will be able to assume all the responsibility or the primary responsibility in the near future," Russell said, "is sadly deluded." But there were still ways out short of complete military victory. He again called for a plebiscite, declaring that he continued to "believe in self-determination in Viet Nam even if they were to determine in a manner that was not in our own best interests." The only other way out was continued bombing of "the dikes that control the rice fields" in the North and a "quarantine on shipping." Starving the North, he indicated, could bring the war to an end in six months.[37]

In 1969, Richard Russell's responsibility in the Senate shifted. Carl Hayden (D-AZ), the most senior Democrat in the Senate, retired that year, leaving Russell the chairmanship of the Appropriations Committee. Because of a Senate rule preventing any member from chairing more than one committee at a time, Russell had to give up his leadership of the Armed Services Committee. Russell remained on Armed Services, though, and was comforted by the fact that the new chair was his protégé, John Stennis (D-MS). The Georgian also continued as head of the Defense Appropriations Subcommittee. Military funding still had to have his approval, but Russell's influence was fading. He remained a critic of American policy in Vietnam during the first few years of the Nixon administration, but his energies were mainly conserved for other matters. His health also continued to decline. It had become hard for Russell to breathe, and he had long, uncontrolled coughing fits. On March 17, 1969, doctors found a malignant tumor in his left lung. He began radiation treatments five days a week while continuing his usual hectic schedule. The treatments worked temporarily. He seemed in good health over the summer but was back in the hospital by fall. Russell held on for another agonizing year. He died on January 21, 1971.

Richard Russell failed as a dove and as a hawk. He was unable to keep the United States from becoming involved in Vietnam or from escalating its commitment there. Once the nation had committed to the fight, he could not convince the White House to make the political and military effort necessary to force a negotiated settlement. Though he reached a position of tremendous power and influence, especially in the Johnson years, the executive policy-making establishment rejected his views of America's place in the world and its strategic role in Vietnam. Liberal internationalists in the Johnson administration had relegated Russell's protectionist, racist positions to the dustbin of history. In doing so, they left behind the prejudice, injustice, and myopic nationalism that had hindered the nation's efforts in fighting the Cold War, but at the same time, they also swept away Russell's careful considerations of strategic cost and culture that might have prevented America's tragic involvement in Vietnam.

Notes

1. Leslie Gelb and Richard Betts, *The Irony of Vietnam: The System Worked* (Washington, DC: Brookings Institution, 1979), 216.

2. William Conrad Gibbons, *The U.S. Government and the Vietnam War: Executive and Legislative Roles and Relationships, Part III: January to July 1965* (Princeton, NJ: Princeton University Press, 1989), 286–88.

3. Calvin Mcleod Logue and Dwight L. Freshley, eds., *Voice of Georgia: Speeches of Richard B. Russell, 1928–1969* (Macon, GA: Mercer University Press, 1997), 290–92.

4. Logue and Freshley, *Voice of Georgia*, 43.

5. George Herring, *America's Longest War: The United States and Vietnam, 1950–1975* (New York: Knopf, 1979), 142–43.

6. Randall Woods, *Fulbright: A Biography* (New York: Cambridge University Press, 1995), 374–75.

7. *Congressional Record*, 89th Cong., 1st sess., 1965, 111, pt. 14:19673–76.

8. "What It Will Take to Win in Vietnam," *U.S. News & World Report*, September 6, 1965, 56–60.

9. Robert Dallek, *Flawed Giant: Lyndon Johnson and His Times, 1961–1973* (New York: Oxford University Press, 1998), 288.

10. Johnson Tapes, WH6503.03, PNO1–2, 3/6/65, 12:05P, 7026–27, Lyndon Baines Johnson Library.

11. Johnson Tapes, WH6509.04, PNO1, 9/14/65, 6:35P, 8859, Lyndon Baines Johnson Library; *Congressional Record*, 89th Cong., 1st sess., 1965, 111, pt. 20:27253–54.

12. Dallek, *Flawed Giant*, 349.

13. Woods, *Fulbright*, 400–409.

14. *Congressional Record*, 89th Cong., 2nd sess., 1966, 112, pt. 3:3135–36.

15. *Congressional Record*, 89th Cong., 2nd sess., 1966, 112, pt. 4:4298.

16. *Congressional Record*, 89th Cong., 2nd sess., 1966, 112, pt. 4:4370.

17. "Senator Russell on Vietnam: 'Go in and Win—or Get Out,'" *U.S. News & World Report*, May 2, 1966, 56.

18. Johnson Tapes, WH6405.10, PNO3–5, 5/27/64, 1055A, 3519–21, Lyndon Baines Johnson Library.

19. "The War in Vietnam: Which Way Now?" *U.S. News & World Report*, January 16, 1967, 11.

20. Herring, *America's Longest War*, 148–49.

21. Caroline Ziemke, "Senator Richard B. Russell and the 'Lost Cause' in Vietnam, 1954–1968," *Georgia Historical Quarterly* 72 (Spring 1988), 54–55.

22. Gilbert Fite, *Richard B. Russell, Jr., Senator from Georgia* (Chapel Hill: University of North Carolina Press, 1991), 454.

23. Fite, *Russell*, 454–55.

24. *Congressional Record*, 90th Cong., 1st sess., 1967, 113, pt. 4:4714–23.

25. *Congressional Record*, 90th Cong., 1st sess., 1967, 113, pt. 9:12279–87, 12471–75, 15756–72.

26. *Congressional Record*, 90th Cong., 1st sess., 1967, 113, pt. 4:4277.

27. Dallek, *Flawed Giant*, 469–70.

28. Herring, *America's Longest War*, 170–82.

29. Fite, *Russell*, 388.

30. Johnson Tapes, WH6405.10, PNO3–5, 5/27/64, 10:55A, 3519–21.

31. Ziemke, "Senator Richard B. Russell and the 'Lost Cause' in Vietnam," 59.

32. Russell to Pendergrast, January 26, 1968, box 33, series 16, Russell Papers, Richard Russell Memorial Library.

33. Russell to Strickland, June 27, 1968, box 32, series 16, Russell Papers, Richard Russell Memorial Library.

34. Logue and Freshley, *Voice of Georgia*, 296–97.

35. John A. Goldsmith, *Colleagues: Richard B. Russell and His Apprentice Lyndon B. Johnson* (Macon: Mercer University Press, 1998), 151.

36. Goldsmith, *Colleagues*, 147–65.

37, Ziemke, "Senator Richard B. Russell and the 'Lost Cause' in Vietnam," 64–65; Wayne Kelley, "A Conversation with Richard Russell," *Atlanta Magazine*, December, 1968.

Conclusion

Richard Russell's friend Rudy Inman sent a letter to the senator in the spring of 1966 that included the following story:

> When I left Georgia, Dad had a small turpentine place in Echols County, below Valdosta. He didn't believe in letting a lard-tailed boy add to it by plumb laziness, so he gave me a 16 gauge Parker single trigger shotgun, a box of shells and said, "Take Old Joe (our best bird dog) and bring in some meat for the table." After that bad day I was dipping sand in my brogans as I passed Clem Higginbottom's house and heard his wife, Eufala, hollering that Clem was akilling her. I dropped the shotgun, busted into the kitchen, kicked the slop hog out of the way and saw Clem slapping Eufala something terrible, so I threw a shoulder block at Clem and knocked him into the bacon grease by the kitchen stove. I ran over to see if he was bad hurt and came to with a hickory knot on my head, the size of a goose egg. Eufala had beaned me with a pot-iron skillet. When I got up, she said, "You quail-shooting skunk, get out of here. This is a private fight."[1]

Richard Russell declared Inman's story "priceless." Indeed, it summed up the senator's criticism of U.S. policies at home and abroad. "Some sweet day," he replied to his friend, "we may learn—and I hope before it is too late—to stay out of 'private fights.'"[2]

In desegregating the South and expanding its role internationally, Russell argued, the federal government had forced its will upon peoples and cultures that were not yet willing or able to bear the burden. The senator believed profoundly that those who experienced social change beyond their ability or will were doomed to disorder, destruction, and tyranny. The senator derived this cautious axiom principally from Southern history. Like his friend, colleague, and occasional nemesis J. William Fulbright, Russell saw the South as an oppressed colony of the North. This instilled in him an intense anti-imperialism, a sensitivity for national self-determination, and a conviction that the social order could not be easily changed at the point of a bayonet.[3] His opposition to American involvement in Southeast Asia, Africa, and other areas around the world was thus a "Southern" thing. But, like other "Southern" things in 1964, it had become an anachronism.

Russell's racist protectionism was out of touch with the mid-twentieth century's overwhelmingly liberal internationalist impulses. He was a pessimist about human progress at a time of tremendous optimism. That Russell's views were misplaced in time did not mean that they were inherently simplistic or backward. While in part based on gross prejudice, Russell's pessimistic racial worldview was tempered with a deep sense of cultural relativism and history. The absence of the democratic spirit was not just a question of blood for Russell. It was also a question of a society's democratic traditions and institutions. Those who had not experienced the orderly transition of power and lived under the rule of law had little understanding of how to preserve democracy and protect liberty. Acquiring these traditions, Russell argued, was a matter of evolution rather than revolution. This understanding provided the substructure for the senator's definition of America's global economic and military interests. While he agreed with the liberal internationalists that democratic traditions should be preserved in the face of aggressively expanding totalitarianism, he did not believe, as they seemed to, that any amount of money or display of military might could force responsible democratic citizenship.

Russell recognized that he lived at a time when liberal internationalist ideas had overtaken his own more traditional, cautious understanding of the world, but that fact never discouraged him, even as his advice was repeatedly rejected by executive branch policy makers. Richard Russell's was never a joyless or defeated personality. He was as comfortable in his position of power as Lyndon Johnson was uncomfortable. He took defeat in stride, recuperated from personal and political tragedy quickly, and rarely cracked under stress. He was certainly overworked, smoked too much, and lived what was by common standards a solitary life, but he loved the work; took time out for dates, Washington Senators' baseball, and University of Georgia football; and found sufficient comfort and companionship among his friends, his extended family, and the Senate. His tremendous capacity for caring and nurturing, moreover, found an outlet in the work he did for young soldiers and their families as head of the Armed Services Committee. And while his view of human nature was pessimistic, he never lost hope. People, he knew, were not on the whole honorable and would lie, cheat, and steal to protect their interests, but he believed that constitutional democracy, when accepted by responsible citizens of their own free will, could allay personal corruption.

Richard Russell did not set the course of American foreign and defense policy in the mid-twentieth century, but he significantly, sometimes even wisely, framed the foreign and defense policy counterpoints of his time. There was much to criticize in Russell's approach. His racism, myopic militarism, and disregard for the killing of enemy noncombatants were derived from a gross prejudice that distorted his views on the most sensitive and contingent national security issues. But there was also much to praise. The senator's acute, even prescient, sensitivity to what would be the results of American intervention in Vietnam; his mediation of the politically explosive MacArthur situation; his carefully considered advice and consent; and his commitment to the defense of American security were valuable contributions. In the end, Russell provides the shadow, the contrast, that helps set Cold War American foreign and defense policies in their proper light.

Notes

1. Inman to Russell, May 3, 1966, box 32, series 16, Russell Papers, Richard Russell Memorial Library.

2. Russell to Inman, May 5, 1966, box 32, series 16, Russell Papers, Richard Russell Memorial Library.

3. *Congressional Record*, 85th Cong., 1st sess., 1957, 103, pt. 8:10775; *Congressional Record*, 85th Cong., 1st sess., 1957, 103, pt. 12:16661; *Congressional Record*, 87th Cong., 2nd sess., 1962, 108, pt. 3:4153; Gilbert Fite, *Richard B. Russell, Jr., Senator from Georgia* (Chapel Hill: University of North Carolina Press, 1991), 337–38, 414; Robert Mann, *The Walls of Jericho* (New York: Harcourt Brace, 1996), 191–99; Randall B. Woods, "Dixie's Dove: J. William Fulbright, the Vietnam War, and the American South," *Vietnam and the American Political Tradition* (New York: Cambridge University Press, 2003).

Bibliographical Essay

Any work on Richard Russell must start with Gilbert C. Fite's biography, *Richard B. Russell, Jr., Senator from Georgia* (Chapel Hill: University of North Carolina Press, 1991). Fite's work was the first to draw on Russell's extensive manuscript collections housed at the Richard B. Russell Library at the University of Georgia in Athens. Fite's coverage is broad but not so deep as to uncover every exciting nugget in the Russell papers. A collection of Russell's speeches edited by Calvin McLeod Logue and Dwight L. Freshley entitled *Voice of Georgia: Speeches of Richard B. Russell, 1928–1969* (Macon, GA: Mercer University Press, 1997) is also very useful. The best piece on Russell and Vietnam continues to be Caroline Ziemke's "Senator Richard B. Russell and the 'Lost Cause' in Vietnam, 1954–1968," *Georgia Historical Quarterly* 72 (Spring 1988). An interesting look into the Russell-Johnson relationship is John A. Goldsmith, *Colleagues: Richard B. Russell and His Apprentice Lyndon B. Johnson* (Macon, GA: Mercer University Press, 1998).

The Roosevelt, Truman, Eisenhower, Kennedy, and Johnson libraries all contain valuable documents on Russell and his relationship with those presidents. The telephone recordings from the Kennedy and Johnson libraries, many of which are now online at www.whitehousetapes.org, are especially rewarding. Russell's work for the Senate Armed Services Committee and other committees can be found in the Senate papers housed at the National Archives in Washington, D.C. And a scant record of Russell's relationship with the CIA is located in the CIA Records Search Tool (CREST) database at the National Archives.

Joseph A. Fry, *Dixie Looks Abroad: The South and U.S. Foreign Relations 1789–1973* (Baton Rouge: Louisiana State

University Press, 2002) and Tennant S. McWilliams, *The New South Faces the World: Foreign Affairs and the Southern Sense of Self, 1877–1950* (Baton Rouge: Louisiana State University Press, 1988) are excellent studies of the Southern approach to foreign policy. Fry's book, in particular, provides some valuable insights into Russell as Southerner.

Biographies of his colleagues in the Senate and general works on Congress and foreign policy offer interesting glimpses into Russell's world. Among them are Kyle Longley, *Senator Albert Gore, Sr.: Tennessee Maverick* (Baton Rouge: Louisiana State University Press, 2004); Don Oberdorfer, *Senator Mansfield: The Extraordinary Life of a Great American Statesman and Diplomat* (Washington, DC: Smithsonian Books, 2003); Robert Dallek, *Lone Star Rising: Lyndon Johnson and His Times, 1908–1960* (New York: Oxford University Press, 1991); Randall Woods, *Fulbright: A Biography* (Cambridge: Cambridge University Press, 1995); James Patterson, *Mr. Republican: A Biography of Robert A. Taft* (Boston: Houghton Mifflin, 1972); Frank J. Smist Jr., *Congress Oversees the United States Intelligence Community* (Knoxville: University of Tennessee Press, 1990); Barry Blechman, *The Politics of National Security: Congress and U.S. Defense Policy* (New York: Oxford University Press, 1990); and Robert David Johnson, *Congress and the Cold War* (New York: Cambridge University Press, 2006).

Many presidential biographies discuss Russell and his relationship to the chief executives. Especially useful are Alonzo Hamby, *Man of the People: A Life of Harry S. Truman* (New York: Oxford University Press, 1995); Chester Pach and Elmo Richardson, *The Presidency of Dwight D. Eisenhower* (Lawrence: University of Kansas Press, 1991); Stephen Ambrose, *Eisenhower Volume 2: The President* (New York: Simon & Schuster, 1983); Richard Reeves, *Profile of Power* (New York: Simon & Schuster, 1993); James Giglio, *The Presidency of John F. Kennedy* (Lawrence: University of Kansas Press, 1991); Robert Dallek, *Flawed Giant: Lyndon Johnson and His Times, 1961–1973* (New York: Oxford University Press, 1998); and Randall Woods, *LBJ: Architect of American Ambition* (New York: Free Press, 2006).

On World War II, see Robert Dallek, *Franklin D. Roosevelt and American Foreign Policy, 1933–1945* (New York: Oxford University Press, 1995); Wayne S. Cole, *Roosevelt and the Isolationists, 1932–1945* (Lincoln: University of Nebraska Press, 1983); John W. Dower, *War without Mercy: Race and Power in the Pacific War* (New York: Pantheon, 1987); Robert Divine, *Second Chance: The Triumph of Internationalism in America during World War II* (New York: Atheneum, 1967); and Gaddis Smith, *American Diplomacy during the Second World War* (New York: John Wiley & Sons, 1965).

For early Cold War defense and foreign policy strategy, see John Lewis Gaddis, *Strategies of Containment: A Critical Appraisal of American National Security Policy during the Cold War* (New York: Oxford University Press, 1982) and *The United States and the Origins of the Cold War* (New York: Columbia University Press, 1972). See also Randall Woods, *Dawning of the Cold War: The United States' Quest for Order* (Athens: University of Georgia Press, 1991) and Melvin Leffler, *Preponderance of Power: National Security, the Truman Administration, and the Cold War* (Stanford, CA: Stanford University Press, 1992).

On military aid, see Chester Pach, *Arming the Free World: The Origins of the United States Military Assistance Program, 1945–1950* (Chapel Hill: University of North Carolina Press, 1991). On Kennedy-era foreign policy, see Michael Beschloss, *The Crisis Years: Kennedy and Khrushchev, 1960–1963* (New York: Edward Burlingame Books, 1991) and Ernest R. May and Philip D. Zelikow, eds., *The Kennedy Tapes: Inside the White House during the Cuban Missile Crisis* (Cambridge: Belknap Press, 1997). On U.S. relations with Africa, see Thomas J. Noer, *Cold War and Black Liberation* (Columbia: University of Missouri Press, 1985) and Thomas Borstelmann, *The Cold War and the Color Line: American Race Relations in the Global Arena* (Cambridge, MA: Howard University Press, 2001). On U.S. relations with Latin America, see Kyle Longley, *In the Eagle's Shadow: The United States and Latin America* (New York: Harlan Davidson, 2002).

On the Vietnam era, see David Halberstam, *The Best and the Brightest* (New York: Penguin Books, 1983); William Conrad Gibbons, *The U.S. Government and the Vietnam War: Executive and Legislative Roles and Relationships, Part II: 1961–1964* (Princeton, NJ: Princeton University Press, 1986); George Herring, *America's Longest War: The United States and Vietnam, 1950–1975* (New York: Knopf, 1979); Fredrick Logevall, *Choosing War: The Lost Chance for Peace and the Escalation of the War in Vietnam* (Berkeley: University of California Press, 1999); and Leslie Gelb and Richard Betts, *The Irony of Vietnam: The System Worked* (Washington: Brookings Institution, 1979).

There are many good books on ideology and American foreign policy. Among them are Michael Hunt, *Ideology and American Foreign Policy* (New Haven, CT: Yale University Press, 1988); Tony Smith, *America's Mission: The United States and the Worldwide Struggle for Democracy in the Twentieth Century* (Princeton, NJ: Princeton University Press, 1994); and Frank Ninkovich, *Modernity and Power: A History of the Domino Theory in the Twentieth Century* (Chicago: University of Chicago Press, 1994).

Index

ABM. *See* missile defense
Acheson, Dean, 154
Adams, Henry, xvi
Adams, John Quincy, 89
Adoula, Cyrille, 102–103, 104
Africa, 79, 89, 99–108, 162
Aiken, George, 129, 140
Anderson, Robert, 57
Antarctica Treaty, 72
Asia, 20–24, 29, 40–47, 89, 113–133,
    137–158, 162
Atlantic Charter, 19
Atomic Bomb. *See* Nuclear War
Australia, 133

Bao Dai, 116
Ball, George, 123, 129, 138, 150
Barkley, Alben, 15
Baruch Plan, 72
Bataan, 20, 22
Batista, Fulgencio,
Bay of Pigs, 54, 81–83, 89, 102, 117,
    118
Belgium, 101, 104–105
Bennett, Tapley, 93, 95–98
Bissell, Richard, 82
Bosch, Juan, 95–96
Bradley, Omar, 44–45
Brewster, Ralph, 15
Bricker, John, 38
Bridges, Styles, 67
British Loan 1946, 35
Brown v. Board of Education, 80, 116,
    117

Bryan, William Jennings, xv, 1, 8
Bundy, McGeorge, 85, 97, 120, 125,
    129, 138
Burma, 115, 118
Byrd, Harry, 60
Byrnes, James F., 24

Cabral, Donald Reid, 95–96
Calhoun, John C., xv
Cambodia, 115, 116
Carmichael, Stokley, 156
Castro, Fidel, 80, 81, 83, 84–91, 96
Central Intelligence Agency (CIA),
    44, 53–55, 81–82, 96, 102, 104, 115,
    118, 127, 129, 132, 138;
    congressional oversight of. *See*
    Senate, CIA Oversight
    Subcommittee
Chaing Kai-shek, 15, 17, 29, 40, 42
Chandler, Albert, 15
Chennault, Claire, 17
Chiari, Roberto, 93–95
Childs, Marquis, 44
China, 17, 39, 40–42, 46, 106, 114,
    115, 123, 124, 125, 142, 143, 146;
    loss of, 40–41
Churchill, Winston, 15; iron curtain
    speech, 29
Civil Rights Act 1957, 62–65, 80
Civil Rights Act 1960, 80, 81
Civil Rights Act 1964, 92, 93, 120,
    122
Civil War, xvii, 1, 2, 3, 12–13, 121, 126
Clifford, Clark, 153, 154

Crisp, Charles, 7
Cold War, xvi, xx, 10, 19, 24, 27, 30,
    33, 39, 40, 48, 54, 63, 74, 89, 114,
    115, 158, 163
Collins, Patricia, 51
Communism, 29, 30–31, 38, 52, 57,
    61, 62, 63, 64, 81, 82, 83, 89, 91, 92,
    95, 96, 97, 98, 99, 101, 102, 116,
    118, 119, 124, 133, 137, 138, 145
Congo, 101–108
Connally, Tom, 43
Conseil National de Liberation
    (CNL) 105
Cooper Church Resolution, 106
Cooper, John Sherman, 140
Crane, Stephen, xvi,
Cronkite, Walter, 153, 154
Cuba, 1, 80, 81, 82–83, 84–91, 98, 115,
    118, 130
Cuban Missile Crisis, 54, 73, 84–91,
    108
Czechoslovakia, 57, 98

Democratic Party, 32, 38, 43, 44, 46,
    47, 48, 56, 60, 64, 69–70, 84, 89
Desoto Missions, 127, 129, 130
Developmental Loan Fund, 63–65
Dien Bien Phu, 116
Dillon, Douglas, 38
Dirksen, Everett, 38, 96, 123, 142
Displaced Persons Act, 10
Dixiecrats. *See* States Rights Party
Dominican Republic, 81, 93;
    American intervention in, 54,
    95–99, 108, 142
Dominican Revolutionary Party, 96
Dulles, Allen, 54, 71, 82
Dulles, John Foster, 55, 57, 62, 116
Dutton, Frederick, 84

Egypt, 57–63
Eisenhower Doctrine, 59–65
Eisenhower, Dwight, 15, 37, 52, 55,
    56–70, 80, 113, 115–117
Ethiopia, 11, 57

Evans, Rowland, 90
Excomm. *See* National Security
    Council

Fair Deal, 35
Fair Employment Practices
    Commission (FEPC), 13–14, 20,
    28, 31, 47, 80
Finland, 9
flexible response, 52, 70
Formosa, 40, 130
Fortas, Abe, 156
France, 12, 57–58, 61, 115–117, 119,
    123
French-Indochina War, 115–117
Fulbright, J. William, 35, 38, 43, 54,
    60, 62, 88–89, 97–99, 105, 106, 123,
    128–129, 137, 140, 142, 143, 148,
    162

Gabon, 102
Galbraith, John Kenneth, 71, 118
Geneva Conference 1954, 116
George, Walter, 5
Georgia, 13, 15, 60, 84, 87, 90, 151,
    161; Winder, 1, 87; University of,
    2, 162
Germany, 12, 13, 22, 23, 29, 86, 103,
    150
Ghana, 104
Gizenga, Antoine, 101, 104
Goldwater, Barry, 82, 128
Good Neighbor Policy, 91, 99
Gore, Albert, Sr., 62
Gould, Stephen J., xvii
Great Britain, 18, 35–36, 57–58, 67, 146
Great Depression, xvi, 6
Great Society, 74, 75, 92, 93, 120, 124,
    125, 147
Greece, 36, 118
Gromyko, Andrei, 73
Gruening, Ernest, 131, 143, 145

Harlow, Bryce, 62–63
Harris, Roy, 7

Harris, William J., 7
Hatfield McGovern Resolution, 106
Hayden, Carl, 157
Herrick, John, 129
Hickenlooper, Bourke, 129
Hill, Robert, 62
Hitler, Adolph, 12, 29
Ho Chi Minh, 114, 119–120, 141
Holt, Pat, 129
Hoover, J. Edgar, 92
House, Edward M., 4
Humphrey, Hubert, 38, 59
Hungary, 52, 87, 92, 104

Iceland, 102
India, 18, 103, 118
Inman, Rudy, 161
Iraq, 61
Israel, 57–58, 61, 62
Italy, 11, 13, 29, 88

Jackson, Andrew, 95
Jackson, Henry "Scoop," 69
Japan, 12, 13, 20–24, 29, 150
Japanese-American Internment, 21
Jefferson, Thomas, 2, 8
Joint Chiefs of Staff, 44, 45, 81, 82,
    116, 118, 137, 147, 150, 153
Joint Committee on Atomic Energy,
    xix, 33, 51, 53
Johnson, Lyndon, xx, 43, 45, 49, 52,
    54, 62, 63, 64, 66, 69, 74–76, 85,
    92–99, 100, 104–105, 107–108, 113,
    114, 118, 119–133, 139, 140,
    142–143, 147, 148, 150, 153–156
Johnson, Lady Bird, 113

Kasavubu, Joseph, 101
Keating, Kenneth, 84
Kefauver, Estes, 48
Kennan, George, 29, 30, 115, 143;
    long telegram, 29
Kennedy, John F., 52, 62, 69–74,
    81–83, 84–91, 100, 101–104, 113,
    117–120

Kennedy, Robert, 85, 149
King, Martin Luther, Jr., 156
Knowland, William, 57, 62
Korea, 34, 35, 40–47, 118, 123, 129,
    138, 146
Khrushchev, Nikita, 81, 83, 84–91

Laos, 55, 114, 115, 116, 117–119, 123,
    127
Latin America, 79, 80–99, 120
Lawrence, Alexander, 155–156
League of Nations, 5, 7, 11, 104
Lebanon, 57, 61
Legislative Reorganization Act 1946,
    33
lend lease, xix, 12, 38
liberal internationalism, xv–xvii, xx,
    4–5, 19, 39, 63, 79, 113, 126, 149,
    157, 162
Libya, 57, 61
Lincoln, Abraham, 121–122
Little Rock Crisis, 65, 67
Lodge, Henry Cabot, Sr., 5, 73
Lodge, Henry Cabot, Jr., 15, 17, 38,
    44, 120
Long, Huey, 8
Lumumba, Patrice, 101–105
Lundahl, Arthur, 85

MacArthur, Douglas, 15, 41–46
Mann, Thomas, 92–98
Mansfield, Mike, 38, 54, 118, 128,
    129, 140, 143
Mansfield Troop Reduction Bill, 151
Mao Tse-tung, 119
Marshall, Burke, 149
Marshall, George C., 44, 45, 46
Marshall Plan, xix, 36, 59
Martin, Joseph, 42
McCarthy, Joseph, 40, 41, 43
McCone, John, 82, 85, 132
McCormack, John, 96
McElroy, Neil, 67
McGill, Ralph, 32
McKinley, William, 1

McNamara, Robert, 74, 85, 87, 100, 120, 122, 123, 125, 129–130, 138, 139, 142, 150–151, 154
Mead, James, 15
Mexico, 91
Middle East, 18, 36, 56–63, 130
military industrial complex, 75–76
missile defense, 65–70; ABM, 74–76, 156
missile gap, 65–76
Mobutu, Joseph, 101, 104–106
Monroe Doctrine, 72, 82, 83, 89, 91
Morse, Wayne, 38, 128, 130, 131, 143, 145
Morton, Thruston, 117
Moyers, Bill, 97, 150
Mussolini, Benito, 11
Mutual Security Act 1957, 63–65

Nasser, Gamal Abdel, 56–58, 61
National Defense Education Act (NDEA), 68
National Liberation Front, 152
National Origins Act 1924, 10, 39
National Security Act 1947, 53
National Security Council, 69, 85, 115; Excomm, 85
National Security Council Memorandum 68 (NSC-68), 34
Neutrality Act 1936, 11
New Deal, xvi, 9, 13, 38, 120
Ngo Dinh Diem, 116, 119–120, 122
Nguyen Cao Ky, 137
Nguyen Kanh, 122–123, 131
Nigeria, 106
Nixon, Richard, 69, 157
Nkrumah, Kwame, 104
North Atlantic Treaty Organization (NATO), xix, 36, 52, 71
Nuclear Nonproliferation Treaty, 74
Nuclear Test Ban Treaty, 73

Nuclear War, 39, 45, 70, 74, 87
Nuclear Weapons, 22–23, 34, 66–76, 84–91
Nye, Gerald, 11

Operation Mongoose, 83
Operation Plan 34 (Oplan 34), 127, 129
Operation Rolling Thunder, 132
Ordaz, Diaz, 91
Organization of American States (OAS), 83, 90, 91, 94, 97, 99

Panama Canal, 72, 80, 93
Panamanian Crisis 1964, 80, 92–95, 108, 121
Pearl Harbor, 13, 22
Phillipines, 146
Pleiku, 132
Point Four Program, 60
Poland, 104
poll tax, 14
Potsdam, 23, 24, 115
Project 100,000, 149
Pueblo Incident, 55
punctuated equilibrium, xvii

Radford, Arthur, 116
Reconstruction, xviii, 3, 80, 126
Reedy, George, 45, 52
Republican Party, 38, 43, 56, 63, 67–68, 84, 128, 142
Rhodesia, 100
Rio Treaty 1947, 83
Robinson, Joe T., 8
Roosevelt, Franklin Delano, 8, 12, 22
Rowan, Carl, 100
Rusk, Dean, 85, 86, 94, 97, 103, 105–107, 118, 120, 122, 123, 125, 138, 144, 154
Russell, Ina (Balinda) Dillard, 2

About the Author

Jeff Woods is an assistant professor of history at Arkansas Tech University. He is the author of *Black Struggle, Red Scare: Segregation and Anticommunism in the South, 1948–1968* (2004).